BIOGRAPHY

THE STEEL REBEL WILLY KORF

Oliver Driesen

Dedicated to my father,
Fritz Driesen,
who flew too close to steel.

Imprint:
First publication:
2005 by Hoffmann und Campe Verlag, Hamburg
A company of the GANSKR VERLAGSGRUPPE:
English Translation by: Chris Abbey
Germany 2022

Contents

Preface to the English translation
Original publisher's foreword
Author's preface and acknowledgements

PREFACE TO THE ENGLISH TRANSLATION

My father's biography was originally published in German by Jürgen Großmann in 2005. For a long time, I have wanted to make it available to an international audience. Now, with this English translation, I have been able to realise that dream.

My special thanks to Chris Abbey, Chris Merritt, Mike Walsh, Susanne Tenzler und Jutta Groen, who all contributed to make this project happen, as well as to my family for their support.

Astrid Korf-Wolman
Chair of the Willy Korf Foundation
https://www.korfsteel.com/

PUBLISHER'S FOREWORD

No one who ever met the man whose astonishing life is the subject of this book will easily forget him. And those who only 'meet' him here will soon realize how desperately we need many more like him.

I still remember my first encounter with Willy Korf as if it were yesterday. It was in the early 1980s, when I was just starting out at the Klöckner Group. A young engineer with a doctorate under my belt, I was attending a social during the VDEh Steel Institute's conference. Many of the big names of the steel industry were gathered there. Among them was Korf, the eternal rising star, someone who never became truly established alongside the long-standing heavyweights like Krupp, Thyssen and Hoesch: a restless firebrand with a string of enormous, intriguingly rapid successes as a steel producer and innovator on the one hand, and a slightly faltering 'empire' on the other.

The stories that preceded him were far more impressive than his physical stature. He was a man who attracted people, ideas and new technologies like a magnet. I was introduced to him by Klaus Didillon, who had managed an electric steel plant in Brazil for Thyssen before joining Willy Korf. When we suddenly found ourselves face to face, we couldn't have been more different: Korf, wiry, in a double-breasted pinstripe suit, standing erect, always looking slightly upwards, about 1.70 metres (5' 7") tall, while I was over 2 metres tall and already on the large side. Korf asked Didillon who I was, and was told that "this young man" had just joined Klöckner. I quickly fetched a tray of beer from the bar and handed out the glasses to Korf and the others standing with him, declaring: "What an honour it is for me, a young engineer, to buy you, a great steel magnate, a beer!" That broke the ice immediately. After chatting back and forth for a while, Korf took his leave of me, saying: "Well, let's see what becomes of you! Maybe we'll meet again one day."

We did indeed meet again, but under more strained circumstances. Being an assistant to the board of Klöckner and head of its technology company, I was in charge of Klöckner's wealth of patents. At that time, steel producers were competing to introduce the latest coal-based direct reduction and scrap melting processes in an effort to get away from expensive, old-fashioned blast furnaces. Klöckner had made great strides in its own technology; in our view, Korf was trespassing on our patch. And so we sat opposite each other in the conference centre at Frankfurt airport, negotiating rights and also penalties for their infringement. It was fascinating to see how light-heartedly Korf dealt with these serious matters, which involved huge sums of money and severe legal consequences. That was Korf down to a T: a player with ideas, a constantly restless spirit, always seeking new frontiers when he should have been taking care of unfinished business. Driven by pure plans and visions, there can't have been many industrialists who were livelier than Willy Korf.

And rarely has there been anyone who injected as much momentum into our sometimes sluggish industry and even metallurgical research as Willy Korf. The honorary doctorate that the self-taught, non-academic Korf received from RWTH Aachen University at the age of 50 for his contribution to the concept of mini steel mills speaks volumes. Korf had a gift for picking up knowledge, developing theoretical aspects, and putting the results into profitable practice. Korf was able to familiarize himself with the finest ramifications of metallurgy with breathtaking ease. And he always found capable engineers willing to implement his ideas with the aim of improving, even revolutionizing the process of steel production, which had remained almost unchanged for a century. He never ceased to encourage his employees, inspiring them to excellence. But he always demanded just as much from himself as he did from others. This was one of the secrets of his meteoric rise in an industry that tended to emphasize its history rather than its progress.

Fifteen years after his death and fifty years after he joined the steel industry, why is the first biography of Willy Korf being published? Because we're living in a time calling out for authentic role models, even if we don't always agree with them. In this book, Willy Korf the entrepreneur and Willy Korf the man are introduced to a wider readership for the first time: his vitality, his vivacious spirit, his unquenchable thirst for freedom, and the living example he set for Germany as he demonstrated what it meant to be a true entrepreneur.

Willy Korf never shied away from risks. He was often one to act first and ask questions later. He paid dearly for his mistakes, but that's part and parcel of being courageous. He never complained, despite his brutal, unfair treatment at the hands of both fate and some of the people he mixed with. Even in a crisis, he always sensed his next opportunity. Willy Korf went through all the ups and downs of being an entrepreneur. He won everything against massive odds, and almost everything was taken away from him again. Down and out, he pulled himself back on his feet and made another spectacular ascent, before being felled by his tragic, untimely death. Even so, the roller coaster of his life suited him, this man who championed the free market more than most in a society increasingly abandoning the market and competition, individual responsibility and straightforwardness, imagination and life's dreams. He was influenced by his early admiration for the highly self-reliant capitalism of the USA, a country where it was no coincidence that he was one of the first German entrepreneurs to be a successful founder and a sought-after 'job creator'.

As both a person and an industrialist, Korf operated without a safety net. He savoured victory and endured defeat. He made friends easily, yet just as many enviers and adversaries. As a business partner, he could be refreshingly inspirational, yet also an awkward associate (just ask Klöckner). Willy Korf, like many great public figures, was someone who polarized society. He didn't try to hide his many internal contradictions, such as ambition to the point of obsession, intransigence to the point of stubbornness, enthusiasm to the point of losing touch with reality. He rarely gave the people around him a moment's peace. But how could it have been otherwise, considering Korf was a man who was only too willing to go through thick and thin with his cohorts?

Nowadays, the German economy may or may not be in economic crisis, but it's definitely in psychological turmoil. Despondency and ossification are all-pervading. Distrust, a lack of prospects, and fear of the future are ubiquitous; even managers and entrepreneurs often set no better example. We're about to lose our technological primacy in a variety of areas; educational standards are declining alarmingly. Bureaucracy and dependency syndrome seem to be flourishing. Whatever our opinion of Willy Korf, if he were alive today, there's no doubt that he'd be the hero of any movement campaigning for age-old virtues like diligence, self-assertion, enthusiasm, clarity and directness. He'd be a living illustration of how the will to succeed is fed by the fun of achievement and the simple joy of discovery. Korf was always a tinkerer, ever since his wartime childhood in Siegerland. Tinkerers are people who know nothing of neuroses because every toy taken apart and examined, every chemical experiment conducted, every page of new formulae studied at night enriches their knowledge and curiosity.

But it shouldn't be forgotten that Willy Korf was also a tough, furious fighter. When he was a newcomer, he refused to be cowed by the efforts of his established, well-known competitors to oust him from the steel market. Later, no one was more vehement than he was in his opposition to what he regarded as the evil of state subsidies, the devastating results of which hit him harder than anyone else. Right until the end, he laid the blame for the collapse of his business empire (to which additional factors also contributed) solely on the billions that his rivals received from the state. This funding was only granted because politicians knew they could buoy their chances at the next election by spectacularly 'saving' at a stroke thousands of jobs that had become unprofitable. In truth, the loss of these jobs was merely delayed until it was too late for their employers and the regional government to catch up with the free market. Good money was thrown after bad, and commercial competition, which is supposed to be a source of guidance for business, was distorted beyond all measure.

Korf, by contrast, received no such state support. His plants employed too few people and operated in too many different regions to qualify. What's more, his flourishing plant in Kehl, Baden-Württemberg, may well have been the target of hungry eyes of which he was unaware. Although Korf carefully cultivated excellent contacts in high political circles and moved with increasing assurance in Bonn and on the international stage, when things got tough, the cosseted ministers and state secretaries refused to grant him the government aid which would have enabled him to start afresh. Being a sharp critic of subsidies, perhaps he'd made himself too unpopular within Germany's administrative system.

The story of Willy Korf, who despite everything still managed to make a new start after all and was sharply on the rise by the time of his horrifying plane crash in 1990, is an encouraging example of someone brimming with confidence, someone defying state obstacles and private complications to go their own way. Sadly, Korf couldn't complete his journey. But he left the steel industry a treasure trove of thought-provoking ideas and innovations described in this book that continue to benefit steelworks to this day. Not all his ideas caught on permanently, but as we all know, it's impossible to make an omelette without breaking a few eggs. This principle, already firmly anchored in the American economy, is another leaf we can take out of Willy Korf's book. As a newspaper cartoon effectively illustrated, this man of small stature successfully wielded his charm and chutzpah to show that the big boys were simply too slow-moving to shoo away pesky insects like Korf – assuming, of course, the little troublemakers had big dreams. Willy Korf, the man of steel, certainly did.

Jürgen Grossmann
Managing Partner
Georgsmarienhütte Holding GmbH

Georgsmarienhütte, May 2005

PREFACE AND ACKNOWLEDGEMENTS

Writing history always means falsifying history, and biographies aren't exempt from this unfortunate rule. Even with the best of intentions, squeezing the life of a stranger between the covers of a book unavoidably means abridging some parts and distorting others. Dramatic events may be overrated, quiet nuances underestimated. By taking their place on a bookshelf, subjective perceptions recalled by friends and foes years later, along with superficial knowledge once reported in the media and now stored in the archives, are all too easily transformed into ostensible facts. Depending on the observer's viewpoint, seemingly impartial figures and statistics, balance sheets and annual reports can be used to interpret a lifetime's achievements in completely opposite ways. Things get even worse and more unpredictable when witnesses, acting out of some sort of obscure self-interest, report misleading information in order to deliberately lay a false trail. Fortunately, this was almost never the case when conducting research for this book. During my countless interviews with Willy Korf's friends, relatives, competitors and observers, I can safely say that everyone told the truth from their own point of view (although I was struck by how different the assessments of the unique Willy Korf could be!).

Therefore, this biography of Willy Korf is a mosaic, a

hopefully not too arbitrary compendium of voices which I inevitably had to evaluate. Any errors or misinterpretations in the presentation of economic data and other facts are solely down to me. I'd like to thank everyone who gave up so much of their time to tell me about their memories of Willy Korf. There isn't the space here to list them all by name; they all know who they are. But allow me to mention a handful of people to whom I'm especially indebted for providing original documents or without whom this project would have been impossible by virtue of their close relationship with Willy Korf and detailed knowledge of him: Helmhold Schneider, who kindly granted access to his private records and photo albums; the municipal archivist in Baden-Baden who didn't mind unearthing documents for me at seven o'clock in the morning; and Astrid Korf Wolman, who agreed to talk about her father despite her perfectly reasonable misgivings. Thanks are also due to Manfred Bissinger at the publishing house Hoffmann und Campe, who so patiently believed in this book. And within these four walls, I would like to thank my wife Christiane Rose for her talent – one of many – as a muse.

O.D.

Hamburg, May 2005

CHAPTER 1

The fall of Icarus

"We're like kamikaze pilots: so completely fearless that people think we're crazy, yet revered for our courage."[1]

In the end, the difference between life and death for Willy Korf was less than 100 metres: an outcrop fatefully located on an Austrian peak.

Mount Kellerjoch, 40 kilometres east of Innsbruck, with an elevation of over 2,300 metres, is notable for some of the most spectacular views in the Tyrol region. No climber looking out from its summit can fail to be entranced by the natural beauty of the Inn Valley, stretching out below against the backdrop of the Karwendel mountain range. For those hiking across Mount Kuhmesser to Gamssteinhaus or the ski resort of Hochfügen, this magnificent panorama is the highlight of their visit.

In winter, skiers are reluctant to divulge the secrets of Kellerjoch. Instead, they prefer to keep their knowledge of its perfect downhill slopes and cross-country trails, as well as its famous toboggan runs and infamous après ski scene, to themselves. Every summer, model glider pilots seek out the powerful thermals that develop in the hot afternoons and long evenings on the lush green slopes.

But in November, the weather on Kellerjoch is anything but conducive to aerial ascent. Low-hanging cloud is a source of sudden snowstorms, occasionally causing dangerous avalanches. On some days, visibility can drop to a few metres in a matter of minutes. And when this happens, the contours of the alpine realm appear to dissolve. Wind-whipped clouds, the expanses of snow, even the very mountains themselves blur into a milky, murky soup, making distances impossible to gauge.

Such were the conditions on Wednesday, 21st November 1990. As fate would have it for a high-altitude drama, it happened to be the Day of Prayer and Repentance, at that time still a public holiday throughout Germany. It was a day on which two men intending to fly together suddenly didn't. One of them, a business consultant named Karl Wienand, backed out unexpectedly in a decision that literally saved his life. The other man – steel industrialist Willy Korf – stuck to his plan.

Karl Wienand had a chequered past. Once the chief whip of the West German Social Democrats, by 1990 his reputation lay in tatters. A political protégé of Herbert Wehner (formerly the minister of relations between East and West Germany), there were times when money, power and connections could scarcely be discussed without mentioning his name. The shrewdness of this apparently down-to-earth man from Siegerland who seemed to have ties everywhere was legendary, even while others spoke of his capacity for backstabbing.

However, Wienand fell under a cloud after the failed vote of no confidence in Chancellor Willy Brandt in 1972. Wienand was suspected of trying to bribe Julius Steiner, an MP from the opposition Christian Democrats, to vote for Brandt. Much later, the 50,000 Deutsche Marks (DM) offered to Steiner would turn out to have been stumped up by the notorious Stasi, the East German secret police. Wienand had successfully managed to conceal his work as an agent with the Stasi, but many years later, it would be revealed and judged in court. At the end of 1974, Wienand, by now in poor health, was forced to withdraw from German politics. He briefly sought sanctuary in an Italian country house on Lake Garda.

On returning to Germany, Wienand embarked on a career in

business and management consultancy, which proved to be as up and down as his political life. His nadir at this time was a fine of over 100,000 DM, which he received for tax evasion in 1975, after failing to declare income from a consultancy contract. His planned political comeback with the Social Democrats in the early 1980s was thwarted by resistance from inside his own party, and as late as 1990 his reputation was still so controversial that his chances of becoming an elected official were slim to none.

Moreover, having recently been arrested for drunk driving, the 63-year-old Wienand now faced a court hearing, putting an end to any dreams he still cherished of standing for local chairman of the Social Democrats in the district of Rhein-Sieg. This humiliating realization was still fresh in Wienand's mind as he took off from Frankfurt bound for Italy on the morning of 21 November 1990, accompanied by the 61-year-old Willy Korf – someone he'd been friends with since his youth – on board the latter's private plane.

Nevertheless, as the twin-engine turboprop took off from the airfield in Frankfurt at 7:58am, defeat was the last thing on the minds of its two passengers, blessed as both of them were with a gift for unrelenting optimism, and the skill to suppress doubt. Ahead of them lay a day that was expected to bring each of them success.

Wienand, a well-versed commercial traveller with a knack for delicate political missions, and who viewed Italy as his second home, had been asked to accompany Korf as an authority on the country. In the town of Udine, near the Adriatic city of Trieste in northern Italy, Korf was due to discuss rolling mill equipment for a state-of-the-art steelmaking operation based on the EOF, or Energy-Optimizing Furnace.

Developed by his engineers, for years Korf had touted this resource-saving furnace as the best in class and the future of steelmaking. He was able to license and deliver the technology, build the plants around the furnaces, and market the products. Whenever there was a hint of interest in the EOF, Korf would immediately jump on a plane to explore the prospect of a sale. His air mile tally was said to be second to only that of Hans-Dietrich Genscher, West Germany's perpetually airborne foreign minister.

Owning a private jet was one of the luxuries that international steel industrialist Willy Korf permitted himself. It was also a reflection of his belief that technology would one day conquer all barriers of space and time. At the height of his business success in the 1970s, he'd already had his own internal business aviation operation for many years. In 1973, his fleet even acquired its first Dassault Falcon 20, a twin-engine medium-haul jet. By 1980, with the Korf Group now over a quarter of a century old, this aircraft type had begun to be replaced by the Falcon 50 trijet, enabling long-haul flights of over eight hours. This put Korf's holdings in Saudi Arabia and his plants in the south-eastern United States within easy non-stop reach of his German headquarters in Baden-Baden. By comparison, Udine was just a stone's throw away, and flying there in 1990 was a fairly unglamourous job, better suited to a propeller plane.

Korf's leased Beechcraft Super King Air 200, with the registration D-IGSW, was one of the most successful types in its class. More than a thousand of them were built for use in business aviation between its maiden flight in 1973 and 1990. Fitted with two Pratt & Whitney turboprop engines, the aircraft had a range of just under 3,500 kilometres (over 2,100 miles) and a top speed of 536 km/h (333 miles per hour).

The Beechcraft was a reliable carthorse of the skies, capable of carrying eight passengers and two crew members, although on this particular day there were only four people on board. With Korf's long-time chief pilot Anton Schulze having just gone on holiday, the plane was manned by the experienced pilot and flight instructor Karl Klauberg, age 47, from Offenburg and his equally experienced co-pilot Werner Görig, 61. The only two passengers were Willy Korf and Karl Wienand.

The journey south was unremarkable, with only a minor

snag of fog on the approach to Bergamo, their stop-off, which wasn't surprising in the Po Valley at that time of year. Since the small airfield didn't yet have an instrument landing system, Karl Klauberg had to rely on visual orientation despite the poor conditions. Among his colleagues, he was considered a confident pilot, but this was a tricky approach for any aviator. However, Karl Wienand, who knew Bergamo well from the air, was happy to assist, and once he'd spotted a prominent monument on the motorway to Milan, he was able to explain to Klauberg the approximate whereabouts of the runway. After a few turns, the runway lights filtered through the haze, and shortly afterwards the plane landed safely in Bergamo.

Was it intuition or simply coincidence that while they were still in the air, Karl Wienand decided not to get back on the plane in Bergamo? Originally, Wienand, a consultant with an expert knowledge of Italy and a network of contacts in international banking, was supposed to have joined Willy Korf in Udine. When it came to money or banks, this was a time when many industrialists sought Wienand's advice. He subsequently explained his maxim to broadcaster WDR: "I accept assignments only when all else has failed – for then can I demand anything I want." Years later, he also declared that he never took a penny from his friend Willy Korf: a claim that others dispute.

There's no doubt that both he and Korf enjoyed the thrill of the chase, whether for small game, the *dolce vita*, or a lucrative business opportunity. But all Wienand would later tell *Bunte,* the people magazine from Munich with a strong interest in human tragedies suffered by the wealthy, was that: "During the flight, we changed our plans." What he neglected to mention was that he'd clashed with Korf on board. To Korf's annoyance, Wienand had told his friend that he felt unable to help him during the tedious discussions about manufacturing details in Trieste, and that he'd decided to disembark in Bergamo in order to deal with some private business of his own – he needed to visit the land registry at the district court in nearby Rovereto regarding his wife's house on Lake Garda.

For Korf, there was nothing for it but to fly on to Udine alone. Wienand agreed to join him again in Bolzano on the way back that afternoon, the plan being that after they arrived in Baden-Baden, Korf would have Wienand flown back to Cologne. And so, the two of them parted company in Bergamo, not realizing they'd never see each other again.

Eight days earlier, Willy Korf had joined a close friend and his wife for dinner at an Italian restaurant in Baden-Baden. The friend, himself a company director who flew his own private helicopter, recalls Korf saying: "Helicopters are too vulnerable. Future generations will be amazed that we were brave enough to fly those things!" Korf preferred to play it safe, which is why he never even used single-engine aircraft; two engines were the minimum for him. Moreover, the Beechcraft was equipped with an instrument landing system, and so wasn't dependent on good visibility.

On the afternoon of 21 November, with the weather having deteriorated considerably, it was impossible to land in Bolzano. But in this era before mobile phones, an alternative meeting place had been agreed for just such an eventuality, and so both Willy Korf and Karl Wienand made their separate ways to Innsbruck Airport. At 4.22pm, Karl Klauberg, having crossed the Ziller Valley, radioed the control tower using his call sign – Delta India Golf Sierra Whiskey – for the last time. It was a routine call, it seems, despite the worsening weather conditions.

On the ground, it was still business as usual. Innsbruck is a provincial airport: not especially large, and with a short chain of command. Someone like Wienand thought nothing of dropping in at the control tower to ask how things were on board D-IGSW. "Everything's fine," he was told. "The pilot's already radioed in." Even so, the air traffic controller asked the Beechcraft to circle one more time because of the weather: it had started to rain in the afternoon, and heavy snowfall had set in at higher altitudes. Visibility was poor, with clouds descending over the mountains and passes. There was a strong south-westerly wind at high altitudes and warmer foehn winds were also rising.

Situated in a narrow valley, Innsbruck is regarded as one of the most difficult aerial approaches in the Alps, even for an experienced pilot of a Super King Air 200. But Korf was used to getting his way – and he was determined to land there and then.

D-IGSW was cleared for an instrument-guided landing on runway 26. In the first phase, according to the accident reconstruction, the heading had to be sharply adjusted above the approved altitude. After another correction by Klauberg, the middle phase began largely as planned. But before reaching the approach fix for the final phase, D-IGSW went into a drastic descent.

That was when the nightmare started. Barely a minute later, the plane dropped off the radar. At first, no one knew what had happened. From 4.27pm onwards, the radio traffic log only showed the steady stream of attempts by the Innsbruck control tower to contact the plane: "D-IGSW, this is Innsbruck. Do you read me?" The same prayer-like call was intoned again and again, but there was no response.

An alarmed Wienand, who always knew the right people to contact in any situation, immediately telephoned Karl Blecha, the former Austrian interior minister, and asked him to launch an official search operation. He also got in touch with Willy Korf's family to tell them the distressing news, adding there was still a slight chance that the plane had diverted to a remote alternative airfield. The terrible wait began.

It wasn't until 17 hours later, at 10am on Thursday, that the crew of an Austrian gendarmerie helicopter finally discovered the wreckage of a Beechcraft in the driving snow on Kellerjoch – above the tree line at an altitude of 2,010 metres, on the eastern slope of the Gratzenkopf peak. The force of the impact had thrust the aircraft up the steep slope from its point of impact 20 metres below. The rear of the plane with its distinctive tail unit had been torn from the fuselage and stood nearly upright, looking virtually unscathed in the thin snow. The wings had been shattered, the flaps were retracted, the trim tabs neutral. The cabin, almost completely charred and burnt out, was still pointing towards the summit, less than 100 metres away. The pilot's logbook, almost intact, lay open in the snow, the pages fluttering in the wind.

Wienand was shown the victims' personal belongings found at the crash site, including Willy Korf's wristwatch. Its hands, to which Korf had always paid meticulous attention, had permanently stopped.

The investigation report by the Austrian transport ministry attributed the accident to a combination of bad weather and pilot error. According to Anton Schulze, Korf's chief pilot, who had been on leave at the time, Karl Klauberg's main mistake was likely to have been that he confused the radio frequencies of two DME (distance measuring equipment) beacons about 8 kilometres apart. In connection with the barometric on-board altimeter and the instrument landing system, this would have led to incorrect altitude calculations. The report sombrely concluded that the crash had been caused by: "Overexertion of the pilot flying alone due to abnormal course correction coupled with challenging control settings in the cockpit."

To some minds, however, Willy Korf's death has never really been fully explained. There was a third man who had originally been supposed to fly to Italy with Korf and Wienand. It was a person Korf liked to have with him as a relative, someone with business acumen, an excellent adviser whenever negotiations were on the agenda. This man had also pulled out of the flight, because he had an important appointment in Hamburg.

Helmhold Schneider, a cousin of Willy Korf's on his mother's side, was the owner – and occasional pilot – of the helicopter Korf had criticized as unsafe just over a week earlier. Schneider, a manufacturer of plastic products in Siegerland with ten plants worldwide in the WERIT group, was the godfather of Korf's elder daughter Astrid. Slightly older than Willy, Helmhold had been close to Korf ever since their childhood days together on the River Sieg: "Back then we were like brothers," Korf had said. Perhaps this was because they had both lost their real siblings early on: Korf's only sister had died very young of a ruptured appendix, while Schneider's only brother had been killed in the Second World War.

Schneider was also the first to write a short book about Korf's life and work two years after his death (*A Life Dedicated to Steel*). When Korf's business operations were wound up following the plane crash, Schneider salvaged a wealth of documents about the steel magnate and his work. He amassed a collection of files, press cuttings, photos and correspondence from the holdings of Korf KG in Baden-Baden that took up over 10 metres of shelving in WERIT's large conference room in Altenkirchen. The contents of the folders are still neatly typed on the spines, just as they were when Korf and his secretaries used them. They were systematically analysed for the first time for this book.

The cabinet in the conference room also contains two rusty samples of a pioneering type of structural steel mesh developed in the mid-1950s. The novel touch was that instead of being welded together, the wire intersections were secured by plastic sheaths that were injection-moulded during trials in Schneider's Altenkirchen factory. In more ways than one, they represented the first innovative bonds in the network of Willy Korf's steel empire, which was soon to expand at breakneck speed in all directions.

Over the years, the business interests of Willy Korf and Helmhold Schneider frequently coincided. In the period before that fateful day in 1990, however, Schneider hadn't been in close touch with Korf for a while. Schneider still ponders in vain over the reasons for the mysterious demise of a man who, like Icarus, had often come precariously close to the sun.

There's clearly plenty of scope for imagination, as the final report of the Austrian aviation authority records a total of no less than seven 'anomalies' in the plane's approach – seven unusual reactions, inexplicable deviations from the familiar pattern. It's certainly puzzling: a flawless aircraft suitable for bad weather conditions, experienced pilots, two of the three scheduled passengers not on board at the time of the accident – and no flight recorder.

Was sabotage to blame? Had the DME beacons been manipulated? Had sinister forces planned to eliminate Wienand, at that time not yet unmasked as a Stasi agent, because he knew too much? There had already been two attempts on his life: shots had been fired at his car near Bonn, and a car bomb in Italy that had failed to explode. Did Korf meet a fate intended for someone else? And yet, none of these theories is substantiated by the official report.

Studies show that most people can roughly estimate their lifespan by unconsciously taking into account hereditary diseases in their family as well as their lifestyle and psychological disposition. Of course, no one can factor in unforeseen tragedies like a plane crash. When Willy Korf celebrated his fiftieth birthday in 1979, his guests expressed the usual wish that 'the other half of his life' would be just as successful. Korf could have left it at that, but in his speech of thanks he struck a reflective tone. Noting that he'd begun his career as an industrialist with the production of structural steel mesh almost 25 years beforehand in June 1955, he continued: "I'd like to say that that's when my life started. In other words, if I've reached the halfway mark on my fiftieth birthday, I can assume I'll live to 75." In the end, his estimate was too generous by 14 years.

Sometimes, premonitions are also apparent in works of art. There is a disturbingly prophetic painting of Willy Korf by Roger von Wackerbarth, an artist from Munich, who presented it to Korf for his sixtieth birthday. Such flattering, venerating works of art usually depict a proud patriarch amidst the trappings of his success. And this picture is no exception, for here, too, we see his villa, one of his steelworks from the air, and a scene from steel production. But the painting also has a ghostly element. Reminiscent of a surreal collage, Korf's likeness is framed by a broken clock face and superimposed by a digital clock showing the time one minute to twelve. Below it, his aeroplane can be seen drifting into a shadowy patch of grey. Korf received the painting on 13 August 1989 – fifteen months and eight days before boarding his Super King Air 200 for the final time.

How could Willy Korf's life have ended so abruptly, and in what *Bunte* described as a "damn stupid death"? Later on, his friend and cousin Helmhold Schneider, as baffled as everyone else, would quote from the obituary by Korf's former employees contained in the collection of newspaper clippings in Altenkirchen: "He died as he lived: in flight, in pursuit of new goals."

CHAPTER 2

Short of stature

"We learn to fly by flying."

Who was Willy Korf? To some, he was legendary, for others, controversial. Among his many attributes, though, this difference of opinion was perhaps most apparent when it came to his height. Over the decades, even this simple, verifiable detail prompted journalists, friends and rivals alike to make wildly divergent claims about him. The only thing they seemed to agree on was that Willy Korf was short of stature.

So short, in fact, that in industry, people mockingly nicknamed him 'Tall Willy' behind his back, alluding to the striking contrast between his lack of height, and his enormous confidence and public persona. And it was for this reason, too, that the media used comparisons like "the Napoleon of the steel industry" and referred to him disparagingly in headlines such as: "In steel, even the dwarfs are tall."

When he was still only 39 years old, a feature on him in the business magazine *Capital* included an early portrait with the caption "As short as Korf, as tough as steel." This was also the first article to disclose Korf's height, still with a certain coy discretion, as "nearly 1.70 metres" (5' 7"). For its part, in 1972, the weekly *Welt am Sonntag* was similarly vague, but nevertheless lopped off almost 5 centimetres: "barely more than 1.65 metres tall" (5' 5"). The following year, according to business weekly *Wirtschaftswoche*, Willy Korf was exactly "1.69

metres short", while in 1976, the Swiss publication *Schweizer Weltwoche,* reporting objectively from its foreign viewpoint, added another centimetre to this. Four years later, *Welt am Sonntag* suddenly revised his height to a dwarfish 1.52 metres (less than 5 feet). In 1983, this crushing estimate was echoed by *Bunte,* the popular German illustrated weekly. At least *Bild,* Germany's leading tabloid and reliable purveyor of truth, would posthumously give Willy Korf a height of 1 metre and 65 centimetres in 1990, which (more or less) came to be the definitive figure.

Assuming official documents don't lie, for once the solution to this mystery doesn't fall neatly in the middle. His last passport, which was issued in the city of Baden-Baden on 19 January 1990 and bore the number 6390073972, recorded that Wilhelm Willy Korf, a German citizen, born in the town of Hamm (Sieg) on 13 August 1929, was actually taller than most estimates, namely 173 centimetres (5' 8"). Mind you, the passport official – like so many other people before him – may well have been dazzled by Korf's personal charisma, which made him appear taller than he actually was, even at the age of 60. And it shouldn't be forgotten that the "steel baron from Baden-Baden" was in the habit of wearing slightly elevated shoes.

If the question of his height alone is so contentious, imagine how much harder it must be to verify his more important characteristics – for example, whether the modestly-sized Willy Korf also came from a modest background. Once again, the answer is contradictory: yes, compared to his later social status, but not relative to the social environment in which he grew up. When Korf told *Wirtschaftswoche* in 1973: "I came from small beginnings," this was a half-truth.

The Korfs had long been successful in business. The family originally came from the Baltic region, where their name was spelled in seventeenth-century records with sometimes one, sometimes two f's. In Latvia, the Korf(f)s held important positions in the trading alliances of the Hanseatic League and, following the advent of the Machine Age, became industrialists.

The first notable economic venture of the German branch of the Korf clan was the cabbage-pickling factory owned by Willy Korf's great-grandparents near the village of Hamm (Sieg) in, of all places, the hilly, bitterly poor Westerwald region. Interestingly, despite or perhaps because of the hardship suffered by the local peasantry in the nineteenth century, Hamm became a focal point of economic history. For example, Friedrich Wilhelm Raiffeisen was born there in 1818. The founder of rural credit unions and cooperatives, he went on to become one of Germany's greatest social reformers, while his banking model in agricultural commerce spread across the globe.

Agricultural commerce was also the line of business of Gustav Korf, Willy's grandfather. In 1878, he teamed up with various partners to launch a business selling building materials and agricultural products in the neighbouring town of Au (Sieg) under the name of Vendel, Korf & Company. It sold everything a rural population needed for building and farming: construction materials from wood to iron, fertilizer, animal feed, flour, salt, fuel, seed and grain. As the firm extended its catchment area to 50 kilometres around Au, so it's clientele expanded to include the surrounding cooperatives. Gustav Korf, almost like the local hero Raiffeisen before him, also became a kind of bank for local farmers. He financed their machinery and building investments and even their harvests against collateral, mainly land mortgages. Dozens of mortgage deeds survived the turmoil of war in the company's iron safe.

Furthermore, the growing venture began to serve the coal and ore industry, the source of raw materials for steel production. The Siegerland region, where steel and armaments industrialist Friedrich Flick was also born in Kreuztal in 1883, contained iron ore mines – and now also railway tracks. The construction of the new line from Cologne via Siegen to Frankfurt had been a key factor in the foundation of the new company, as the high demand for building materials combined with the strategic feature of a promising trade route.

The yield from the mines on either side of the River Sieg

also prompted Gustav Korf briefly to operate a small mine in the village of Pracht, the Weinstock mining company remaining in business until the Great Depression in the 1920s. The ore also contained a high level of manganese, making it attractive to foreign customers. Meanwhile, several iron and steel works were drawn to the region by the quality of the ore from Siegerland, including in Willy Korf's birthplace Hamm, and also Wissen (Sieg). The plant in Hamm did not survive the nineteenth century, although the one in Wissen lasted until the end of the Second World War. But thousands of people were once employed there, so it is perhaps no wonder that the regional construction industry also flourished, generating additional revenue for Gustav Korf. Around 1930, the family business had several quarries nearby, and later acquired a brickyard and a flour mill.

Gustav Korf reigned over the company for half a century until his death in 1932, and paid more corporation tax than anyone else in the Altenkirchen district. He and his wife Emilie (Willy Korf's grandmother) had five children. But in 1919, at the age of only 46, Emilie died of typhoid fever, which she had caught while caring for soldiers on hospital trains in the First World War. Gustav Korf's second wife, Frieda, became the foster mother of the children, including Arthur, Willy Korf's father.

Ten years after the death of his grandmother Emilie, Willy Korf was born on 13 August 1929. His mother Margarethe ('Grete'), Arthur Korf's wife, was too mindful of her social status simply to be a housewife. Indeed, the family's standing was evident from the fact that they spent three weeks every summer on the exclusive island resort of Borkum. Although a lady of leisure, Willy Korf's mother was also a strong woman. He loved and revered her, and she was a great influence in his life until she died in 1979.

Despite this power, not even she could prevent her son from acting up at times, like so many other adolescents. There are a few anecdotes from Willy Korf's childhood that reveal something of his later business acumen, his fascination for technical innovation, and his formidable spirit. For example, on Sundays and national holidays, his family often visited their 'new' grandmother Frieda, had lunch together, and then returned to Au in the evening. Following her husband's passing, Frieda became the authority figure in the family and was determined for her grandson to have the same religious upbringing as she herself had had. But Willy could not be coaxed to attend church regularly. So, Frieda Korf hit on the idea of only giving him his pocket money once he'd been to the service – a simple move that quickly motivated Willy to become an eager churchgoer.

He also showed an urge to rise up in the world when he was still very young, sometimes literally. On family outings with his grandmother, uncles and aunts to Königswinter, they would often stop off at a teahouse on the Rhine promenade. Willy, instead of sitting demurely on his chair, would obstinately climb onto the neatly laid table and refuse to get down, despite the pleas and remonstrations of his family. As a result, his family regularly had to leave the teahouse amid caustic comments from neighbouring tables. This was a metaphor for things to come, for no one would find it easy to halt Willy Korf on his ascent – or to oust him from the terrain he'd conquered.

In retrospect, some who knew Willy claimed – not altogether seriously – to have spotted his later involvement in the wire industry early on. He once used a very long piece of wire to connect an electric fence surrounding a meadow in Siegerland to the iron railing of a bridge spanning the river. The bridge was frequently crossed, and the cries as people touched the electrified railing were a source of mischievous delight to little Willy, safe in his hiding place. Later on, he would use wire to shock many more people.

Experiments always gave Willy Korf a thrill; the riskier, the better. He often visited his cousin Helmhold Schneider in the neighbouring village. Helmhold's hobby was chemistry, paving the way for his subsequent career as a plastics entrepreneur. When Willy was sixteen, Helmhold told him that he had just learned how to make gunpowder at school. He explained to

Willy that all you had to do was carefully mix 10 per cent sulphur, 75 per cent saltpetre and 15 per cent charcoal in a mortar. The two cousins proceeded to blow up dead tree trunks by drilling holes, filling them with homemade gunpowder, and attaching a fuse. But this wasn't enough for Willy.

In an early signal of his grand ambitions, he couldn't help wondering how much more exciting it would be to blow up the ruins of the bridge across the Sieg in Au. Even though the bridge had been destroyed in the war, its pillars were still in place – complete with the necessary blasting holes. And so, a few months later, there was a huge blast in Au, breaking numerous windowpanes in the vicinity. Criminal charges were brought and Willy Korf, the self-styled demolition expert, found himself in serious trouble, because the bridge had just been prepared for reconstruction.

Korf's other pursuits included football and handball, popular activities among energetic teenagers, and it was there that he met Karl Wienand, destined to become his lifelong companion (as well as a Social Democratic politician who courted considerable controversy of his own). Wienand later recalled why they became friends despite the differences in their sporting prowess: it was because, unlike almost everyone else, Willy refused to snub him for the Wienand family's opposition to the Nazis. Moreover, he didn't look down on Wienand because of his working-class background. Grete Korf, Willy's mother, also took a liking to the young Karl, even warning him to be wary of her son, because he always wanted too much at once.

Meanwhile, Willy was developing another trait for which would later come to be known: his constant, impetuous mobility. At first, this was limited to his daily commute to Betzdorf grammar school, invariably doing his homework at the last minute on the train. As the years passed, however, he switched to other, more exciting means of transport. It wasn't long before Willy and his cousin Helmhold both had motorbikes.

Later on, in times of economic scarcity, the young Willy

Korf drove a genuine Mercedes-Benz: a wine-red pre-war 170V limousine. But filling it up with petrol was out of the question, for that would have required bribing British or French occupation troops. However, the lack of fuel didn't bother Korf. Instead, using his technical acumen, he installed a gas generator in the vehicle's boot, which ran on sack-loads of dry waste wood, causing the engine to smoke and crackle. Adding the correct amount of air was crucial, otherwise the engine immediately began to stutter, at which point the driver had to stop and poke the embers to restore the right gas pressure – a humiliating procedure which somewhat undermined the prestige of owning a Mercedes.

While trying to get the most out of his makeshift propulsion system, Korf made another lasting friendship with Edgar Georg, a factory owner's son from nearby Neitersen, who knew all about wood gas generators. Georg's father was friends with Willy's uncle Hugo, and also built truck trailers, which he sold to Gustav Korf OHG. At that time, vans in particular were powered by wood gas. Years later, Edgar Georg, who by that time was a qualified mechanical engineer, would be appointed to Korf's supervisory board.

Turning up with their prototype eco-Mercedes, Willy and his cousin Helmhold were the stars of every village fete and wine festival on the Rhine and the Moselle. The girls flocked around the two lone knights of the road, while the boys without their own sources of fuel didn't get a look-in. "Whenever we stayed the night anywhere," said Helmhold Schneider, "all we had to say by way of an excuse when we returned home the next morning was that the wood had got wet!"

By 1939, Gustav Korf OHG had grown into a well-known commercial enterprise with its own production setup, buoyed by good transport links thanks to its location in Au (Sieg), an important railway junction. However, the Second World War had drastic consequences for the company. Almost all the commodities it traded in were managed by the state, business was regulated by quotas and ration coupons, and its vehicle fleet was partly requisitioned by the Wehrmacht. In December 1944, the warehouses and administration building were destroyed by British fighter-bombers. Amidst this chaos and even after the war, with bartering and improvisation now common, Willy – although still at high school – was expected to help out in his father's business. He later described it as "the ultimate commercial apprenticeship".

Wednesday, 20 February 1946 proved to be a historic day in Willy Korf's life. Frieda, the second wife of his grandfather Gustav Korf, was laid to rest. It rained and snowed alternately during the funeral in Rheinbrohl, with temperatures hovering around freezing. That day and its unusual weather are so accurately recorded in the Korfs' family history because, by a tragic coincidence, it gave double cause for mourning.

In the post-war German landscape of bombed-ravaged ruins, lines of refugees, and the occupation regime, any journey – even if only to a funeral in the neighbouring town – was fraught with unpredictable danger. When the wake in a restaurant in Rheinbrohl concluded late that evening, Arthur Korf, his brother Hugo – with whom he had run the company since the death of their father Gustav, 14 years earlier – and Hugo's wife Otti set off for home in Au in a rickety pre-war delivery van.

The only bridge over the Sieg that was still intact after the war was in Rossbach, a town divided by the border between the French and Belgian zones of occupation. The border guards did everything they could to keep warm, including resorting to alcohol – but intoxicated sentries and live ammunition are a perilous mix. With thick snow falling, the van reached the barrier an hour before midnight. Hugo, who was driving, climbed out to attract attention, but no one could be seen through the driving snow. No sooner had he got back inside the van and begun to drive on, shots suddenly rang out, for a night-time curfew was in force. Otti, seated in the middle of the cab, was hit in the arm. To her right, however, Arthur Korf suffered a far more severe injury.

Hugo braked and ran around the truck to open the passenger

door, and his brother, covered in blood, collapsed into his arms, dead. Arthur Korf had survived the war as an officer in the Wehrmacht, only to be shot through the heart by a drunk Belgian border guard.

Willy Korf was informed of his father's death early the next morning. Arthur Korf's only son was 17 years old and still enrolled at the grammar school in Betzdorf. The second-generation agricultural trading business, which had existed for over 80 years, was suddenly without its principal director. The family had doubtless planned to put Willy in charge of the business one day – but not so soon.

At first, he wanted to study economics in Cologne, while his grandmother would have preferred him to become a pharmacist. But although Willy's uncle Hugo, himself childless, was a hard-working partner and assistant, he lacked the vision to lead Gustav Korf OHG to prosperity in the long run.

And so, at the end of 1948, after two more years at college in Cologne and with a successful commercial baccalaureate under his belt, Willy Korf took the helm of Gustav Korf OHG in Au (Sieg), at the age of 19, as a partner with personal liability for the firm. This might have seemed like a giant step for someone who was still a teenager. But, for a young man forged in the fires of ore and coal, regional business was to prove far too small a playing field.

CHAPTER 3

New kid in town

"Baden-Baden is our air base. This is where we take off, and this is where we return from our sorties day and night."

On 20 June 1948, the Deutschmark currency was introduced in western Germany, which was still under Allied occupation, and the old Reichsmark was abolished. Damages suffered by the company premises during the war aside, this reform finally allowed business to get back to normal again for Gustav Korf OHG. One of Willy Korf's first decisions as the new man at the helm of his grandfather's business was to focus more strongly on the firm's role as a builders' merchant. After all, by 1950, the country was seized by a wave of reconstruction.

Nowhere was the need for timber, roofing tiles and reinforcing steel greater than in the Ruhr Valley, which had suffered particularly badly in the war, prompting Korf to expand his activities there. Moreover, he extended his commercial feelers to south Germany, sourcing truckloads of timber from the sawmills of the Black Forest and Bavaria. But with reconstruction in full swing throughout the country, there was another commodity in short supply and high demand: reinforcing steel.

Wire mesh was required to add stability to the prefabricated concrete elements used in ceilings and walls. In 1951, Korf began importing reinforcing steel from Lorraine in France.

Several thousand tonnes was used on an especially prominent building: the new Federal Audit Office in Frankfurt.

Given the mushrooming volume of freight transported by Gustav Korf OHG, Willy Korf found himself having to purchase more and more lorries. He made sure no trucks travelled empty during the construction boom, so lorries bearing timber from southern Germany were then dispatched to other destinations with building materials and steel on board. It was in this favourable climate that, in 1951, Willy Korf founded the first company of his own: Korf-Transport GmbH.

Initially acting solely as an in-house haulage company for Gustav Korf OHG, the firm soon evolved into a transport contractor catering to external clients. This entailed buying long-distance transport permits – an investment that repaid itself many times over. In turn, this new enterprise paved the way for further growth – since any business with both its own transport and products to deliver was unlikely to remain local for long.

Willy Korf was a director of Korf-Transport GmbH, and it remained the apple of his eye for the rest of his life. It would become the nucleus of several phases of expansion, reorganization and restructuring in his business empire. Moreover, with the company name emblazoned on its fleet, it was a rolling – and later floating and flying – advertisement for all his commercial ventures. Perhaps most notably, Korf-Transport GmbH was the only firm established by Korf to remain profitable until the end.

In 1953, Gustav Korf Company marked its seventy-fifth anniversary. By this time, Willy Korf had gained enough experience to feel confident steering his grandfather's company into new territories. At that time, wire mesh was still a new concrete reinforcement product for the construction industry, but it already held huge potential. Assuming Korf had enough in stock, nothing would stand in the way of his expansion. The ideal solution would have been for Gustav Korf OHG to have its own production plant, but this seemed out of reach. However, it wasn't long before Korf was introduced to a potential partner who, on the face of it, seemed an ideal match.

Herr Liedtke had arrived as a refugee from East Prussia after the war. Now based in nearby Fredeburg, he was also a manufacturer of steel mesh for use in construction. He had a modest production operation, modest capital – and no idea of the great things Korf had in mind with his new business partner. Moreover, there was something about him to which Korf was irresistibly drawn, for Liedtke was an outsider, a David fighting a Goliath – a characteristic that was to be a regular leitmotif in Korf's own career.

Liedtke was one of the first mid-level businessmen who was willing to take on the far more powerful Baustahlgewebe GmbH in Düsseldorf – a joint enterprise originally set up in autumn 1929, in which the major German steel corporations cynically colluded to sell their wire mesh at inflated prices to the desperate building industry. Its unspoken motto was: If you don't like our terms, you can find another way to stabilize your concrete. Any manufacturers or dealers planning to defy what was essentially a cartel had to be mindful of just how powerful their opponent was. Korf was about to find this out for himself.

Since Liedtke had nothing like the financial clout of Baustahlgewebe GmbH, Korf decided to acquire a silent partnership in his firm. Basically, Korf became his own customer: he bought Liedtke's entire output of welded wire mesh and took on sole distribution. He also dedicated two of his own employees to restructure Liedtke's "totally disorganized" operation in Fredeburg.

Although concealed at the time, this far-reaching involvement allowed Korf's corporate historians to report years later that "the Liedtke company quickly developed from an initial monthly output of only 600 tonnes into a powerful supplier on the wire mesh market." Nevertheless, this "powerful partner" soon ran out of steam. This was the first sign of a recurring pattern in Korf's business undertakings.

As Korf, a brilliant salesman, surged ahead, the penniless

Liedtke fought to keep up with the rapidly increasing sales by building a second factory making steel mesh in Medebach, another Sauerland town. The outcome of this venture was reported (with Korf's approval) in the account of his business activities *25 Years of Korf* as follows: "However, the Liedtke company ... could not cope financially with its rapid growth ...". This assessment sits is in stark contrast to Korf's ongoing tendency to ignore the same issue in his own commercial dealings.

Because Liedtke wasn't nearly as good at buying steel as Korf was at selling the finished mesh, delivery obligations increasingly fell behind. Korf's customers were unhappy and threatened to desert him for Baustahlgewebe GmbH, which had a far higher delivery capacity. In turn, Korf sued his partner for damages, before settling out of court and ending their collaboration. His main takeaway from all this was that "the business had to be continued without fail. I'd invested a lot of money in building up a sales organization and found a very good market in the south of Germany."

With Liedtke having failed as a supplier and a partner, Korf decided to start making wire himself. He saw this as an opportunity, for manufacturing goods was a desire he had quietly nurtured for a long time. A factory needs capital, not to mention a good strategic location, and Korf, blessed with plenty of ideas but not enough money, realized that the best course of action would be to somehow combine these two requirements.

After a fruitless search in Bavaria and Baden-Württemberg, he decided to set up his wire factory on a piece of ground littered with bomb craters in the town of Kehl on the Upper Rhine. Separated only by the waters of the Rhine from Strasbourg and Alsace in France, Kehl gave the impression of a deserted wasteland, now that the prolonged Allied occupation was over. Two world wars had ruined the town's early industrial prosperity, with its port facilities and a cellulose factory, and the associated evacuations scattering inhabitants as far as Lake

Constance. In fact, until the Washington Agreement on the Clearance of the City of Kehl was signed in 1949, the town had still been at risk of annexation by France. Gradually, over the next few years, the town and the port were returned to the people of Kehl by the French occupation regime. To some, however, the departure of the French seemed to signify the final stage of economic collapse for this battered region.

Other investors might have turned their noses up at the ravaged port, yet Korf saw only advantages there. The south German market he'd successfully tapped was right on the doorstep. There were plenty of workers, unemployed after years of post-war austerity, queuing up in the area for jobs. And, crucially, Kehl was far removed from the reaches of the 'robber baron' steel producers based in the Ruhr. The factory would be located directly on the Rhine, the biggest transport artery for heavy industrial goods in Europe. Raw materials would arrive from France, and the factory's output could easily be shipped by water, first to the Ruhr region and then to Hamburg.

Luckily for Korf, the unusual location even held the promise of fresh financial capital. To set up his new company and finance the initial investments, he needed the sum of 300,000 marks. At first, he tried to interest Hugo Stinnes Jr – son of the legendary industrialist who'd been the world's biggest employer in the 1920s, and heir to his coal, glass and chemical empire – in contributing the necessary resources. But Stinnes declined, regarding Korf, still only 23, as someone far too young to be his business partner. Instead, Willy Korf explored sources of state funding.

A special aid decree enacted by the Federal Ministry of Finance offered tax breaks and long-term loans to employers willing to invest in Kehl, while the regional government of Baden-Württemberg also provided some assistance. For the first time, Korf had to deal with politicians to receive funds that, strictly speaking, clashed with the principles of the free market. Somewhat ironically, in his later years, Korf would become a harsh critic of policies relying on state subsidies.

Just seven months later, Korf's wire factory, built with public funding on a disused industrial site in the port of Kehl, was largely completed. The drawing, straightening and mesh-welding machines were ready to start, and promised to manufacture up to 1,200 tonnes of wire mesh every month. The factory's administrative block overlooking the Upper Rhine was three storeys tall. A company brochure boasted: "Steel construction mesh from Kehl. Suitable for reinforcing concrete. State-of-the-art production." In April 1955, the wire-manufacturing business SÜDRA was entered in Kehl's company register. And on 23 June 1955, Willy Korf began to make his own welded wire mesh in Kehl.

It wasn't long before SÜDRA had over a hundred employees. Trudpert Müller, at that time the mayor of Kehl, was introduced to Korf, 8 years his junior, and immediately took a liking to the newcomer. Korf divulged his future plans to the mayor: "I'm going to build a steel mill in the port of Kehl, just you wait and see!" At first, Müller took this as the boast of a young high-flyer; many other entrepreneurs had promised him similar things. "But I quickly learned that Korf was usually true to his word." Müller also learned that Korf, a new resident of Kehl, was living "in a one-bedroom flat in social housing". Apparently, there was a lively atmosphere at his home: "Alcohol was drunk, and sometimes he had female company." This was Willy Korf's proof, to be repeated many times throughout his life, that being an entrepreneur didn't have to mean a dreary 24-hour job. For him, 16 hours of work a day was quite enough.

Willy Korf would sometime visit his friend Edgar Georg from Siegerland, who was now studying mechanical engineering in Stuttgart, and speak of his intention to graduate from making wire mesh to manufacturing steel. By now, Korf had his gaze fixed on Germany at the national scale. He already employed eight freelance sales representatives to distribute his steel mesh: four covering the south of the country, four in the north. This irritated the established competition in the Ruhr, and the corporations largely controlling steel decided to make Korf aware of his limitations by going for his Achilles' heel.

A wire mesh plant is reliant on rolled steel. And hardly any of the steel corporations like Krupp, Hoesch, Thyssen or Klöckner were keen to sell it to their young competitor. Only one steel mill on the Ruhr agreed to supply him with the precious commodity – but this was barely enough to meet 5 per cent of Korf's demand.

It was just as well for the newcomer that the European Coal and Steel Community (ECSC) had come into being in 1952, abolishing import tariffs on steel between its member states. In early 1956, Korf began buying wire rod from two French mills in Lorraine, Europe's oldest coal and steel region, far more cheaply than would have been possible in Germany. The French President Charles de Gaulle, determined to fight French inflation, had introduced price caps. And under ECSC rules, the same domestic prices had to be offered to foreign buyers as well.

This was an opportunity too good for Korf to miss. A contract with Hugo Stinnes' branches ensured the efficient distribution of his welded wire mesh made from French steel. The Stinnes corporation, which had just been returned to German hands from US supervision after the war, was to become an important partner of Korf over the next few years, and was to handle the sole distribution of steel mesh from Kehl in southern Germany.

In 1955, with SÜDRA still in its first year of business, Korf tried to find new products to supplement his range and make him less dependent on steel mesh for the construction industry. Working with a Wiesbaden company specializing in prefabricated concrete ceilings, SÜDRA developed a new lattice truss bridge made of drawn wire for concrete reinforcement. It began manufacturing these truss bridges in the Kehl factory in 1956 under the Omnia brand. Omnia truss bridges were eventually sold under long-term supply contracts to about a hundred concrete plants throughout Germany.

In his efforts to further disrupt and undermine the wire mesh cartel in the Ruhr, Korf also attempted to optimize welded wire mesh. Ever since the European steel market had been opened up by the ECSC, the cartel had endeavoured to grind down the ten or so medium-sized outsiders among German manufacturers with a succession of lawsuits involving over-inflated claims. When that didn't succeed, Baustahlgewebe GmbH pulled another weapon out of its armoury: patenting a particular variant of welded wire fabric with fewer longitudinal wires on the sides to allow overlapping without wasting steel.

This 'reduced-edge weldmesh' was made out of smooth-drawn wire like all other types of steel mesh, and so claiming it was a patent-worthy innovation was merely a pretext to exclude competition. Korf sidestepped this gambit by working in great secrecy to invent another type of mesh made of ribbed wire. Its improved bonding to concrete reduced the specific consumption of steel in construction by nearly 20 per cent. The Düsseldorf cartel tried in vain to stop the building authorities from approving this new mesh, before finding itself forced to adopt the technology. In 1957, it finally agreed to a 'peace deal' allowing the two rivals to use ribbed steel mesh.

The fact that Baustahlgewebe GmbH now put up with Korf's offensive market strategy for the first time granted him special status compared to the other independents. This paved the way for Willy Korf to build two more production plants in 1958: one in Göppingen making welded wire mesh, wire nails and barbed wire, and the other in Hamburg turning out steel mesh for use in construction. Together, the three factories produced up to 70,000 tonnes of mesh per year, accounting for a tenth of the West German market. The diminutive Korf had become the biggest of the outsiders, thanks to his sharp focus on innovation and diversification.

However, his approach wasn't restricted to new wire products. For the first time, Korf moved into an entirely different material with a bright future: plastic. The company Südwest-Plastic GmbH, which he founded for this purpose in Kehl in 1957, started by making plastic pipes. But it soon branched out into motorboats made of fibreglass with polyester resin. This early lifestyle product naturally also stemmed from its inventor's enthusiasm for any means of transport combining speed with glamour. In Kehl, he could often be seen furrowing the waters of the Rhine on a speedboat with an outboard motor. Indeed, the nautical fleet of Südwest-Plastic would likely have flourished had its technical director not been killed in an untimely accident, taking his irreplaceable knowledge with him and putting an end to the company after just three years.

Bizarrely, this tragedy also led to a new personal friendship. When Korf dissolved Südwest-Plastic, he sold off his remaining stocks of motorboats in newspaper advertisements for just 400 marks each. One day, someone called him who was interested in buying three boats, but was only willing to pay 1,000 marks. The potential buyer so keen to drive a hard bargain was Franz Burda, the son of a famous publisher from Offenburg. It might have been a clearance sale, yet Korf had no intention of lowering the price any further. After a tussle on the phone, Burda finally had to give in, and he agreed to buy two boats for 800 marks. "After that phone call", the publisher's son recalled, "neither of us thought much of the other." It wasn't until years later that a mutual acquaintance introduced the pair, starting a lifelong friendship between two bon vivants with a zest for life.

Despite Korf's passion for the water, powerboats were no substitute for his chief indulgence: aviation. A flying fanatic for many years, in 1958 he decided the time was right to treat SÜDRA – and himself – to a company aircraft. He plumped for a Dornier Do27, known for its short take-off and landing capabilities. Korf leased a field especially for the Dornier in Au, near the headquarters of his grandfather's company. And he developed a habit of commuting by air between the Sieg and the Upper Rhine, between business and factory: a 90-minute flight.

It goes without saying that Willy Korf was keen to show off his new acquisition to all and sundry. Later on, the press would emphasize his proficiency as an amateur pilot who "acquired a pilot's licence after the war" (*Wirtschaftswoche*). Flying seemed to be an inevitable pastime for this intrepid self-made man.

Indeed, he did everything he could to reinforce his image as a natural-born a daredevil aviator.

The following year, Korf joined forces with Claus Kühl to set up an aviation company called Deutsche Taxiflug GmbH. Once again, Korf had managed to find a dependable business partner who was just as enthusiastic as he was – and had financial muscle besides. Kühl, originally a bookseller from Hamburg, had come up with the idea for the legendary Burda Squadron – an aerobatic display team which promoted the Burda publishing house by flying advertising banners. Consisting of five Piper A18 propeller planes, the team was a regular sight at air shows throughout the country. Claus Kühl, a pilot who'd won a string of awards, was the squadron leader from 1954 to 1958. The planes were stationed at an airfield in Offenburg, where Franz Burda, the publisher's founder, was based.

Deutsche Taxiflug, on the other hand, was based in Mannheim. It's a city associated with several firsts in German air transport, such as the first regular service for holidaymakers from the mainland to the Frisian Islands. Korf and Kühl even introduced scheduled flights to the Oberammergau Passion Play Festival. Although Kühl was a professional pilot, while Korf was merely an amateur aviator who would later employ others to fly him, the public regarded them as equals, at least as far as their piloting skills were concerned. As late as 1979, the monthly aviation publication *Fliegermagazin* carried an outrageous article headlined: 'When Willy Korf still flew to stroke seals' and accompanied by a photo of Korf in the cockpit (admittedly in the co-pilot's seat) of a Do 27. In the article, Korf was lionized like the Red Baron himself:

> The hour was already late when Willy bet a big shot from the Rhineland ten bottles of champagne that he could land his Dornier on a sandbank at any time and stroke a seal's tail. The very next day, Korf and Kühl boarded their Do 27, accompanied by an 'aerial witness', and took off for the small island of Memmert, a wildlife reserve off the north coast of Germany. It was low tide, and many seals could be seen lying

on a sandbank. The two pilots landed their D-ELON on the beach, right next to the seals. Willy jumped out and crawled on all fours up to the last seal. Before it could slip into the water, he reached it, gently stroked its tail, and yelled: "Thank you very much – I've won the bet!" The victory party that evening at the North Sea Hotel is still talked about to this day.

Is this just another tall story from the world of aviation? Seemingly not. The bet really did take place, although Korf never honed his skill as a pilot beyond flying a Do 27, and even failed to renew his sports pilot licence a few years later. "But Korf still understood so much about flying that he could have completed a visual flight at a pinch," declared his chief pilot Anton Schulze. Previously a non-commissioned officer and fighter pilot in the German armed forces, Schulze began his career in civil aviation with Deutsche Taxiflug, and flew large business jets for Willy Korf's operations for more than 25 years.

Willy Korf, meanwhile, not only encouraged fare-paying businesspeople and other wealthy passengers to travel on his aircraft, but also took every opportunity to impress his clients and business partners with a free ride on the Do 27 owned by SÜDRA in Kehl.

On one occasion, in 1960, Korf picked up a married couple – friends of his from the United States who were on holiday in Europe – along with their copious luggage, in the Swiss town of Lugano, in order to fly them to SÜDRA in Kehl. The flight required crossing the Alps at high altitude – and clear visibility. However, the weather deteriorated badly during the flight. After the Dornier had barely made it in one piece over the St Gotthard Pass, despite the rough conditions, Korf sneaked through valleys and along rivers and railway lines over the Black Forest to the Rhine Valley near Freiburg. "From there it was only a stone's throw to Kehl, where we landed safely at our small factory airfield," Korf later recalled. Unaware of the danger they had been in, the American passengers "disembarked as if nothing had happened. Afterwards we spent a delightful evening sampling Alsatian cuisine at the Crocodile restaurant in Strasbourg." Apparently, the treacherous flight hadn't spoiled anyone's appetite.

Deutsche Taxiflug's commercial services got off to a flying start. Carrying 11,000 passengers in its first year, this figure more than doubled in 1960 to 24,000 passengers. The number of flights also doubled to more than 9,000, with the Dorniers averaging 2.5 passengers per flight. Six additional Do 27s were acquired, making a fleet of ten aircraft, and other new purchases including an Italian twin-engine Piaggio P.166 and a Twin Pioneer.

Apart from its base in Mannheim, Deutsche Taxiflug aircraft were stationed in Frankfurt, Hamburg and Munich. In 1961, Korf planned to use twin-engine Do 28s to fly business travellers to and from the Hanover Fair daily from cities such as Stuttgart and Kiel. He even considered the possibility of starting a helicopter taxi service between the exhibition centre and central Hanover.

However, the dream of commercial aviation would not last long. The Piaggio caused a serious accident on a flight between Zurich and Milan; two other accidents involving Dorniers heading for an island in the North Sea, as well as a crash during take-off in snowy Geneva, resulted in multiple deaths, with prominent foreigners among the victims. This flurry of disasters ruined Taxiflug's reputation in no time at all. Passenger numbers fell sharply, and it seemed increasingly unlikely that the company would reach breakeven point.

Korf managed to merge Deutsche Taxiflug with Air Lloyd AG, an aviation company in the Gerling Group, before selling it lock, stock and barrel to Gerling in 1963. From then on, Korf flew solo. Alone above the clouds, accompanied by his professional pilots, he didn't need to fear for the safety of paying passengers anymore. The only lives for which he was responsible in the air were his own and those of his staff.

By the time he turned thirty, Willy Korf had already founded three companies and run them simultaneously

(SÜDRA, Südwest-Plastic and Deutsche Taxiflug) while also working for the family business in Au and the affiliated Korf-Transport. His portfolio of commercial ventures was impressive: manufacturing welded wire mesh, producing plastic motorboats, and aviation. And so, on 1 November 1959, a few weeks after his thirtieth birthday, he decided to set up his first holding company for the dual purposes of centralized control and accounting benefits. It was to be the first of his many such umbrella companies.

Korf chose to locate his new holding company in Baden-Baden. This was not a random decision, but – as always with Korf – the product of a well-thought-out and brilliantly executed negotiating strategy. For the bon vivant Korf, the sophisticated spa town with its magnificent views of the Black Forest had always been his preferred location. Yet, with his entrepreneurial mind, Korf was also determined to extract as much as possible in return.

A letter dated 25 September 1959 to Walter Holdermann, the mayor of Baden-Baden, was full of attempts at beguilement, subtle implication, and self-confident showmanship of the sort that Korf was inclined to exhibit whenever a business relationship or a pecuniary advantage was in the offing. Korf mentioned that he had already proposed siting his holding company in Baden-Baden "in the right circumstances" – naturally, as long as he could rent suitable office space in the town and find a plot of land to build a family home. The question now was, would the mayor be able to help? As Korf noted: "The holding company will unify all my businesses, which will have a total turnover next year of about 50 million marks. Of course, this will generate a certain amount of corporation and other taxes for the city, too." To prompt further discussion, he also extended an offer which he would come to use often in future: "why don't we pick you up with our plane in Baden-Baden and fly you here in order to show you my main business operation?"

The letter certainly had its intended effect in the economically depressed town. On the reverse of the document, the mayor's office noted: "The visit took place on 30 November. Mr Korf has gained a firm foothold with his company in Kehl. Mr. Korf's project in Baden-Baden absolutely deserves our support."

The umbrella company Korf Handels- und Verwaltungsgesellschaft GmbH & Co. KG took up residence on Ludwig-Wilhelm-Strasse. In 1962, it was renamed Korf Industrie und Handel GmbH & Co. KG. For the next two decades, it served as the headquarters for the procurement of raw materials and the sale of finished products. It was Willy Korf's tax-efficiency scheme and securities account rolled into one. Significantly, it was also a reflection of just how much the Korf Group revolved around its eponymous leader. Despite all subsequent corporate adjustments, shareholdings and external involvement, and regardless of various supervisory committees and boardroom disputes, in the long run only one man – Willy Korf himself – ran the show and carried responsibility for failure.

But alongside this business milestone, November 1959 also turned out to be a fateful month in Willy Korf's private life. On 16 November, there was a naming ceremony for a ship owned by Stinnes in Hamburg, to which Willy Korf had been invited. Also in attendance was the young Brigitte Kaiser from Frankfurt, whose father owned the best-known brand in prefabricated concrete ceiling construction. Brigitte had travelled to the port of Hamburg for the event, without much enthusiasm and only at the insistent bidding of her mother. At the champagne reception, Willy Korf was determined to be introduced to the beautiful blonde woman who had captured his attention, and so met his future wife for the first time.

Later that week, he wrote a formal letter to Brigitte Kaiser's mother, requesting permission to see her daughter again. In the months that followed, he spared neither effort nor expense in his pursuit of Brigitte. Concrete ceilings reinforced with wire mesh proved to be the beginning of not just a corporate relationship, but also a romantic one.

Brigitte, who always appeared a few centimetres taller than

Willy Korf because of her fondness for high-heeled shoes, had been an only child, just like him. Months of persistent courtship (it wasn't until the following year that his intended finally visited Korf in Baden-Baden for the first time) were followed in 1962 by a glamorous wedding at Königstein Castle in Taunus.

That same year, their first daughter, Astrid, was born, to be followed by another girl, Sylvia, in 1965. Their mother was an attractive, extrovert woman, who was ever mindful of her image. Henceforth, she would become an important part of Korf's public persona – a focus for press photographers and an elegant companion whenever Korf attended receptions and visited statesmen across the world. Although she had no influence over his business, in many respects Korf's life revolved around Brigitte, the 'first lady' at the centre of his steel empire.

As the Korfs honeymooned in 1962, however, fresh trouble was already brewing for Willy on the steel front, despite the earlier appeasement of his competition. Wielding its 'reduced-edge weldmesh' patent, Baustahlgewebe GmbH had already tried in 1960 to force independent producers into a licensing system that would bind them to delivery quotas and fixed prices. Willy Korf, despite cultivating an appearance of standing up to the cartel, hadn't been as defiant as it seemed.

At times when he had still traded exclusively for Gustav Korf OHG, he himself – via an intermediary – had been indirectly dependent on the steel mesh cartel. Indeed, it was only through Baustahlgewebe that he'd entered the steel business in the first place. As he watched more and more small producers sign the licences, Korf stubbornly resisted, all the while driving up the price of his own agreement. In 1961, he finally sold all three SÜDRA plants for around 20 million marks to Klöckner, one of the shareholders in Baustahlgewebe, keeping just the company and parts of its manufacturing operation in Kehl for himself.

The 20 million price tag seemed like a good investment to the big boys in the Ruhr, because Korf also contractually undertook not to produce or trade in 'spot-welded reinforcement mesh' in Germany for ten years. Their troublesome competitor finally seemed to have been paid off and eliminated. Korf was 32 years old and suddenly very rich: "From then on", he told *Welt am Sonntag* in 1980, "I could have retired and lived off the interest."

But Korf's talent for retaining accomplished legal experts, such as Otfried Lieberknecht, had been underestimated in the Ruhr. This shrewd antitrust lawyer had been involved in the wrangle with Baustahlgewebe GmbH and the sale of SÜDRA's production plants. Acting on Lieberknecht's advice, Willy Korf had allowed Baustahlgewebe GmbH to include the phrase 'friction-locked connection of wires' in the wording of the agreement as a distinguishing feature of spot-welded mesh. Korf was barred from producing not only wire mesh of this type, but presumably of any type, since there was no other economically viable method – until he personally devised one.

To do so, he teamed up with his cousin Helmhold Schneider in Altenkirchen, who already had some experience as a plastics producer. "Willy arrived here", Schneider recalled, "with his cheque from Düsseldorf still uncashed, shouting: 'I've got an idea! Suppose we …?'" Indeed, they could – and together they set about manually developing 'composite steel mesh'.

Whereas crossing wires had previously been secured by spot-welding them together, Korf and Schneider achieved the same effect by means of plastic extrusion – without the need for a 'frictional connection'. The resulting stability was sufficient to cast the mesh in concrete; nothing more was needed, for the internal strength was provided by the setting process. Korf had the machines for the new process developed in his recently established mechanical engineering department at what was left of SÜDRA in Kehl, and then built by a company in Krefeld. The production of steel mesh could begin again.

As Schneider later recalled, it must have given his cousin enormous pleasure to show the mesh cartel once again that he was more innovative than the major players. After all, his innovation was more than just a ploy to circumvent a contract, as was subsequently claimed for decades; it was genuinely pioneering. The fact that this method of connection was novel and also functional, especially for large wire diameters that couldn't easily be spot-welded, was finally confirmed when it was approved by the building authorities.

Naturally, lawyers from Düsseldorf were quick to use every trick in the book to contest the new production process. But Korf's long-standing rivals were no longer able to resort to the legal threat of the 'reduced-edge weldmesh' patent. Even so, the dispute led to arbitration proceedings that dragged on for years. And despite its potential, Korf's composite steel mesh was not ultimately a commercial success.

His competitors had hoped that Korf, now a multi-millionaire, would quietly retire and live off the interest of his SÜDRA plant sales. But Willy had other ideas. He had been completely immersing himself in the world of steel, devouring every book and expert opinion on the industry. Meanwhile, his entrepreneurial imagination continued to fire on all cylinders.

Between 1962 and 1964, he took over several branches of Hugo Stinnes OHG following its collapse, including the one in Munich, and also Walzstahl AG in Basel, which would become the centre of Korf's activities in Switzerland. But 20 million marks offered him even greater possibilities. He could fulfil a long-cherished dream and become a steel manufacturer himself – assuming he was crazy enough to challenge this most traditional of all industries.

CHAPTER 4
On dangerous ground

"We're not afraid of thunderstorms, air pockets or turbulence. That's what makes flying fun!"

No one could say that Willy Korf hadn't been warned. However, his experience with the cartel Baustahlgewebe GmbH had only been a taste of the flaws and idiosyncrasies of the West German steel industry, with its scorn for free-market transparency. The dominant manufacturers and suppliers were neither innovative, cost-effective or customer-friendly, as might be expected of market leaders. Instead, they were characterised by inflexibility, inefficiency, and arrogance.

The bastions of the established players seemed utterly impregnable. Trusts and traditions, collusion and conventions, price agreements and production quotas were the order of the day. This was an environment where wheelers and dealers thrived, and where political influence always trumped simple economics. The price of a tonne of rolled steel was anything but fixed for industrialists who lived by free market rules.

Economists believing in competition had long been horrified by what went on in the steel industry, and the control exerted by its main actors. In the nineteenth century, blast furnaces were built next to iron ore and coal mines, steelworks and foundries were added to them, which in turn attracted machinery factories. As if by magic, the conglomerates making up heavy industry emerged – a sector which was to dominate economic activity for over a century.

By the 1930s, heavy industry accounted for about 80 per cent of total industrial turnover in Germany. No wonder then, Korf once wrote in a published article, that the steel sector and its managers considered themselves the masters of the economy – especially since steel, originally a raw material for weapons, had such high political significance.

Korf had no illusions about the industry he was breaking into. He understood that, because of the conglomerates' monopoly status, "in the steel industry, instead of being competitive, people were used to simply distributing their products. Whenever sales dropped during economic crises, action was quickly taken – at least in Europe – to find a remedy by means of cartels."

The ramifications of this market interference were also of a technological nature, for this was hardly a climate conducive to innovation. The blast furnace, still the main piece of equipment used to make iron out of ore, was already about 130 years old when Korf entered the sector. Even modern 'converters' were merely modifications of the time-honoured smelting units invented by Gilchrist Thomas and Henry Bessemer, the only difference being that as the apparatus grew larger, so, too, did the sluggishness of the steel corporations.

Who could possibly disrupt a structure like this or capture market shares that had long been divvied out among the existing participants? The capital outlay required to build a new, integrated steelworks with an annual capacity of several million tonnes and the necessary sales network was so enormous that it was out of the question even for newly wealthy challengers like Korf.

Moreover, with the exception of a few specialist products, steel was a high-volume basic commodity with few distinguishing features to make the output of one steel mill better than another. Expressed in economic jargon, this meant that its price elasticity of demand was close to zero. In other words, if the price of a tonne of steel went up or down by 100 marks, the quantities purchased hardly changed. Production had to take place anyway – no more and no less. (Compare this to a luxury good like Coca-Cola, for example, more of which is drunk when the price drops.)

This situation alone was virtually an invitation to the industry to hand out market shares to its principal members and let them set their own prices. And it explains why the steel industry had been tightly organized in syndicates from the mid-1920s until the end of the Second World War (a topic meticulously described by the journalist and steel expert Helmut Uebbing in his book *Stahl schreibt Geschichte*, or 'Steel Writes History').

In 1926, eight hitherto independent industrialists on the Ruhr merged their plants to form Vereinigte Stahlwerke (United Steelworks), one of the initiators being August Thyssen, creating a huge steel trust employing 200,000 workers and producing almost 7 million tonnes of crude steel and 26 million tonnes of hard coal annually. Vereinigte Stahlwerke proceeded to claim prescribed sales quotas (i.e. enforced market shares) of between 46 and 89 per cent (depending on product class) in the steel industry's sales organizations. However, there was almost nothing in terms of new developments, improvements or streamlining in this mega-network. Instead, Vereinigte Stahlwerke plodded through the Great Depression, Hitler, and then the war, before being broken up by the Allies.

For a few short years during the post-war reconstruction boom, the West German market was temporarily free of cartels and sales syndicates. At this time, demand was so high that manufacturers quickly sold everything they produced. But the Treaty establishing the European Coal and Steel Community (ECSC) reintroduced complex regulation of the market, including extensive scope for state and industry intervention. And, to make matters worse, just as Korf was planning his own steelworks in the mid-1960s, Germany was drifting towards another carve-up of its own market.

In autumn 1965, the economy went into recession, reducing

the demand for steel. Exports to countries outside the ECSC were only possible with massive price dumping, because steel on the world market was far cheaper than in the price bubble of Europe, which was protected by trade tariffs. By summer 1966, incoming orders were well down on the previous year, and this lower revenue was compounded by significant wage increases which bore no relationship to productivity or performance.

Against this backdrop, representatives of the West German steel industry told the government and the ECSC of their intention to get a grip on falling prices by means of sales syndicates. There was no objection from the European Parliament. Karl Schiller, the Minister of Economic Affairs, and the rest of the cabinet also agreed. They hoped that the planned Rolled Steel Syndicates would serve as "training centres for new steel mergers", because larger corporations with more market power would bolster Germany's position on the world stage. 'Big is beautiful' was the motto, and visionaries dreamed of giant steelworks producing 10 million or possibly 20 million tonnes year in, year out. Even the trade unions, fearing further job losses in the crisis-ridden steel industry, gave their backing to the syndicates.

The steel industry proposed that 38 companies, ranging from the large corporations in the Ruhr to the smallest steel mills, be subsumed within four limited liability companies to be known as 'Rolled Steel Syndicates', one for each of the main locations of the steel industry in West Germany. Syndicate West was dominated by Thyssen, Mannesmann and Krupp, Syndicate Westphalia by Hoesch, Syndicate North by Klöckner and the state-owned Salzgitter-Werke, and Syndicate South by Arbed in Saarland. While the member companies would still be allowed to sell certain specialist products on their own account, from now on their wire rod and reinforcing steel could only be sold via the Rolled Steel Syndicates. As a result, when it came to these and many other products, the choice available to buyers was reduced from over thirty to just four suppliers at a stroke.

In February 1967, this anti-market system received the

blessing of the High Authority of the European Coal and Steel Community in Luxembourg. The corporate masters breathed a sigh of relief: they now felt safer from price erosion, and also safer from the threat posed by undesirable upstarts and newcomers. The coordinated pricing policy, coupled with their centralized, modernized production, would quickly bring to heel anyone who dared to make steel more cheaply.

However, this strategy was not strictly legal. Back in 1957, a new competition law of the European Economic Community (EEC) came into force. In the spirit of maximizing free trade, it had banned cartels and syndicates, much to the acclaim of a new generation of economic theorists. One of them was a young professor of civil, economic and employment law at Ruhr University in Bochum named Kurt Biedenkopf – a pupil of Franz Böhm from the Freiburg School of economic thought and an associate of Ludwig Erhard, the West German Chancellor between 1963 and 1966.

Biedenkopf was appointed rector in 1967, and was destined for a long political career, including the premiership of Saxony after German reunification. A champion of the free market, he was a sharp critic of European coal subsidies. But of course, he was also aware of the counterargument: "The steel industry invoked the Treaty of Paris [the Treaty establishing the European Coal and Steel Community], which didn't treat distortions of competition as strictly as the subsequent rules of the European Community. Although the Treaty of Rome was already in force, the Treaty of Paris was still applied to coal and steel because it was much more generous towards such entities as Rolled Steel Syndicates." Biedenkopf would later join Willy Korf in the campaign against distortions of competition in the steel industry.

The clear breach of the new European antitrust laws led to a series of cat-and-mouse games between the Rolled Steel Syndicates and industry watchdogs. At this time, Renate Höing was a secretary at Rheinstahl Hüttenwerke in Essen, which was part of Syndicate Westphalia dominated by Hoesch AG. Höing worked for Rheinstahl's sales director, so she saw what went on behind the scenes. "Because it was a cartel, everything was very secretive," she explained.

> The Federal Cartel Office had no idea what was happening. The managers' meetings were held in great secrecy at the Federation of the German Steel Industry in Düsseldorf. They arranged the quotas among themselves: if someone couldn't keep up and others had surpluses, adjustments were made so that no one would go under. That was the whole point: prices were coordinated. We rented a basement in Dortmund near Hoesch's headquarters. Occasionally, we caught wind of the fact that the Cartel Office was about to send someone over to check up on us. All the files that no one from the Cartel Office was supposed to see had been marked, and they were immediately carted away to the basement in cars. However, the third time this happened, inspectors from the Cartel Office discovered the basement just as our estate car was on its way there with a mountain of files. Fortunately, the driver received our warning just in time and the documents were left in the car. It was like a scene from a James Bond film!

Meanwhile, Willy Korf had already made great strides in planning his own steelworks. His idea was to deploy a 'magic triangle', consisting of two advanced technologies and a resulting revolutionary steel mill concept, to break the stranglehold of the established steel corporations. This approach would enable Korf to produce the two standard products – rolled steel and rebars – cheaply and efficiently, and also to deliver them to his customers so quickly that he'd be able to wrest market share even from the powerful cartels.

The first side of the magic triangle was the electric arc furnace – a cheaper, more efficient alternative to the monstrous blast furnaces of old. Blast furnaces, which are between 25 and 30 metres tall, are charged from the top with coke, ore (iron oxide), and additives such as limestone. Within the furnace, oxygen is removed from the iron oxide in the coke-fired smelting process, reducing it to 'pig' iron. The molten iron is regularly tapped, allowing it to flow out through an opening called a taphole. Crude steel is then produced using the LD (Linz-Donawitz) process, which involves blowing oxygen through and the addition of constituent alloying elements.

The electric arc furnace (EAF) has a diameter of 7 metres and a large lid which is swung off in order to fill the furnace with raw material, usually scrap, and lime (which together form the 'charge'). A huge electrode protrudes through the closed lid into the furnace. Between it and the charge at the bottom, a hot arc with a temperature of around 1,600 degrees centigrade is formed when the circuit is closed. The charge takes about 30 minutes to be transformed into liquid crude steel, which is then tapped. A furnace like this consumes a vast amount of electricity – 65,000 kilowatts or more , therefore an electric steel plant operation is heavily dependent on the price of electricity. Ultra-high power (UHP) electric arc furnaces use additional natural gas/oxygen burners. In Korf's early period, the input material for all electric arc furnaces was scrap, a problematic raw material due to its fluctuating supply, price, purity level and consequent quality. However, Korf already had a plan in mind to solve these snags.

The second side of the triangle was continuous casting, which was developed in the mid-1960s. This process eliminated the need for an expensive ingot mill, which was only economically viable if at least half a million tonnes of semi-finished casting products were rolled per year. In traditional ingot casting, the crude molten steel solidified in moulds, which necessitated lengthy secondary shaping involving a combination of mechanical and manual intermediate steps. In continuous casting, however, the molten steel is shaped into a strand with thin, solidified walls, which is then supported and transported by rollers. During cooling, the vertical strand is curved by the rollers to bring it into a horizontal position. Oxyacetylene torches are then used to cut the strand into manageable semi-finished units known as billets, which are then ready for final rolling.

Korf was the first person in Germany to realize that scrap fed electric arc furnaces could be combined with the continuous casting process, enabling a completely new manufacturing system which was the antithesis of the Ruhr corporations' enormous integrated steelworks. The mini steel mill was the final side of this magic triangle. Suddenly, small was beautiful.

The pioneers of the mini mill concept were based in northern Italy. The industrial region around the city of Brescia, provincial capital of the Lombardy region, had been home to family steel businesses for centuries. Elsewhere, they were mocked for their small scale of operation, disparagingly referred to as 'Bresciani', but their pedigree spoke for itself.

Once the largest armourers in Europe, the Bresciani had weathered their first crisis after the Thirty Years War, when central Europe no longer needed the weapons they produced. They stayed in business, and their descendants were just as successful. When it came to making reinforcing bar and rod, the modern Bresciani had the lowest costs and the leanest administrative structures imaginable. Hydroelectric power generated on the south side of the Alps was cheap, and in the typical family business, the father took delivery of scrap (the raw material) at the entrance and weighed it while the mother paid the suppliers in cash and wrote the invoices for outgoing rebars. Using the simplest of means, a handful of assistants produced wire rod from steel reclaimed from sources such as old railway tracks. However, this did not mean the Bresciani rejected innovation: while father Giovanni was still a master craftsman on the small rolling mill, son Luigi was already a qualified engineer and had introduced an electric furnace to make production even more efficient.

Korf had made contact with the Bresciani through his Munich-based Korf Eisenhandel company, which he had acquired from Stinnes in 1964. This trading subsidiary imported reinforcing steel from several of these Italian mini steel mills, and Korf wondered how they managed to make high-quality rebars with scrap sourced almost exclusively from southern Germany while undercutting the German corporations, despite the enormous freight costs involved in crossing the Alps twice (to import raw material and export the finished products). He visited many Bresciani and realized that the solution was simplicity. The Bresciani limited their output to a few common products, which also reduced the size of their rolling mills. Moreover, their administrative structure was pared down to the barest essentials.

With this model in mind, Korf set out to find a site for his reinforcing steel plant. Since 1955, he'd already had a foothold in the port of Kehl, where he still owned parts of the wire mills. He also knew that the Ruhr industry had little use for its scrap metal, and so sold it. The broad Rhine flowed slowly past his factory gates, and since large quantities of scrap were shipped from the Frankfurt–Mannheim–Karlsruhe conurbation to Basel, he nicknamed the river the 'scrap stream'. It would be central to his plan.

Korf's scheme was as follows: In Germany, about 450 kilos of scrap accrued per inhabitant each year. A mini steel mill with a capacity of 400,000 tonnes of crude steel (his plant had a similar capacity at first) needed about 450,000 tonnes of scrap. This in turn required a catchment area of a million people – one Korf didn't have to share with others. As he later wrote: "I planned to halt the scrap in Kehl, convert it there into steel products, and then sell them north of the Alps without having to spend the considerable freight costs incurred by the Bresciani." The port authorities in Kehl found the plan so compelling that they made another 100,000 square metres of land available to Korf, for no one else with such entrepreneurial spirit was interested in their wasteland.

However, the problems began almost immediately. There was certainly enough land, but not enough cheap electricity to run the electric arc furnace. Korf also needed more modern machinery and a better operating cost structure than the Bresciani, who paid significantly lower wages. Badenwerk AG, a state-owned power utility, was inflexible and not ready to deal with industrialists who wanted to take a different approach from the competition in this hitherto remote region. Only after the regional government in Stuttgart had intervened did the arduous negotiations over electricity prices finally reach a compromise at the end of 1967. By that time, the rolling mill for reinforcing steel had long been up and running (having taken just eight months to build), supplied with billets from French and German steel manufacturers until such time as the company's own electric furnaces went into operation. Time was running against Korf: amid the onset of a new economic crisis, the Rolled Steel Syndicates' cartel on the Ruhr had opened for business in February.

Despite working at great speed, another ten months passed before the two furnaces and an additional rolling mill were erected and Germany's first-ever scrap-based electric steel plant produced its first wire rod and reinforcing steel. On 1 January 1968, Korf merged all his Kehl enterprises to form Badische Stahlwerke AG. Instead of going public, ownership of the company was shared by Korf and a bank (Frankfurter Investitions- und Handelsbank), which held a 50 per cent stake.

Korf appointed Otfried Lieberknecht, the antitrust lawyer who in the meantime had moved to Düsseldorf, and Bert Pfluger, another legal expert, to the supervisory board. Pfluger, an auditor from Karlsruhe and consultant to other family business entrepreneurs, initially served as Korf's tax advisor, but soon also gave him the benefit of his expertise in corporate law. As fate would have it, Korf had found both his future executor (Lieberknecht, who, however, had nothing to execute after Korf's death) and the future trustee of his estate (Pfluger) early on.

In addition, a third advisor was already involved, albeit someone who didn't yet have a seat on any of Korf's boards. In his new Düsseldorf law firm, Lieberknecht's partner was a corporate lawyer named Max Kreifels, whose clients included Willy Schlieker – another risk-taking outsider like Korf. Being an authority when it came to devising the best strategic corporate structures, Kreifels rapidly became the legal architect of Korf's business network. But his influence on the aspiring steel entrepreneur was set to become far greater.

This steel mill in the port of Kehl, the first of its kind in Germany, was nothing less than a full-scale provocation. Why hadn't any of the key players, with their top engineers and strategists, come up with this idea? Why hadn't anyone tried their hand at small, scrap-based steel mills with continuous casting and an electric furnace?

Essentially, the idea of working with electric arc furnaces was nothing new, not even in Germany. "Electric furnaces were common long before Korf," recalled Dieter Spethmann, who later rose to become Thyssen's CEO.

> There were several of them at Deutsche Edelstahlwerke AG, where I was chairman from 1964. However, they were employed to produce special alloyed steels, not mass-produced steels. Korf's ground-breaking idea was to use them for reinforcing steel. This was only viable where three factors coincided: cheap scrap, low electricity prices, and favourable processing costs. And that was the case in Kehl.

Under these favourable conditions, mini steel plants were also more flexible because they could be switched on and off as required. Integrated steelworks with blast furnaces, by contrast, were tied to the continuous running times of chemical processes taking place in the pig iron stage. Thyssen, Krupp and the other companies additionally smelted the pig iron in 'converters' – cylindrical vessels in which the pig iron extracted was converted into steel. Iron from a blast furnace isn't yet steel, but more like cast iron: it can't be forged or rolled, and it breaks easily – because it's contaminated with carbon up to saturation point from the coke used as fuel. To eliminate most of the carbon, it has to be burnt out by blowing oxygen into the fire of the converter – only then is usable steel formed. The converters greatly complicated the chemical and operational processes before the final product was ready. Korf, on the other hand, by using scrap as his raw material, made do without a blast furnace or converter. And he was therefore able to significantly shorten the time following smelting, cutting his costs and increasing the plant's efficiency.

Korf's use of scrap was also one of the psychological reasons why the steel newcomer was regarded as an outsider by the Ruhr barons from the outset. Herbert Gienow, who later spent many years as chairman of the board of Klöckner, and at that time was involved in the groundwork for the foundation of Ruhrkohle AG, summed up the view of the big corporations in those years as follows: "The scrap-based electric steel process isn't really steel production as scrap is already steel. It's more akin to recycling, just supplemented by a small amount of molten pig iron or iron in some other form. In the eyes of the industry, the mini steel mills weren't really steel mills at all."

Accordingly, the big industrialists didn't deem people like Korf to be serious competitors, let alone potential members of their own elitist club. Indeed, electric steel from such mills actually had serious disadvantages because its quality was liable to fluctuate with the scrap used. But these reputational issues wouldn't matter to Korf, for whom the technology's key feature lay elsewhere.

The revolutionary advantage of mini steel mills (as their name suggests) was their small dimensions. "What people failed to realize," said Gienow, "is that mini steel mills slashed the previously insurmountable market entry threshold for newcomers like Korf. They just needed a tenth of the capital required for a blast furnace. This was soon to be a real game changer for both production and the market."

The established industrial players with their far wider product ranges also had misgivings about the continuous casting process, which was still in its infancy. Despite being adequate for reinforcing steel, it wasn't yet up to the demands of more complex products like spring steel. This didn't matter to Korf, however, because he only made reinforcing steel and wire rod.

Both technologically and ideologically, he was the new outsider, and he embraced this role. He did, however, make a half-hearted attempt to join the establishment in May 1968, by becoming a member of the Federation of the German Steel Industry in Düsseldorf, the official club of the powerful industrialists. But he only remained for five months, leaving in September after asserting that it merely served the interests of big corporations. To Willy Korf, this seemed to be proven by Syndicate West and Syndicate North letting him down when he tried to order steel billet feedstock for his rolling mills. Representatives of Syndicate South, for their part, even tried to persuade him to join their ranks, but in vain. Korf simply wasn't cut out for market regulation.

Although Korf and the syndicates tried to reach a compromise regarding raw material feedstock, in the end his terms couldn't be met, as they would have called into question the entire construct of this anti-competition structure. Talking to *Capital,* Korf, expressed angrily that: "After that argument we had there, after what I experienced and saw in those negotiations, even if they'd promised me God knows what and offered me twice the price, I'd always have declined. It's so phoney what's going on there, I would never consider joining a syndicate again." The man who loved being an outsider delighted the American readership of *Business Week* by summarizing the purpose of the Steel Federation as follows: "It exists to prevent competition. In the US, they'd put you in jail for something like that."

Just five years later, Korf would be swept by the tide straight into the establishment he so derided and quietly rejoin the Federation. But this was perhaps just another example of the ambivalent attitude to power he had always displayed.

Korf was the *enfant terrible* of the German steel industry even before he'd really started producing in earnest. In spite of everything, he'd garnered up to 20 per cent of the reinforcing steel market in northern German without joining any of the Rolled Steel Syndicates. A thorn in their side, he was perhaps similar to Friedrich Flick, also from Siegerland, who hadn't joined any of the syndicates either with his Maxhütte steelworks. But Flick preferred to profit quietly from his existence in the shadow of the controlled market; he wasn't one to give interviews or statements criticizing the powerful.

However, Korf was a different breed: he broke the unwritten rule that as long as everyone makes a living, there's no need to rock the boat. He ridiculed and pilloried the big players for their illegality. It's hardly surprising that the attitude to him at the Düsseldorf headquarters of the ultra-traditional Federation of the German Steel Industry, was somewhat hostile. On visiting the boardroom of Syndicate West, Korf was greeted with the brash question: "Are you sure you're welcome here?" Korf wasn't at all sure.

At least outwardly, though, the cartel sought to maintain decorum. "It's not nice to say unpleasant things on the phone about someone," a reporter from *Capital* was told in response to his question about Willy Korf. And one manager would do no more than reveal that: "Everyone sees Korf in their dreams – but actually they're nightmares!" The secretary Renate Höing remembered the fortnightly management meetings of Syndicate West: "Korf was always on the agenda because he constantly undercut their list prices. He was described as a very clever chap. Somehow they admired him, despite their disagreements."

The conflict came to a dramatic head on 23 November 1968. That day saw the official opening of Badische Stahlwerke in Kehl – the first time in more than 50 years that a German entrepreneur had founded a brand new steel mill of his own. And being Willy Korf, it was inevitable that he would use this occasion to denounce his fellow industrialists, in front of hundreds of guests of honour, on board a specially chartered ship. In his missionary zeal, he even went so far as to mock the "grandpas in the Ruhr". The "grandpas" might not have been very fond of each other either, but they also had eyes and ears on board, and they decided to set aside their differences, join forces and strike back.

The attack, however, didn't take place "that very day" as Korf later repeatedly alleged, recounting his role of David fighting multiple Goliaths. And it wasn't levelled because the Rolled Steel Syndicates felt threatened by additional competition, even though Korf had already announced on 22 November his intention to build a further steel and rolling mill with American partners in the port of Hamburg. What had caused the syndicates to snap was simply that the upstart, acerbic Korf had crossed a line with his verbal attacks. It seemed that only humiliation on this scale was capable of forging at least a temporary coalition among his maverick opponents, as they turned their attention away from their own deals in favour of sweet revenge. The castigation in Kehl was so deeply etched in the minds of the Ruhr barons that some of them refused to speak to Korf again for years.

Two weeks later, on 5 December 1968, the syndicates suddenly took concerted action, reducing their prices for reinforcing steel by 24 per cent to 305 marks per tonne, undercutting Korf by a vicious 85 marks. Syndicate West, with Thyssen, Krupp and Mannesmann at its head, consolidated its entire rebar production from fourteen to a single line. The syndicate's members were therefore able to superficially prove that they'd reduced their costs accordingly. The sole point of this endeavour was not, apparently, to streamline their business, but to take revenge on Korf.

Willy Korf now found himself in a quandary. In a losing battle of mutual underbidding, the big corporations would be able to hold out longer than he would with his new plant in Kehl. A manager of Syndicate West exclaimed – albeit somewhat prematurely – that down in Kehl they were "squealing like scalded cats". Crisis meetings in Baden-Baden went on day and night – until Korf hit upon the idea of turning to the court of public opinion again, where Davids usually receive more sympathy than Goliaths.

All of Korf's customers were invited to attend a gathering in

Offenburg, where Korf gave another rousing speech deploring this "attack against free competition". He even appealed to his customers to voluntarily pay higher prices and keep buying from him. Korf, the steel renegade, received academic and political support for his reasoning from Kurt Biedenkopf, the competition law expert at Ruhr University in Bochum, and simultaneously in Brussels from Ernst Albrecht, who at that time headed the Directorate-General for Competition at the European Commission, and later became the premier of Lower Saxony.

With Biedenkopf's assistance, Korf made a great show of posing before customers and the press as the victim – a strategy which was very well received in Brussels. Korf, who was a friend of Biedenkopf's wife, saw in the belligerent young competition law expert a kindred spirit. He found the support he'd been hoping for: "My aim", said Biedenkopf decades later, "was to allow the man to develop and not be driven out by big industrialists who appealed to the state for subsidized coking coal while selling their products below cost.

After studying the figures proving that the syndicates had distorted competition, Biedenkopf decided not to play the Cartel Office card, as that would have taken too long. Instead, he paid a visit to Franz-Josef Strauss, the Minister of Finance, whom he knew vaguely from meetings with the circle of advisers to Josef Abs, the head of Deutsche Bank. Biedenkopf explained to Strauss that businesses in receipt of government subsidies were undercutting Korf in order to oust their rival from the market, something that clearly clashed with his economic and financial policy. Strauss must have been impressed, for behind the scenes he even threatened to cut coking coal subsidies, a warning which did not go unheeded. Although the Rolled Steel Syndicates preferred to remain out of the limelight, they were dragged through the mud by the press, politicians and foreign governments. Even the Bundestag began debating what had come to be called the 'rebar war' against Korf.

Meanwhile, the European Community in Brussels was

preparing to sanction Syndicate West for the first time for breach of competition law. When news of this leaked out, Syndicate West raised its prices for rebars between 20 January and April 1969 to 335–350 marks per tonne, depending on its grade. But its members weren't off the hook. They'd encountered sizeable logistical problems by concentrating the entire output of several corporations on the same production line, causing nationwide delivery issues. Because of these shortages, orders were switched to foreign steel producers and the few German outsiders, above all Korf, and the price for reinforcing steel rose to giddy heights of up to 800 marks.

At the same time, an unexpected, unprecedented construction boom began in Germany – yet the syndicates were contractually obliged to keep selling their steel at their list price of 305 marks until the end of the year. Korf, originally supposed to have been forced out of the market, instead found himself able to cherry-pick the most profitable niches. He had successfully banked on the business press being behind him, as well as public opinion, and relied on his ability to convincingly play the victim, alongside his backing from free market economist Kurt Biedenkopf. Korf made sure he thanked him effusively for this, telling Biedenkopf that he had "saved his life" in the rebar war.

But Korf had been victorious partly because his suppliers and customers were convinced that his way of producing simple steels, taking inspiration from the Bresciani, was the future of the industry. Now Korf could pour scorn on those who had put so much pressure on him. He explained to *Industrie-Kurier* that if the bargain price of 305 marks per tonne had never been offered, steel prices would never have risen to the record levels that followed. Owing to artificial shortages and the concurrent construction boom in 1969, however, there had been additional demand for steel of 300,000 tonnes which, aggravated by dealers' empty warehouses, had taken the total shortfall to as much as 700,000 tonnes. The losers of this cut-throat competition were the consumers who had paid far more than the 'reasonable' price on the market in autumn 1968. But according to Korf's calculation, the initiators of this unfortunate saga also ended up paying over the odds: "The reinforcing steel campaign cost various plants at least as much as they paid in dividends. This price war was completely unnecessary and can only be explained in purely emotional terms."

Additionally, it heralded the early end of the Rolled Steel Syndicates. In July 1971, they were replaced by four Rationalization Groups, whose primary aim – instead of focusing on joint sales – was to restructure manufacturing locations and unify the corporations' investment planning. But even before they could get established, they were overwhelmed by the events of the following years. The syndicates' legacy (apart from the above-mentioned "training ground for mergers") was, essentially, nothing.

The lesson Korf took from this failed experiment was his David-and-Goliath strategy, which he pursued even more aggressively from that point onwards: "Don't be afraid of size. They can't unscrupulously slam the little guy up against the wall because that would cause public disgrace."

Years later, Korf's assessment would be confirmed by business weekly *Wirtschaftswoche:* "Ever since the steel companies tried it on, Korf has been a symbol of the fight against the giants." And David, defeater of the Goliaths, continued to repeat his refrain of guileless modesty into every microphone proffered to him: "We're just playing a little game, albeit a cheaper one."

CHAPTER 5

Land of the free

"We fly west to take advantage of the time zones and gain a few precious hours. Stretching the day to 30 hours or even longer is simply delightful!"

Korf was never a man to do things by halves. In his determination to explore boundaries – and push through them – he always sought to go one step further than his previous accomplishments. When Korf became frustrated with the parochialism of Germany and its steel industry, he began to look beyond its national borders. Where in the world could he satisfy his overwhelming desire for freedom, his yearning for travel, and his naively optimistic belief in the free market? The answer was obvious: The United States of America, self-proclaimed 'Land of the Free'.

To appreciate Willy Korf's empire-building success, it is essential to understand his relationship with the USA. Korf first travelled to the motherland of capitalism in 1957, as part of an organized study group. Having arrived, he immediately felt at home. This vast country of opportunity, where everything was bigger, taller, and wider than in Europe, cast a spell over Korf – just as it had done to many visionary capitalists before him. He became, and remained, a lifelong supporter of the United States.

A photo taken during that first trip shows 27-year-old Korf on board a ferry, with a pensive expression and hat in hand, against the backdrop of a majestic bridge. It was during this visit that he resolved to become one of the first post-war German entrepreneurs to invest and manufacture in the USA. But Korf knew he wouldn't succeed without local advice and assistance. Before long, he was making frequent trips to the USA, using his customary skills to develop contacts across the country. This network would shape his business activities for years to come.

Just at the right time, the name of a particularly adept lawyer was brought to Korf's attention. He was based in New York and, being of German-Jewish origin, spoke Korf's mother tongue. The recommendation came from Julius Hoffmann, the German consul general in New York. And so, in 1958 – just one year after first stepping onto American soil – Korf found himself in the modest offices of Otto L. Walter, whose address signalled his intention to rise up in the world – for Wall Street was no place for those lacking ambition.

1950s New York was full of German-Jewish law firms; indeed, German was the unofficial second official language of jurisprudence. Hitler's campaign of terror had triggered a wave of immigration from Germany and Austria in the 1930s, and many of the best legal minds had managed to escape to America just in time. Walter was one of these émigrés, as was his Viennese secretary, known to everyone as simply Elsie. Korf later recalled the lawyer's clear eyes and the sense of "calm, fatherly care" he exuded which "didn't really suit a native of Bavaria!" Born in Hof, Walter even had relevant industrial experience: during the war, he'd been placed in charge of a smelter in New Jersey. As a lawyer and consultant, he specialized in tax law and mainly served German clients seeking to gain a business foothold in the USA. He was ideal for Korf.

Korf quickly realized that Walter (whom he'd soon simply call Otto) was "the right adviser for our American interests". The lawyer turned out to be a shrewd judge of character, able to tell whenever proposed business deals seemed overly optimistic – a skill that Korf sadly lacked. Walter was therefore usually the first to rein in Korf's exuberance, but he also became the main voice to which Korf listened.

Some 30 years after they first met, Korf was asked to contribute to a commemorative volume marking Walter's eightieth birthday. He expressed his gratitude to him in the preface: "On one occasion, he managed to dissuade me at the last minute from going into partnership with people who were obviously financed by the Mafia." For a non-Jewish German entrepreneur, a 'goy', it was an outstanding honour to be asked to pay tribute in this way to a Jew who, like so many of those persecuted by the Nazis, had lost family members in German concentration camps. This alone speaks volumes about the reputation Korf earned in the USA over a matter of decades. In the meantime, Walter's simple offices had expanded into the law firm Walter, Conston, Alexander & Green, with chambers on the prestigious Park Avenue. Partner Henry Conston in particular had long since become a trusted aide in Korf's pursuit of the American dream.

Incidentally, Otto L. Walter and his wife Fran were the American couple with whom Willy Korf had stared death in the face when he'd personally flown them over the Alps in a propeller plane, in disastrous weather conditions, during their summer holiday in 1960. In a letter written to Korf in 1989, Walter thanked him for his kind words, adding his own recollection of the near-tragic flight: "Experiencing sudden danger on all sides, overcoming it, and returning to business as usual would make a great template for a biography of Korf!" Of course, Walter had no idea what lay around the corner for his friend, flying in treacherous weather, just a year later.

At the end of 1959, just over two years after his first overseas visit, Korf (with Walter's assistance) acquired three American business partners from Chicago, who gave him the necessary capital injection to set up his first US company. As was customary in the USA, it carried a name that spoke of big dreams: Trans-American Steel Corporation, or TASCO for short. This was an early indication that it would not be enough for Willy Korf to pursue isolated undertakings here and there in the

USA – he wanted to unfurl his entrepreneurial spirit right across the American continent. Already in control of three businesses and a recently founded holding company in Germany by age 30, he arrived on the American scene with the zeal of a would-be conqueror.

Korf and his three partners began producing steel mesh for the construction industry in the small town of Kenosha, in the northern state of Wisconsin, due to its proximity to Chicago. Drawn wire – the primary material for the new factory – was supplied by SÜDRA in Kehl. However, this bold venture with highly complex logistics for an industrialist with limited experience was ill-fated from the outset. Not much is known about Korf's first foreign enterprise; he himself spoke only of "a chain of unfortunate circumstances". What is certain, though is that Korf didn't give up at this hurdle.

Despite the problems, in 1961, he paid off his former partners and simply relocated the factory a few hundred miles southeast to North Carolina, which at that time still had a largely undeveloped industrial structure. In the nondescript town of High Point, which had never anticipated large-scale industrial investment, those in charge offered him building land on very favourable terms, and there was also an abundance of cheap labour in the area. Seen thus, the conditions were similar to those under which Korf would set up his first mini steelworks in Kehl a few years later. Once established, the wire mesh plant at High Point, with its railway siding on the edge of huge coniferous forests, began slowly to flourish. But it was not to be Korf's only project in the hospitable south-eastern states.

The same tiny town was also home to a long-established spring factory, the National Springs Corporation, which also had a branch in Tupelo, Mississippi. National Springs produced spring cores for the US furniture industry. In 1962, Korf initially used a loan to buy out the ailing company and straightaway made TASCO its supplier of drawn wire for spring production. Korf described this as the "clean-up phase" of his first American operations. But it was at this point that the German market took up his attention for a few years, as his battle with Baustahlgewebe GmbH continued to rage and his plans to open his own steel mill in Kehl neared completion.

To manage his activities on both fronts, Korf's subsequent routine amounted to flying back and forth across the Atlantic, living around meetings and appointments in different time zones as he tried to be everywhere at once. For the time being, as far as his transatlantic connections were concerned, he was still entirely reliant on the scheduled services of major airlines – and the telephone, on which he would continue to hone his communication skills.

The technological synergy between the two countries on either side of the Atlantic soon materialized. Korf's model plant in Kehl, opened in 1968, wasn't just the first mini steel mill in Germany (there were already dozens in the USA by that time, or as Korf put it: "America is a paradise for mini steel plants") – it was also intended to become less dependent on scrap metal as a raw material as soon as possible. True, scrap made it possible to dispense with blast furnaces and converters in steel production. But scrap was beset by three snags.

Firstly, its price went up and down all the time like any true commodity. Secondly, the German steel companies, which controlled the scrap market, maintained their strategy of making life difficult for the burgeoning competition from electric steel mills by manipulating the price of scrap, while simultaneously profiting from long-term supply contracts with iron ore mines abroad. And thirdly, the quality of scrap metal was almost as volatile as its price due to impurity variations.

"scrap is a crazy commodity, with price fluctuations of up to 100 per cent and open to manipulation," pronounced Korf. When the trade journal *Rohstoff-Rundschau* asked him how he thought the scrap price might develop, all he could say was: "The price of scrap is just as impossible to predict as the price of gold, the stock market or the dollar exchange rate." After his plant in Kehl had been running for a year, Korf noted that scrap had gone up in price by 50 per cent, reaching 180 German marks per tonne. By contrast, the price of iron ore, the traditional raw material of the steel industry, had stagnated or even declined slightly on the world market. The steel companies in the Ruhr were laughing all the way to the bank.

Korf told his engineers to find an alternative to scrap that didn't need a blast furnace and could hence be used in mini steelworks. Back in 1963, when the plant in Kehl was still just a blueprint in Willy Korf's imagination, they came across a promising technology: direct iron ore reduction (DRI). Steel strategists all over the world had been working on this method for decades, the very first experiments having been carried out in 1936. Hundreds of patents had been filed, and almost every German steel company had trialled some form of direct iron ore reduction or other – but no reliable method had yet been devised. Whereas in a blast furnace, the oxygen is only removed from the ore or iron oxide when it reaches molten state, reducing it to liquid pig iron, in direct reduction (as its name suggests), reduction takes place 'directly', i.e. in a solid state. This creates porous 'sponge iron' – iron lumps that look like sharp-edged sponges due to their pores. Sponge iron only contains very small amounts of oxygen and almost no slag; experts refer to a high degree of metallization. Sponge iron is therefore highly pure and, just like scrap, can be directly processed into crude steel in an electric arc furnace.

Iron ore used in the direct reduction process should ideally be in the form of pellets with a diameter of about one centimetre. These pellets are converted into sponge iron with the help of reducing gas at a temperature below 1,000 degrees, i.e. far below the melting point of iron. This results in ore with an iron content of about 50 to 65 per cent and a degree of metallization of roughly 95 per cent, which can then be used as raw material to make crude steel in an electric arc furnace.

Alongside its independence from scrap and blast furnaces, another advantage of the direct reduction process is that an electric arc furnace can be charged continuously instead of only in batches (as with scrap) allowing for computerized process control. Moreover, unlike a blast furnace, a reduction plant doesn't produce any toxic waste gases, merely water vapour, thereby offering more flexibility over its location. But Korf was equally aware of the direct reduction plant's key disadvantage, namely the scale of its output, which is only about a tenth to a sixth of a blast furnace's crude iron production.

All this had been theoretically researched and established as a feasible alternative to both the blast furnace process and the use of scrap in an electric steel plant. But where could any successful practical examples of the technique be seen? Once again, Korf turned to the USA for answers. In 1967, during one of his regular visits there, he heard about the Midland Ross Corporation from Cleveland, Ohio, which operated a laboratory in Toledo called the Surface Combustion Division. Working largely in secret, this lab had developed what was known as Midrex direct reduction in a project headed by engineer Donald Beggs. Midland Ross put its first commercial plant into operation at the steelworks of the Gilmore Steel Corporation in Portland, Oregon. Korf decided to get in touch with them.

Right from the start, the 'chemistry' between the development engineers of Surface Combustion and Willy Korf was excellent. They shared a determination to be the first industrialists in the world to operate an economically efficient direct reduction plant – and to use it for steel production in both the USA and Europe. They had every chance of success, because the Midrex process had a key advantage over other direct reduction concepts: its cost.

It used the method of 'gas reforming', where the waste gas from reduction was combined with natural gas and then completely recycled to produce fresh reduction gas, cutting costs considerably. However, with natural gas being the main reduction agent, there was the risk of a new dependency. Korf, having managed to move away from both coke and scrap, underestimated this risk. Although future energy crises weren't yet foreseeable, it was inevitable that reduction plants running on natural gas would eventually be hit, given the price link of gas to oil. At the start of this venture, though, natural gas was cheap. For Korf, the prospects were too good to ignore.

Consequently, far-reaching partnership agreements between the cutting-edge Americans and the ambitious German were soon signed. And hoping to benefit from this new production method, in October 1967 Korf founded the Georgetown Steel Corporation in Georgetown, South Carolina, with Midland Ross taking a 25 per cent stake. Again choosing an east coast state with limited industrial infrastructure, yet close to his processing plants in North Carolina, Korf built his second mini steelworks – with an upstream Midrex direct reduction plant, of course.

The 'magic triangle' consisting of the electric arc furnace, continuous casting and a mini steel mill had, in conjunction with direct reduction, become the most advanced steelworks concept of its time. According to Korf's calculations, the Midrex mini steelworks had a 50 per cent advantage over large integrated steelworks in terms of investment and production costs. This signified an economic revolution, since until then the only way to cut costs had been to raise production volumes. In those years, demand for steel was widely expected to increase, and the existing large steelworks were already operating at full capacity. Because of the vast investment costs involved in building new blast furnaces, the additional ones needed to meet this rising demand would only go onstream in four or five years at the earliest – and even then there wouldn't be enough. Moreover, they'd require an enormous infrastructure and huge sites, while the failure or even shutdown of a blast furnace due to any disruption always meant a small disaster for the steel plant. Flexible mini steel mills like the one in Kehl, commissioned in less than a year and switched on or off almost at will, could therefore neatly fill the gaps in demand, whether in Germany or the USA.

As in Kehl, the US plant was to produce reinforcing steel and wire rod using the electric steel process. The was a strategic decision because, as in Germany, Korf wanted to make his operations less dependent on external supplies. And he chose South Carolina simply because he wanted the new plant to be on the Eastern Seaboard of the USA, preferably halfway between New York and Florida.

Never before had a foreigner dared to open a plant in the biggest steel manufacturing country in the free world – and so far away from the traditional mining regions in Pennsylvania and the Midwest. Despite the large steel markets in the south-eastern states, steel companies in Europe had never been tempted to invest in America, chiefly because they were deterred by the significantly overvalued dollar, worth about 4 marks in 1967, which made local labour costs exorbitant. Instead, they relied on a thriving export trade, since the Americans themselves could never produce as cheaply as in Europe. But this was a fallacy that would unravel within in just a few years as the dollar exchange rate slipped slowly but surely downwards.

As usual, Korf had judged his leap across the Atlantic far more optimistically than the German traditionalists, who had all condemned it as too risky. Either the dollar would drop significantly in the not-too-distant future, he reasoned, melting away the Europeans' export advantage, or the US government would introduce import tariffs to encourage domestic production.

Korf also included other monetary gains in his calculation, such as the generous support from South Carolina, which granted him investment and training subsidies, and also stepped in to broker low electricity and gas rates. The regional electricity utility even laid a mains electricity cable with a length of 2½ kilometres (1½ miles) to Korf's plant and installed a transformer at the end of it – all at its own expense. Furthermore, the newly incorporated Georgetown Steel was exempted from corporation tax for ten years. Korf had clearly used his smooth-talking skills acquired in Kehl to successfully lobby local politicians. He also persuaded the town to slash the asking price for the building plot by half a million dollars, by which point, it was almost being given to him for free!

Construction proceeded swiftly, and in August 1969, after just nine months, Korf saw his labours come to fruition in the form of the first US steel produced in Georgetown. The plant had an annual capacity of 300,000 tonnes. Sited in Winyah Bay, it enjoyed almost direct access to the Atlantic and hence unlimited transport options by water (as was the case in Kehl with the Rhine). In addition, to provide Georgetown Steel with its own wire-making plant based on the Kehl model, Korf founded the Andrews Wire Corporation just 30 kilometres (18 miles) away in Andrews, South Carolina. Its main product was high-quality spring wire. Willy Korf had finally arrived in the USA.

When Georgetown Steel was officially opened on 17 April 1970, the Midrex plant was not yet part of production, although it had already been under construction for several months. Nevertheless, there was no shortage of pomp and ceremony at the official opening – and in this regard, too, Willy Korf and the USA were a perfect match for each other. He'd invited 250 guests, many of whom were flown in on wide-bodied Boeing jets from Germany, France, the UK, Austria, Switzerland and Brazil. Two US federal senators, as well as a congressman, and the governor of South Carolina were on hand. There were also representatives of Kehl and Badische Stahlwerke, along with a member of the Bundestag and a state secretary. However, the best-known German politician to attend was none other than Korf's old pal Karl Wienand, the chief whip of the Social Democrats.

If the US dignitaries had been expecting words of gratitude from the German entrepreneur they'd welcomed into their midst, they weren't disappointed. The USA was a country where hard work and good ideas paid off, declared Korf, who'd previously lauded the land of unlimited opportunity in the German media: "It's a country with free competition and fair rules."

Speaking in English, Korf explained to his audience that his local small steel mills would strengthen resilience to economic crisis. He also expressed his desire for a harmonious relationship (a clear reference to fair competition) with the established steel corporations. Adopting a statesmanlike manner, he added that this was a chance to reinforce the already friendly ties between Germans and Americans; just 25 years after the war, this was no cliché. Korf saw himself as a trailblazer for German interests, and a pioneer who would be followed by others. In giving this speech, it was apparent that Korf felt almost as American at heart as the Americans themselves – safe in the knowledge that he'd already been granted honorary citizenship by Georgetown.

However, in addition to his solemn words, Korf also had a special treat in store for those who'd come all the way from Europe. He laid on a four-day recreation programme of river cruises and sightseeing, taking his guests on a journey through three centuries of local colonial history. He immersed them in the past of South Carolina, which was somewhat more glamorous than its present, at least for those with money.

According to a German reporter: "Comfortable, spacious holiday homes for the bourgeois upper class alternate with half-ruined wooden shacks where only curtains and geranium pots in the windows confirm that they are still inhabited." Another member of Korf's retinue was shocked to read signs in shop windows declaring: "We accept food stamps." Korf, on the other hand, evoked anew a grandeur that had long since faded: the style of mansions on the rice plantations. "Today," wrote the above-mentioned reporter, "the old mansions are summer residences of wealthy managers relaxing from their labours in fairy-tale parks." Korf had rented just such a domicile not far from his new factory as the official guesthouse of the Georgetown Steel Corporation. It would impress many a visitor from overseas in the following decade.

Unsurprisingly, perhaps, the Georgetown Steel venture didn't turn out to be quite as secure as the epic opening speeches and sightseeing programme had promised. The Georgetown region was part of the hurricane-prone coastal zone of the USA. The rural area also had virtually no trained steel workers, so in the first year almost all the skilled positions had to be filled by Germans, shipped across the Atlantic at high expense. And then there was the question of who would manage Korf's US activities, since Korf himself never spent long dealing with day-to-day matters once his investment projects were up and running.

Setting up the entire plant had been overseen by a German named Wolfgang Jansen. Although barely 30 years old, Jansen was no newcomer to Korf's empire. He first made Korf's acquaintance in a very different part of the world during Korf's first commercial quest abroad. It is worth briefly dwelling on this episode – not just to shed light on Jansen's background, but also to discover more about the distinctly 'American' spirit of adventure that Korf took with him to the United States.

On 1 October 1960, Nigeria gained its independence from the UK. A friend by the name of Herbert Summ, a philologist with no business experience whatsoever, put the idea into young Willy Korf's head of moving into the unoccupied markets for nails, steel mesh, wire fencing and reinforcing steel in this populous, post-colonial African country. Summ persuaded him that there were at least 55 million consumers ready and waiting. And so, with initial capital of 700,000 marks, Willy Korf set up West African Steel and Wire Ltd. (WASCO) in Ikeja, an industrial area 22 kilometres (14 miles) from the capital Lagos. Production began in mid-1961, even though the factory only received its first telephone two years later.

Chief Ben Oluwole, a tribal chief aged 77, had a 6 per cent share in this bold enterprise and was made a director of WASCO. Aside from Korf's interest in the chief's his tribe's history and customs, Oluwole's appointment – as a Nigerian – was essential to secure development aid from Bonn. Meanwhile, Herbert Summ was made Korf's general agent in Nigeria.

At first, Korf's African business boomed, with turnover doubling every year between 1961 and 1965. The tax-free profits were reinvested, and the share capital was regularly increased. A British competitor appearing in the country in 1962 was neatly eliminated by agreeing to a one-third stake in WASCO in return for pulling out of the market. Another third was acquired by a well-known German company headed by the Cologne industrialist Otto Wolff von Amerongen.

But then a period of unrest began in Nigeria. Two military coups in 1966 brought construction to a halt. WASCO's products were suddenly unsaleable for years, and the situation did not improve until 1969. Korf decided to expand his product range so as to reduce his dependence on the ups and downs of the building industry. When his two British and German partners didn't follow suit, Korf accused them of lacking courage and began to plough his own furrow with the assistance of his trusted associates, Oluwole and Summ. And so, his African workers started making goods as diverse as enamelled pots, buckets, ballpoint pens, oil tanks, razor blades, wood preservatives and paint.

For the many plastic products in the newly expanded range, Korf and his cousin Helmhold Schneider imported disused injection moulding machines from the WERIT factories in Altenkirchen, while cheap plastic was obtained from East Germany. One of Korf's bestsellers in Nigeria was chamber pots; allegedly, a million of them were bought by the Yoruba tribe alone. The main selling point of the chamber pot – previously unknown to locals – was that rural inhabitants no longer had to leave their huts at night to use the toilet, avoiding the risk of snakebite.

Up to 2,000 Nigerians and 20 Europeans worked for Willy Korf at that time. He exported his range of department store goods as far as Ghana, Senegal and Gabon. Taking a leaf out of Gustav Korf OHG's book, he also took a 60 per cent stake in the country's second-largest builders' merchant – and thus became one of the biggest tycoons in Nigeria. He even opened a Lufthansa agency in Lagos; thanks to his activities, Nigeria had become attractive for the airline as a business destination. The Nigerian Korf Group was also the largest steel processor in this new, sometimes volatile state, with little history or experience of free market capitalism.

A crockery factory was also planned, but the outbreak of the Nigerian Civil War thwarted Korf's intention to find a German partner or banker. Undaunted, he wooed Czechoslovakian financiers: the state export company Pragoinvest, which subsequently supplied all the machinery for the crockery factory. Naturally, he couldn't resist the temptation to plan a Nigerian mini steel mill with a direct reduction plant, electric arc furnace and continuous casting. However, the Nigerian government, like many other regimes of the time, had dreams of a huge, integrated steelworks, even though its cost was likely to be prohibitive.

All in all, further expansion in the crisis-ridden state became increasingly unpromising. State institutions treated contracts as lists of optional clauses, delivery assurances weren't kept, and bureaucracy and corruption began to take over. The complexity of a newly independent African state came crashing down on Korf. But he refused to let this dampen his optimism until the very end – an end which was to begin somewhat insidiously.

In November 1972, the United Bank for Africa suddenly gave Korf just 21 days to repay a loan of 11 million marks. But because WASCO was insolvent, Korf was immediately joined by an officially appointed administrator, causing panic among his financial backers. A total of 33 creditors swiftly demanded repayments from WASCO totalling around 100 million marks. A spokesman for Wafios, a machine-building company based in Reutlingen, summed up the general consternation: "We all trusted in the good German names Korf and Wolff and delivered on credit." But in the meantime, the two partners had fallen out over the question of who ultimately owned WASCO. The business interests of Korf and his partners had become almost too convoluted to untangle – a portent of much greater confusion to come.

To make matters worse, there was also the failure of Korf's friend Herbert Summ as his representative in Nigeria. According to press reports, he was responsible for allowing building projects with a budget of 12 million marks to spiral up to two and a half times that amount. Otto Wolff von Amerongen had had enough and wanted out of his partnership with Korf; the latter, who wanted a completely free hand anyway, agreed.

On 13 February 1972, negotiations took place at the Dom Hotel in Cologne, at which Korf (who by this point had almost no liquidity) bought out von Amerongen on behalf of an anonymous silent partner. Regrettably, only the first instalment was received, after which the cheques dried up. At Wolff's insistence, Korf finally revealed the supposed identity of the mysterious investor: Cyprus's UNICEF representative in Paris, Anastasios G. Leventis, operator of a chain of department stores in Nigeria. But Leventis denied ever having approved the purchase, claiming that a manager who'd long since been fired had probably taken the initiative without his knowledge. Thus ended the African adventure for Korf and Wolff: in disagreements, unpaid invoices, burnt bridges and a tarnished reputation.

But there was one man who managed to get out in time and fall on his feet: Wolfgang Jansen. Korf "attracted people of a certain kind" recalled David Yarborough, one of Korf's US managers. "They reflected his personality." By setting up the plants in Nigeria, the young Jansen had distinguished himself as someone who could faithfully render Korf's visions – and, moreover, as someone who was tough enough for the 'combat' of the pioneering days. Korf always recognized loyalty. And this same Jansen was now at Korf's side in the USA when Georgetown Steel was launched and then formerly opened a year later.

Jansen had been appointed president of Georgetown Steel not long after Korf had commissioned him to find a site for the US steelworks as early as 1967. Jansen had proven himself an efficient, energetic founder, able to tap sources of finance and sales markets. The question was whether he would be capable of steering Korf's US interests in a solid, profitable direction over the long term. Ahead of him and his newly assembled team, there now lay the austere years of carefully calculated startup losses. Was this really a job for a pathfinder hurling himself into the fray – or rather for somebody with a cool head?

Testing times soon came: 1971 was the year in which the Midrex plant in Georgetown finally went into operation, yet the initial euphoria about the German steelworks in the small town soon gave way to growing anger, when locals began complaining about water and air pollution. The regional environmental authority gave Korf an ultimatum to install the necessary filters. Civil rights groups and trade unions accused the management of not employing enough black foremen and appointing too few black people to management positions, although it would have been difficult to do otherwise given the qualifications and experience in the local workforce. Furthermore, despite tough negotiations since the factory's establishment, a collective pay agreement still had not been reached by 1971. There were breaches of health and safety regulations, several injuries, and, according to press reports, even a death in the factory.

Starting on 25 August 1970, a three-month strike broke out. There were numerous clashes between union activists and strike-breakers. The latter had been lured by the management under Jansen with above-average wages, while Jansen and his executives preferred to operate the hoists and other machinery themselves rather than give in to a walkout. In the end, they succeeded in breaking the strikers' resistance. But their intransigent attitude drew the ire of American steelworkers with their hatred of foreign investors. "It's not good that we're allowing a German company to bleed American workers dry," *Rheinische Merkur* quoted one striker as saying.

The newspaper went on to identify a real "anti-Korf campaign", the target of which spoke out in return: the existence of such a campaign was inconceivable, and the fact that the Midland Ross Corporation had increased its shareholding in Georgetown Steel from 25 to 49 per cent was proof that Korf was not planning to desert America, despite rumours to the contrary. It was simply the same ownership structure that had prevailed in Korf-Midland-Ross Holding AG in Baden-Baden, a joint venture founded in 1969. The strike and subsequent war of words prompted Korf to realize – not for the first time – that trying to hold together an empire spanning thousands of miles was no small challenge.

In response, Korf tried to simplify and stabilize matters by setting up another holding company. Korf-Midland-Ross Holding emerged from a shell company which Korf (as the majority shareholder) and his potent US partner Midland Ross (with a 49 per cent stake) had acquired in 1969: IBAG Internationale Baumaschinen AG in Neustadt an der Weinstrasse. Its factory was spun off and merged with another new acquisition. What prompted the American partners – who had no experience of their own in the steel industry – to get involved in this German-American project was their desire to make the Midrex process fit for the world market, by teaming up with a modern steel producer. Korf's main interest in this new partnership, apart from the Midrex innovation, was the US giant's cash resources, which he needed to finance his new startups and expansions.

IBAG was soon renamed Korf-Midland-Ross Holding, while IBAG's engineering arm became Korf-Midland-Ross Engineering. The main driving force behind this was a painful realization on both sides that in Georgetown and in Kehl, the two partners had made the same discovery: external plant suppliers might have good machinery for sale, but were obviously incapable of planning or even fitting out entire mini steelworks. Perhaps that was no wonder, since plants running on Korf's 'magic triangle' concept – with upstream direct reduction and modern continuous casting – simply hadn't been built yet. Determined to convince the world of their benefits, however, Korf sought out this space in the market for his own engineering activities.

At that time, there was a young industrial engineer who had been working for Korf for three years, initially as an assistant to the board in Kehl, where he'd helped erect the steelworks and the rolling mill. Otfried Forssman's name preceded him: his father was a cousin of Werner Forssman, the famous doctor who'd received the Nobel Prize in Medicine in 1956, after a legendary experiment in which he'd passed a catheter into his own heart. For his part, the young Otfried suddenly found himself at the forefront of the new German-American steel fraternity through his boss, Korf's technical director Heinz Schmidberger.

Otfried and Heinz flew to Toledo together to negotiate the organizational details of the engineering joint venture with Midland Ross. The US partners presented their own ideas; Schmidberger explained the German proposals, some of which had been worked out by Forssman. He was amazed by the Americans' flexibility: "Three weeks after we'd returned home, we received a huge manuscript from them by post. They'd knocked all the previous plans on the head and completely come round to our organizational ideas."

The first joint project was to be a Midrex direct reduction plant in Europe. After lengthy meetings to shortlist possible locations, which included the North Sea ports of Delfzijl and Rotterdam in the Netherlands as well as Shannon in Ireland, it was decided to opt for a 'big solution': Korf would build his second German steelworks using American Midrex technology in the docklands of Hamburg – a distant no-man's land in steel production terms. Korf had already announced his intention to build a steel plant there in late 1968.

As far as the headquarters of Korf-Midland-Ross-Engineering itself was concerned, the tranquil Neustadt an der Weinstrasse wasn't chosen after all. Forssman pushed through the selection of Düsseldorf because of its proximity to the steel giants of the Ruhr. Korf immediately made the young industrial engineer an authorized signatory at the new head office in the capital of North Rhine-Westphalia. Forssman was destined to go far.

Standing on the threshold of the 1970s, Korf was full of optimism. He was more fascinated than ever by the American way of life, by the people who'd welcomed him with open arms and not doubted his abilities. He found the Americans wonderfully straightforward. In those years, almost everything that the US economy and its political system produced was a source of inspiration in Korf's eyes. As he gushed to *Wirtschaftswoche:* "You can still work freely there. Those with ability and talent still have every opportunity." This contrasted with the not-so-free market economy in Old Europe, especially Germany: "That's not capitalism; it's cronyism." And he knew what he was talking about, having been on the receiving end of its worst practices.

Korf thought it was wonderful that I.W. Abel, a well-known steelworkers' union leader in the USA, agreed to appear in an image campaign for the US steel company United Steel. It showed that it was still possible for employers to talk to their workers. Abel stated in the $29,000 double-page ad in *Business Week:* "I appeal to every American to join the crucial battle to improve our lagging productivity. ... The union is also aware that to get more, we must achieve more." Capital and labour working hand in hand – the USA seemed like business heaven to Korf. As he wistfully put it: "I wish this willingness to cooperate were still possible in Germany today – on both sides."

The Anglo-Saxon press, not given to exuberance, took a fairly restrained view of Korf's ascent in the USA. After he'd been on the US stage for a few years, the British *Financial Times* noted his dapper appearance, but also described him as "elusive". The paper had tried to get Korf to say something concrete about his stream of new projects, but in vain. The journalist wrote that it seemed to be very important to Korf to always keep "personal control", but wondered how long he would be able to do so.

A once-prominent politician, who kept tabs on Korf's activities for many years, observed this about his fixation with the United States: "He always thought and acted big. That's why he was influenced by the fast, high-yield deals that the Americans had. And he always despaired over how long it took in Germany for the necessary permits to be issued." A top manager, who used to be the head of a well-known German company and later moved to the USA himself, perhaps knew his friend Korf a little better: "He was much more romantic than the Americans. They focus on numbers and results. Bold plans are all well and good, but what takes priority is the bottom line. In that respect, Willy Korf wasn't an American. He wasn't a dreamer, exactly, but certainly something along those lines."

Korf hadn't yet run up against the dark side of the US system: the brutal pressure exerted on managers and industrialists by the stock market when high expectations and confident forecasts were not met. The man whose stubborn optimism made some believe he had his feet firmly on the ground and others think he had his head in the clouds found himself crossing the Atlantic more and more frequently. Initially tied to major airlines' schedules, it wasn't long before he began using his own planes to bridge time and space.

Spending seven or eight hours on board with nothing but thousands of square miles of water beneath him, condemned to inactivity, not even being able to use the telephone he loved so much, must have been unbearable for Willy Korf. The above-mentioned politician, who once joined him on a transatlantic flight, recalled: "He could barely wait to use the phone again in America. He found the time on the plane when he couldn't work non-stop to be excruciating." In the 1970s, whenever Korf and his entourage had finally landed and undone their seat belts, he always rushed off to the nearest payphone in the terminal, quarters in hand. "He stayed on the phone until the connecting flight," said a fellow passenger. Many years later, that associate was to buy Korf a gift that was to become indispensable: one of the very first mobile phones on the market.

CHAPTER 6

A free man

"We're jump jets, we're highflyers, we're supersonic!"

Willy Korf may only have been American in spirit, but he fully embodied the values core to American life and the USA's national image. Much like the land of the free and the people who lived in it, Korf possessed a strong sense of independence, combined with a desire to take risks, work hard and live life to the full. Of course, these characteristics also required to Korf to be able to set aside his emotions. After all, an industrialist with ambitious expansion plans, yet extremely thin equity cover, was bound to encounter difficulties sometimes. Fortunately, Korf had a skill for turning major setbacks into minor inconveniences, and even opportunities.

This capacity was demonstrated in an episode recounted by Otfried Forssman when he was still an inexperienced assistant to Korf's technical director Heinz Schmidberger: "One day, in 1968, there was a crisis meeting with the banks in Düsseldorf. It seemed like everything was collapsing around our ears." When the meeting broke up in the evening after heated negotiations about loans that had matured as well as additional cash injections without an agreement in sight, Korf signalled that Forssman should join them: "We're going to Zum Csikos, a Hungarian place in town. They have Budweiser on tap. Why don't you join us?"

Later on, standing at the bar, Forssman said to Korf: "That was awful today!" But Korf had put it all behind him: "You're right, but let's not dwell on that now. We can't do anything about it this evening. We'll wait and see what happens tomorrow. Let's change the subject. Did you know that Csikos came here as a refugee after the war and built up this wonderful bar?" And amid the dim lighting, with Hungarian accordion music in the background, the conversation shifted into areas where money wasn't involved. This taught Forssman a lesson for life: "If you don't feel great but can't do anything about it today, don't take your troubles to bed with you. You still need a good night's sleep so that you'll be fit enough the next day to dive back into the fray." Korf certainly didn't take his troubles to bed with him. The next morning, after a very short night, he was back to his usual dynamic form. And once again, he persuaded the banks not to cut off his credit.

During these years, Korf met two people who would figure prominently in his business ventures, in both good times and bad. One of them was Horst Weitzmann, assistant to Hermann Brandi, at that time the technical director of August Thyssen steelworks. Brandi was fascinated by Korf's mini steel mill in Baden-Württemberg and travelled to Kehl in 1969 to see it first-hand. Korf was only too willing to show his plant to an envoy of the Ruhr barons: he regarded Brandi's visit as a nod from the Ruhr, paving the way for the normalization of their tense relations.

Brandi, who'd brought his assistant Horst Weitzmann with him, was initially disappointed by what he saw. The factory had an air of Heath Robinson improvisation about it: transformers were temporarily covered with corrugated iron, building materials were strewn around the factory floor, and the continuous casting plant wasn't working yet. Nonetheless, what Brandi understood by the end of the tour was that Korf had what it took to get the mill up and running. Not only that, but Korf's production process would be so cheap that he might well put Thyssen, with its expensive pig iron, out of business. Brandi graciously conceded that Korf was a strong competitor, who was growing more powerful by the day.

At this time, Korf was also planning to build the first commercial Midrex plant at his US plant in Georgetown. But the German steel industry now also had a direct reduction process of its own, albeit one that still required some work. It was called Purofer, and had been developed in Germany by Ludwig von Bogdandy, head of research at the steelworks in Oberhausen, which had recently been taken over by Thyssen.

Although the Purofer plant was not yet ready for the market, Bogdandy already held a raft of patents in the field of direct reduction, which he planned to use to paralyse Korf's rival operation. At the end of Brandi's visit to Kehl, Korf invited him to dinner and complained that Bogdandy was giving him a hard time over alleged patent infringements, which in reality were groundless. The benevolent Brandi advised him to discuss the matter with his assistant Weitzmann, who would see what could be done. As Weitzmann recalled: "From that moment on, I had Korf clinging to my coat-tails."

However, Weitzmann soon disappeared from Korf's radar for a few years. After parting company with Thyssen, he went on to build a career for himself in the USA – where, despite the country's vast size, he and Korf would bump into each other again one day.

As luck would have it, Korf's other new acquaintance destined to play a significant role in his life was a friend of Weitzmann's, Klaus Didillon. He was an engineer who, while working for Thyssen, had built a pioneering electric steel mill in Brazil. However, Thyssen was determined to install one of Bogdandy's Purofer direct reduction plants upstream, despite some serious problems, including how to secure the necessary gas supply.

Purofer wasn't a bad method, but the iron reduced in this way was supposed to be fed hot into the furnace immediately afterwards – and that didn't work yet. Even though the plant ran imperfectly, Bogdandy cared less about improving it than he did about alleged patent infringements by his rivals. The enduring Purofer problems caused the whole steelworks to fall considerably behind schedule, and Thyssen eventually gave up and pulled out – as did Didillon.

It was at this point that Korf, who'd always kept a close eye on the market for capable steel managers with experience abroad, stepped in. His charm and enthusiasm fell on fertile ground (not for the last time), especially in view of his generosity to new managers. In 1971, the gifted technician Didillon joined Korf for the first time – and later did so permanently.

Meanwhile, Willy Korf continued to cultivate his David-versus-Goliath image ("I live off the mistakes of the big players," he once told *Wirtschaftswoche*) and pushed hard to diversify his group during this phase. But even he was susceptible to mistakes.

In 1969, Willy Korf took over a second mechanical engineering company alongside IBAG, Mohr & Federhaff AG in Mannheim. It built bulk material handling systems, cranes, dust collectors and processing equipment for the industrial sector. It also made testing and measuring equipment. The official reason for Korf's diversification was that entering the mechanical engineering business would create valuable synergy and expansion opportunities. Unofficially, Korf had been urged to do so by his main bank, IHB (Investitions- und Handelsbank AG), even though Mohr & Federhaff wasn't necessarily a good fit. "Otherwise, it wouldn't have granted him the necessary loans to build up Badische Stahlwerke and his other assets," said Korf's long-time financial director Carl-Theodor Meinecke, for whom the ailing Mannheim firm was a perpetual thorn in his side and bad news for his balance sheet. "The bankers wanted Korf to take Mohr & Federhaff off their hands."

Besides these bold acquisitions, Korf also returned to his erstwhile core business, the production of wire mesh. The year 1971 marked the end of the now legendary ten-year period during which he'd been contractually prohibited from manufacturing 'spot-welded reinforcement mesh' after selling his production operations to Klöckner. With the alternative 'composite steel mesh' (in which the wires were held together with extruded plastic) failing to catch on, Korf quietly resumed making good old spot-welded mesh. He did so not only in the old production plant in Kehl, which was good for 60,000 tonnes per year, but also using new assets acquired especially for this purpose: at BESTA Betonstahl in Lübbecke, Westphalia, and Isar Baustahl near Augsburg, resulting in another 180,000 tonnes annually. Korf was on his way to becoming the largest wire processor in southern Germany. Another reason for acquiring these wire plants was to boost the sales of his growing number of steel and rolling mills.

A little over a year earlier, on 9 December 1969, the first pile was driven for HSW – Korf's new steelworks in Hamburg on a former allotment site in the docklands expansion zone. The location had been prudently selected: masses of scrap (the steel mill's raw material) passed through the port, and as far as exporting steel was concerned, well, Hamburg prided itself on being the gateway to the world. The city leased 150,000 square metres of land to Willy Korf for the first construction phase at the ridiculously low annual rent of 2.10 marks per square metre. Access to the plant for seagoing vessels was enabled by extending the Köhlfleet canal, which included a new quay wall more than 220 metres (720 feet) in length. The state of Hamburg alone invested 25 million marks in infrastructure for the new plant, with the intention of creating up to 900 jobs.

Korf founded Hamburger Stahlwerke GmbH with initial share capital of 20 million marks, just under half of which was owned by Midland Ross. The first Midrex plant on German soil was planned to go into operation in the plant's second phase, during which the annual production volume of 300,000 tonnes per year was sent to double. The Hamburg plant would produce semi-finished casting products, and most of these billets – steel bars up to 14 metres (46 feet) long and with a square cross-section – were to be processed into steel bars and wire rod in the company's own rolling mill. Nevertheless, Willy Korf wouldn't have been able to build HSW without support from Hamburg's regional development bank, which took a one-third stake in it.

Moreover, the project would never have come to fruition without Willy Korf's legendary negotiating skills. When it came to the vexed issue of electricity tariffs for the plant's electric furnaces, Korf found himself sitting opposite Helmuth Kern from the Social Democrats – Hamburg's economic affairs senator and deputy mayor, not to mention the political godfather of the steelworks project. Korf found the electricity rates he was being asked to pay absurdly high.

In his typical unrelenting manner, Korf gently took the senator to task: "Let me tell you how we dealt with this problem in Georgetown," he began, brushing aside objections that free-market US electricity prices weren't a suitable model for the pricing structure of public monopolists in Germany. After much persuasion, Korf succeeded in having his future electricity bills halved. He would later savour this moment in his own inimitable way to the press, explaining that in Hamburg he "also had the advantage of the favourable energy procurement options for natural gas and electricity offered to us under Hamburg's forward-thinking energy policy."

This was all good progress, but it still wasn't enough for Korf. He continued chipping away and finally managed to convince Hamburg to accept the commercial risk for this venture. Only many years later did it transpire that the city had taken on guarantees for HSW that even exceeded the investment costs totalling 200 million marks.

As the project continued, Korf not only pushed for public funding, but also pushed the pace. According to his ambitious schedule, the plant was to start partial operation before the end of 1970, and this pressure inevitably led to some mishaps. For example, when the ship loader was commissioned, a subcontractor had forgotten to attach safety clamps to the trolley. It tore loose, was catapulted over the railway tracks, and sank into the harbour basin, where it had to be recovered by divers. Furthermore, one of the main steel supports for the factory, dispatched by the French supplier failed to arrive on time, despite express delivery by rail. The girder had been inadvertently routed by the German railway operator to Hamm in Westphalia. It finally reached Hamburg via Osnabrück.

Thankfully, there were no more serious hitches, and HSW's rolling mill was successfully commissioned by Korf's deadline. In July 1971, an initial electric furnace and the first continuous casting plant went into production. This was followed in October by the debut of the direct reduction plant. The new mini steel mill was thus almost ready, and it was time for Willy Korf to blow his own trumpet in the media again: "In future, there'll be the big players. And there'll be the small players: they'll be able to choose their location based on their sales strategy, and they'll have benefits in terms of raw material supplies or a cheaper site."

In Korf's opinion, the integrated steel mills might as well shut up shop because of their huge workforces: "Larger plants lead to greater social problems. They mean impersonal working conditions for many employees." His mini steelworks, by contrast, were more manageable, more agile, and simpler to control: "It's easier to ensure a small plant is utilized optimally – regardless of economic fluctuations – than a large plant," explained Korf enthusiastically. "I can walk through the plant and at once I can see what's going on everywhere. That takes the executives in the big steel corporations days, if not weeks." Time was the decisive factor in Korf's pitch: "We deliver faster, we deliver overnight, we can change our quality and rolling programme instantly. The big players can't change their output easily because their rolling programmes are fixed for a month in advance and then computer-controlled."

But not everything in life can be controlled by computer. In the summer of 1971, Korf's plans and his group of companies were knocked sideways when Midland Ross, the US partner which had joined him only a few years earlier, and become so important to him, unexpectedly pulled out. This unexpected shift was the result of a decisive change in US law, which had come into force in the spring of that year.

Whereas beforehand, only shareholdings of 50 per cent or more had had to be consolidated in the parent company's balance sheet, this limit was reduced to just 20 per cent. Midland Ross had a 49 per cent stake in Georgetown Steel and Korf-Midland-Ross-Holding. Any start-up losses suffered by the partnership, which hitherto went unreported, would henceforth spoil the balance sheets. These legal changes led to enormous pressure from the stock market, which insisted on Midland Ross's promise of quarterly profits being met each time. Midland Ross couldn't afford to wait any longer to sit out Georgetown's initial heavy losses, and it no longer had the patience to wait for the jointly planned adventure of HSW to start making a profit. At a stroke, the Midland Ross partnership was over.

Had Korf's American dream been shattered? Despite having been left in the lurch, he proved – not for the last time – that in order to make the best of even the most devastating situation, there was no point complaining or showing outrage. Instead, mustering all his financial resources, he bought back the American shares with the help of IHB bank. Putting in a brilliant negotiating performance, Korf had already managed to get hold of the licensing rights to Midrex for Europe, the Soviet Union, Africa and the Middle East – which he intended to exploit as profitably as possible by granting sub-licences. The Mitsui Group secured the coveted rights for the Far East; Midland Ross only reserved North America and Canada for itself.

Rumours immediately began to circulate that the Midrex process was perhaps not quite as sensational as Midland Ross and Korf had always insisted. Did the Americans not believe in their own system? The question was never satisfactorily answered, even though the claim it contained was vehemently denied by all sides, and subsequently refuted by the continuing success of Midrex (thanks to Korf), which also benefited Midland Ross for many years.

What was certain was that, at the end of 1971, Korf

was suddenly bereft of his most important business partner. Midland Ross's interests in the joint holding company and Georgetown Steel were now held by KIH (Korf Industrie und Handel), although Midland Ross was still tied to Georgetown Steel by long-term supply contracts. And a Midrex plant had also been operating at the Hamburg steelworks since the autumn. Midland Ross's involvement wasn't over quite yet.

Aided by his corporate lawyer Max Kreifels from Düsseldorf, Korf immediately set about erasing the name of his old partner from his group's organizational chart. At the beginning of 1972, Korf-Midland-Ross-Holding was renamed Korf-Stahl AG. Korf now held just under 60 per cent of the shares through KIH based in Baden-Baden, and IHB owned 40 per cent, with a tiny remainder in free float. The holding company's capital was raised from 16 to 60 million marks. Korf-Stahl was now the parent company of the two steelworks in Kehl and Hamburg as well as Korf Engineering in Düsseldorf (formerly Korf-Midland-Ross-Engineering) and the mechanical engineering firm Mohr & Federhaff based in Mannheim.

The boards of the new Korf-Stahl AG were soon appointed. In addition to Korf as chair, Heinz Schmidberger served on the executive board as director of technology, Carl-Theodor Meinecke, the authorized signatory and head of finance at KIH, was promoted to Korf-Stahl's chief financial officer, and Horst Rennau became head of sales. With his expertise and authority, it was only natural for Korf's lawyer and advisor Max Kreifels to be made chair of the supervisory board, which included some high-calibre names. Otmar Emminger, vice-president and later president of Deutsche Bundesbank, as well as Diether II. Hoffmann, spokesman of the management board of Bank für Gemeinwirtschaft, IHB's main shareholder, were both members for a time. An old friend of Korf's from his youth also joined the supervisory board: Edgar Georg. After graduating in mechanical engineering, he'd made a career for himself in the medium-sized metal industry, and might therefore be able to solve the difficulties posed by Mohr & Federhaff.

To the outside world, the opaque structure of Korf's corporate empire wasn't made any clearer by the fact that he deposited the shares previously owned by his American companies with a newly founded 'oberholding', Costaal B.V. in Amsterdam. For a few years, this holding company had a managing director with no real authority, a secretary, a telephone and a letterbox. Some queried why this outpost existed. For Korf, the purpose was obvious: tax efficiency.

Korf travelled to the official opening of HSW in Hamburg on 25 April 1972 – not by road or rail, but on a company jet chartered by Korf-Transport, an Air Commerz Viscount 808. Frankly, there was no other option. After all, he had an extensive entourage from the Baden region in tow: dignitaries from Kehl, Baden-Baden, and the nearby banks. After leaving the airport by coach and stopping off for a brief visit to the infamous Reeperbahn, the 600 international guests invited to the opening ceremony sailed across the Elbe to the district of Finkenwerder. The group included a large US delegation, featuring the governor of South Carolina, who had all been flown across the Atlantic on another plane chartered by Korf.

On board the ship were the senior executives of the big German steel corporations, almost all of whom had already paid exploratory visits to their competitor's new plant beforehand without attracting attention. This time, there was no scandal like the one several years earlier when Badische Stahlwerke was opened in Kehl. Korf had learned his lesson: he didn't want to cause any trouble, and if any of the top managers felt uncomfortable and didn't want to complete the trip, they could always 'escape' on one of the launches that constantly circled the ship. The tour of the "most advanced steel mill in the world" (Korf's wording) and its two electric furnaces was kept rather short, allowing more time for the speeches of praise and thanks during the cold buffet on the ship afterwards. Helmuth Kern, the economic affairs senator, publicly exclaimed: "If only there were a few more Willy Korfs!" The gentlemen from the

Ruhr barely raised an eyebrow.

In Korf's eyes, the only thing he now lacked was a new industrial partner for his plant, which had been half-orphaned by Midland Ross's exit. This remained the case until the end of the year, when rumours suddenly surfaced that the Duisburg-based Klöckner Group wanted to "take a significant stake in the Korf Group." Korf immediately told *Handelsblatt* that Klöckner was only considering cooperating with the Hamburg steelworks. HSW already supplied Klöckner's Haspe plant with the semi-finished casting products exceeding its own requirements after the Klöckner steelworks nearby had been shut down. Klöckner was interested in securing HSW's wire rod or wire mesh production in the long term. Apart from economic efficiency, however, there was another personal factor behind why Klöckner wanted to get involved with Korf: Ludwig von Bogdandy.

Although the inventor of Purofer had since moved from Thyssen to Klöckner's executive board, he had been forced to leave the rights to his direct reduction process at Thyssen. Bogdandy was therefore hoping to access Korf's competing Midrex process on behalf of his new employer – partly in order to put one over on Thyssen, the company in which the ambitious Bogdandy's ascent had been thwarted. Korf, having shrewdly recognized this desire, made use of it in the ensuing cooperation negotiations over possible collaboration, but left no one in any doubt that he would refuse to give up his majority shareholding in HSW.

In March 1973, Klöckner bought a 49 per cent stake in HSW. It took another 49 per cent shareholding in the Düsseldorf based Korf Engineering GmbH, demonstrating that its interest in Korf's empire went beyond his steelworks. Klöckner had its entire stake in HSW financed by regional development bank Hamburgische Landesbank, under a bizarrely one-sided contractual arrangement that deprived Klöckner of almost its entire voice – with fatal consequences, as it would later transpire.

Right from the start, the unequal partners at HSW wouldn't even give each other the time of day. Arbitration proceedings over the terms of the supply contract for semi-finished products that Klöckner had imposed on HSW dragged on for years, and Korf felt that he was at a considerable disadvantage. Meanwhile, behind the scenes, Klöckner was complaining that Korf's KIH was diverting liquidity involved in the purchase of scrap for the joint plant, and in the sale of products, towards Korf-Stahl AG's expansionist ambitions, while Klöckner was stuck with any losses. Dieter Ameling, who joined HSW as plant manager in 1973, later rising to head of the steelworks before becoming the president of the Federation of the German Steel Industry in Düsseldorf, summed up the whole dispute in a nutshell: "Korf behaved as if he owned 100 per cent of the shares and Klöckner as if they held 51 per cent. We always said that together they had 151 per cent. Both partners were entirely focused on their own advantage." It wasn't a good omen for the future of the nascent plant.

Korf began the second half of the year by appointing someone who would prove more formative for his group of companies than almost any other addition to the staff before or since. On 1 July, Wolfgang Bernhardt started work at Korf-Stahl AG as deputy chair of the board and Korf's general manager. At just 37, Bernhardt was relatively young to take on such senior roles. But he was no run-of-the-mill executive.

After studying law and starting his career in a prestigious Düsseldorf law firm, he had been recruited by Germany's largest conglomerate at the time: Friedrich Flick KG. There, he rose to the position of managing director and general manager of the intermediate holding company, responsible among other things for tax matters. Bernhardt was only one of twelve managers at the top of Flick, but when he joined Korf, he was second in command right from the start.

Bernhardt and Korf had been introduced a few years earlier. At that time, Bernhardt sat with Flick's chief technician Mr Vogels on one side of the negotiating table, Korf and his aide

Bert Pfluger on the other. They discussed the possibility of Korf acquiring a stake in Flick's Maxhütte steelworks, now that Korf felt he was in a position to do so. Korf's extraordinary ability to access anywhere he wanted was already legendary: "He can get inside any Bedouin's tent within 24 hours," board member Carl-Theodor Meinecke is said to have once told a newspaper. And Bernhardt added in retrospect: "Korf could open any door. I've never known anyone who could enter any room in any country on the planet with a broad smile on his face like he did."

Although Korf didn't invest in Maxhütte after all (leaving Klöckner to seize this supposed opportunity much later), contact between the two companies had now been established. Even so, Korf and Friedrich Flick, despite hailing from the same area and both considered 'steel industry outsiders', did not know each other personally. When Flick died in 1972, thus ending an era, this was also a reason for Bernhardt to seek new, larger responsibilities. After months of talks with Korf and especially Kreifels, who virtually begged him to join, he agreed and tendered his resignation. Flick's personally liable partner Otto A. Friedrich – later president of the Federation of German Industries – wrote Bernhardt an appreciative letter which described Korf as an "extraordinary entrepreneur who occasionally reminds me of Dr Friedrich Flick in his younger years."

The prospect of being second to Willy Korf in his new position fascinated Bernhardt. Admittedly, the move to provincial Baden-Baden wasn't easy for him or his family after their years in Düsseldorf. But ample recompense beckoned. Above all, Bernhardt described receiving "full personal power of attorney from Willy Korf that went as far as it was possible to go: I could have sold the business lock, stock and barrel!" Bernhardt's decision to change employers was a subject of great interest, and immediately filled the newspapers' business sections.

But why had Korf brought in this highly regarded recruit at such expense? There were two main reasons. Firstly, Korf, who was often away on business, needed a kind of 'minister of the interior' at his Baden-Baden headquarters, as Bernhardt himself described his job at the time. This included the less glamorous managerial tasks, such as maintaining work discipline and efficiency. These were jobs that Max Kreifels, the legal advisor and chair of the supervisory board, couldn't do effectively from Düsseldorf, particularly given his legal impartiality; after all, he represented entrepreneurs from other family businesses. More than once in their many years together, Korf tried to persuade Kreifels to join his company – but in vain. Bernhardt, by contrast, with an independent spirit alongside his proven loyalty, discretion and stringency, seemed predestined to be the 'interior minister'. Kreifels once cryptically called his comrade-in-arms Bernhardt "Korf's good conscience".

Korf's other – perhaps less deliberate – motive was that together, Kreifels and Bernhardt seemed just about strong enough to pull him and his lofty plans back down to earth and rein him in (although Bernhardt always disagreed with this assessment). Their brief was to filter out the good, feasible ideas from Korf's somewhat more unrealistic ones, and then implement them with their full effort. "Korf had a hundred ideas every day," recalled a banker who had long been a friend of the company. "About ninety-eight of them could be binned straightaway – but the two remaining ones were compelling."

The triumvirate of Korf, Kreifels and Bernhardt was quickly forged and, without exception, weighed up all important decisions in the company together, before the boss ultimately made his choice. A dynamic highflyer, a brilliant analyst and a strict strategist: as different as the characters were, their synergy was of a level rarely seen among management teams. The fact that banks reacted almost instinctively to the names Bernhardt ("he was with Flick") and Kreifels by loosening their purse strings was a highly agreeable side effect of this reputation.

But a 'minister of the interior' couldn't expect to win popularity contests among the staff in Baden-Baden. It didn't take long before the ascetic, unapproachable Bernhardt, who was regarded as strictly religious, became the subject of wild rumours in Korf's company headquarters. "He's more Catholic than the Pope," warned some. "He prostrates himself at the feet of the Virgin Mary every day in church!" others claimed. Nevertheless, everyone felt a sense of respect, if not trepidation, in Bernhardt's presence. "He had a steady hand on the tiller," said Werner Marnette, who spent a year as development engineer for Korf in the 1970s, eventually becoming CEO of copper producer and recycler Norddeutsche Affinerie in Hamburg. Bernhardt also acted with a certain severity to put a stop to sloppiness and unnecessary privileges. For instance, he streamlined the organization of mechanical engineering company Mohr & Federhaff and stripped certain executives of their luxurious company cars. Manfred Berner, for many years head of finance and accounting in Baden-Baden, described this as "the beginning of cost-cutting" – an unusual phenomenon in Korf's business.

Even so, whatever the balance of power behind the scenes at Korf's headquarters, there was still only one person in charge, and his name was Willy Korf.

In December 1973, Willy Korf enjoyed a taste of what it would be like to finally be accepted into the pantheon of major global steel figures when *Wirtschaftswoche* declared him Manager of the Year, complete with a nine-page article and a smiling Korf pictured in a leather armchair on the front cover. However, Korf was aware that too much of a 'personality cult' could be detrimental to him.

Certainly, when asked about his steering role in the company, he couldn't resist commenting that: "Once I've perished, the momentum is bound to slacken." But he quickly added: "That's not to say the group wouldn't be consolidated without me. I'm not the only one holding it all together. It's a well-balanced organization. All my companies are run by independent management teams, and I'm joined by four other people on the board at the head office in Baden-Baden." The word 'consolidated' uttered by Korf deserves to be remembered, and not only because he used it so rarely. Korf may have described his business as "well-balanced", but his relentless personal approach to work was quite the opposite, as those who worked with him soon discovered.

In the hymn of praise that *Wirtschaftsblatt* sang to "probably the most successful of all German self-made men" in the post-war period, the theme of freedom once again stands out. Willy Korf explained his entire industrial career with this clear sense of purpose: "It emerged out of my efforts to make myself independent, because the wire processing plant relied on the wire rod supplier. Once we had our own rolling mill, we depended on suppliers of billets and semi-finished casting products. That's how I came to build the electric steel mill. But then I was dependent on scrap again. That's why I turned to direct reduction." Korf had previously told *Die Welt* that his real goal was "personal freedom", and that all his work boiled down to "fighting for and maintaining independence again and again."

After this accolade from the press, more and more observers tried to decipher the character and secrets of this industrial leader, and his struggle for freedom and independence. This resulted in Korf being described, for instance, as "nimble as Kissinger, barely taller than Napoleon, and as self-confident as Helmut Schmidt" (*Der Spiegel*). *Frankfurter Allgemeine Zeitung* added that he had the "typical stubbornness of the inhabitants of Siegerland." A host of other clichés were used to label him. But they weren't really accurate, or only up to a point.

There was something else that distinguished Korf above all: a well-concealed, dry, yet always effective charm that men and women alike found captivating. He made them do his bidding while hardly ever resenting his hot-tempered, bossy or even erratic episodes. It had something to do with Korf's exuberance and creativity, which he was able to pour into clear, precise, yet inspiring messages. There was probably still something confusingly boyish in this small, disciplined man which people disregarded, but subliminally perceived as highly magnetic.

Normally, only little boys think that the whole world belongs to them, and that luck will help them as long as they try hard. When they grew up, they learn to accept their limits and reduce their expectations. Not so Korf. Like no one else, he could make everyone in the room feel that they all belonged together there because they shared a great vision, that they were pioneers working on something genuinely new. Reservation, doubt and objection did not feature in Korf's vocabulary. His confidence and strength of his personality enabled him to take charge, whatever the situation. After all – and this is what distinguished him from those who talked the talk but couldn't walk the walk – he'd proven that he could achieve the impossible. And he would do it again.

For the time being, the old 'top dogs' of the steel industry remained sceptical, even dismissive of Korf. They still considered him something of an upstart, too much of a showman. However, the fact that the old guard kept their distance spurred Korf on even further, especially with the tailwind from the booming economy. Dieter Ameling, now plant manager at the HSW steelworks, took Korf on a tour of the facilities during one of his inspection visits. Korf seemed very impatient, demanding that production be stepped up.

In 1974, crude steel production in Germany reached a record 55 million tonnes. In that same year, after the first oil price shock in 1973, a slowly worsening steel crisis set in on the world markets and wasn't overcome until the late 1990s. And by that time, the continuous casting process, which produces far more product tonnage from less crude steel, had long since been adopted across the board. In 1970, for example, 45 million tonnes of crude steel was produced in Germany, a quantity not reached again until the year 2000 – when 20 per cent more rolled steel was made from the same quantity thanks to continuous casting and higher purity.

In the record year of 1974, the Korf Group celebrated turnover of well over a billion marks for the first time – with a "fat profit", as Korf already predicted in the middle of the year. The leap in turnover – if not necessarily an accompanying explosion in profit– was expected, and there was still room for additional growth with Korf rapidly expanding his group worldwide.

In the USA in 1974, Midland Ross, still under pressure from its shareholders to produce quick profits, also withdrew from the remainder of its former partnership with Korf: the distribution of the Midrex process on the American market. Korf promptly acquired world rights to Midrex and bought the entire Midrex division from Midland Ross. As part of the deal, it was agreed that Midland Ross would continue to receive licence fees for its former process for another ten years. Korf then founded his US holding company Korf Industries in Charlotte, North Carolina, and set up a research and development facility there for the direct reduction process, under a new company name: the Midrex Corporation.

Last but not least, in this eventful year 1974, Korf and his US manager Wolfgang Jansen also laid the basis for another mini steelworks in the USA by founding the Georgetown Texas Steel Corporation in Welcome, North Carolina. The plant was located 1,600 kilometres (1,000 miles) from North Carolina in Beaumont, Texas. Korf and Jansen were attracted by the deepwater port on the Gulf of Mexico, not to mention the local oil industry with its high volume of scrap. But as soon as the steel plant opened in 1977, there were substantial teething troubles: the new electric furnaces didn't work properly, while subsidized cheap imports from Europe caused problems for US steelmakers – a group of which Korf was now a member.

In France, Korf was about to open another plant. Otfried Forssman from Düsseldorf had already been sent there in 1971 to seek a French partner for the project, which could only be managed with external financial assistance. His choice fell on SMN (Société Metallurgique de Normandie) from the Franco-Belgian Empain-Schneider Group, whose CEO was Baron Empain, and which owned, among other assets, the shipyard in Dunkirk. Korf joined forces with Empain-Schneider to found

Société des Aciéries de Montereau.

After examining the course of the Seine, Forssman decided to site the plant in Montereau, some 80 kilometres (50 miles) south-east of Paris. Aware that the French plant was a golden opportunity for promotion, he diligently practised his French and helped draw up the business plan. When the contract was signed in 1972, everyone attending the signing ceremony was given a bottle of Calvados from the mirror-image vintage of 1927. Three years later, the plant was opened with Forssman in charge – "at the worst possible moment", he later stated, "because the market was completely in the pits." Montereau would run at a loss for years to come.

In 1975, Willy Korf entered the uncharted territory of South America when he arrived in Brazil. The continent had everything an aspiring industrialist could hope for: iron ore, good logistics, very low energy costs, an eager workforce, and a firmly established steel industry. Korf bought a stake in the tiny steelworks of the long-standing company FI-EL near São Paulo. But his expansion plans were thwarted by the owners, a large family of German-Brazilian descent, who refused to allow him to increase his shareholding. Korf sold his stake and instead acquired an interest in Companhia Siderúrgica Pains in 1977. The plant was located in Divinópolis in the state of Minas Gerais, 140 kilometres (nearly 90 miles) west of the state capital Bel Horizonte. Meanwhile, in order to build up a technology business in Brazil, too, Korf founded IKOSA in São Paulo, which stood for Indústria de Aço Korf.

None of this would have been possible in Brazil, which was unknown to Korf, without a German consultant. This was Ralph Weber, an engineer who was well acquainted with Brazil and the manager of the Ferrostahl Group. Korf quickly poached him and, after familiarizing him with the Midrex process at HSW in Hamburg, made him his main man in Brazil. The young Brazilian metallurgist Dalton Nosé helped Weber arrange his visit to the Korf Group in Germany, and proceeded to make a career for himself as a development engineer in Weber's team at Pains. At that time, Pains was still using outdated Siemens-Martin furnaces. There was clearly plenty of work to be done there.

Around 1975, Willy Korf had six of his own steel plants in operation or under construction on three continents, a situation that posed a constant logistical challenge for him and his staff. His four-storey administration block in Baden-Baden on Ludwig-Wilhelm-Strasse was bursting at the seams. The building grew ever more crowded owing to the constant stream of new employees; soon there were over a hundred people working there. Finally, in the early summer of 1975, they moved into more suitable premises.

In anticipation of such growth, Willy Korf had already been pushing ahead for five years with a project to build a spacious administrative building in Baden-Baden. He was supported by the architect Kurt E. Walker, who was also a Liberal councillor – one of Korf's few personal friends on the city council. Walker had built hotels for the Steigenberger Hotel Group, and also erected the Burda headquarters in Offenburg in 1962. He had given Korf architectural advice on the planning of mini steelworks all over the world, which consisted of functional modules.

Now, based on his plans, a modern white administration building made of glass and steel had been constructed in a disused quarry on Moltkestrasse on the outskirts of Baden-Baden, with a fairy-tale view over half of the Black Forest. It was leased from a Munich bank. At the topping-out ceremony, Korf and Walker were joined by his party colleague, Hans Friderichs, Germany's minister of economic affairs. Korf's new headquarters for about 150 employees was officially opened on 2 June 1975.

What went on at Korf's HQ, especially on the fifth floor, didn't always live up to the image of a solid, respectable company on the crest of success. Closed office doors concealed chaos, frustration, and perhaps even a trick or two, according to some.

On 15 February, Hellmut Schulte-Derne took up his post as Korf's new sales director. These were tough times; the steel business was in the doldrums.

In March, a managing director of a plant construction corporation demanded to see Schulte-Derne urgently, and told him about an earlier transaction which now had to be settled. "I made a deal with Korf last year so that your balance sheet would look better," he explained. "I ordered 20,000 tonnes of steel from him, which was invoiced but not delivered. We agreed not to discuss what I really want to buy from you until 1975." After this meeting, Schulte-Derne was "so shocked to have joined a company with fake accounting that I immediately wanted to resign. But I wasn't able to find a comparable position due to the economic slump. I approached Korf about the transaction. He said: 'That's none of your concern, that was before your time. Don't worry about it.'"

Schulte-Derne stayed with Korf, but whenever the board of Korf-Stahl AG tabled proposals he regarded as unfair, he protested angrily. On one occasion, a new, cost-saving smelting process was under development at BSW in Kehl, and talk turned to the construction of a new furnace prototype. Innovations like this were substantially subsidized by the German Ministry of Economic Affairs, as long as the company had already invested in the technology. But all BSW had done was provide space for the furnace. As Schulte-Derne later recalled: "Korf, beaming with joy, told us at a board meeting that he'd come up with a solution: HSW would invoice us for the corresponding research so that we qualified for the subsidy without actually doing any work. I objected that that would be fraudulent." Schulte-Derne's concerns were supported by Carl-Theodor Meinecke, the financial director. The matter wasn't recorded in the minutes and was never brought up again. Unsurprisingly, perhaps, Schulte-Derne's relationship with Korf was always "very impersonal and detached".

What the new procurement and sales director also quickly realized was that Korf had no lasting business ties at all during the slump and seemed to rely on speculative ad hoc deals. But since purchasing and sales were based at KIH, a largely autonomous subsidiary over which the board of Korf-Stahl AG had no legal influence, to all intents and purposes Schulte-Derne did deals for years that weren't legally binding. "I sold hundreds of thousands of tonnes in that way," he stated.

But in 1975, Korf-Stahl AG started making huge losses: steel that had been priced at 750 marks per tonne in the previous boom year now had to be sold off at a world market price of 480 marks. When it came to purchasing scrap, however, of which Korf-Stahl AG needed about 1.3 million tonnes annually, Korf only paid with bills of exchange. Schulte-Derne was shocked by the business practices of his new employer: "After six months, I felt the company could suddenly blow up in our faces." Fortunately, for the time being, it didn't. The competition was struggling with the same problems, and using similar methods to circumvent them.

Secretary Renate Höing had come across Willy Korf while working for Rheinstahl (part of the Syndicate Westphalia) in the 1960s, at a time when her bosses were becoming increasingly concerned by their new, young competitor. At the end of 1976, she was looking for a new job but hadn't had much luck, despite possessing references which undoubtedly qualified her to work for many top executives. By chance, Höing was offered a job interview at Korf's head office in Baden-Baden.

Höing recalls the moment she came face to face with Korf: "He looked at me scrutinizingly for a long time. You could hear a pin drop in the room!" A few minutes passed before the interview began. Renate Höing, who was instantly impressed by Korf's aura, knew straightaway that she wanted to work for him. He appeared to her "not at all conceited, but rather benevolent. When he finally spoke, he was clear and precise. He already knew he wanted to hire me. He was very sympathetic when he heard what I'd been through in my previous jobs. I found that exceptionally good on a human level."

Renate Höing began as Willy Korf's secretary on 1 February 1977 and remained with him for over thirteen years. After her successful interview, she rarely found her boss to be "sympathetic", receiving praise from him on just one occasion. In her previous job, her gross monthly salary had been 4,000 marks; Korf paid her 800 marks less. In return, she worked unpaid overtime, sometimes until 10 or 11 p.m. Her boss seemed to live in the office when he wasn't overseas:

> In the evenings he would drive over to his house shortly before eight and watch the news, then come back at nine or nine-thirty and ask how much progress we'd all made. Once he brought me a sandwich from home that his 10-year-old daughter Sylvia had made. Then we carried on. Somehow, we were carried away by his enthusiasm. It wouldn't have been possible otherwise.

It wasn't unusual for Renate Höing, who lived alone, to drive home after midnight – and be back at her desk before eight the next morning. Many people in this tightknit community that Korf had formed did the same – even on Sundays, if necessary. And since Höing's office was opposite Korf's, on the other side of the building, she didn't even get to enjoy the panorama of the Black Forest.

Korf was a workaholic who churned out letters, memoranda and strategy papers non-stop. Höing and her colleagues could hardly keep up with him:

> He dictated like there was no tomorrow. We had no time to think, the work kept piling up. Korf once called me from Kuwait on a Sunday afternoon: he wanted to dictate something to me 'later'. Fine, I was in the office anyway. At 11 p.m., after I'd gone home and gone to bed, he called me again and started dictating. He needed the document at Frankfurt airport at ten o'clock the next morning, so I went to the office at the crack of dawn to type it up. I just hoped the numbers were right for once – Korf usually got them wrong!

Korf seemed to be everywhere at once. Höing transformed the instructions that Korf left for her on the plastic discs recorded on his old-fashioned dictation machine into meticulous schedules for the coming weeks. The unedited Dictaphone orders for a day chosen at random from thirteen years' records highlight Korf's almost unbelievable dynamism and mobility. However, his plans would never have come to full fruition without Höing's input:

> First of all, I'd like to tell you that I've dictated an immediate fax to Miss S. for Mr H., whom I urgently need to speak to regarding the letter of comfort for the loan to CSC. ... Then you'll find some Aer Lingus flight documents on your desk, which Mr B. will pick up. ... You'll see all the folders which I've taken out of the conference room – you can put them back in the conference room when the lawyers have left. ... B. will give you some documents that I need for Mr K. on Tuesday in London. ... Then all my travel documents for India will arrive, so all I have to do now is tell Mr K. which flight I'm taking to Calcutta on Monday. ... Then we have to confirm the appointment with Ambassador S. ... The hunting invitation is also OK. Then you can call H. (Lanvin Paris) and tell him to use a thin blue fabric of about the same quality. Just see that he makes the shirts as quickly as possible and sends them to me, and please tell him to make the cuffs white, too. ... We must definitely send Hermann D. a telegram. Think up something nice in my name and from my wife, but you absolutely have to send it today as he's 85, how remarkable. ... I can't attend the talk by the US ambassador on 27 April. ... The GTZ German Corporation for Technical Cooperation meeting on 11 May is exactly where B. is having his dinner – I can't attend either, even though it's important, but I simply can't. ... Then there was an interesting programme on RTL TV, a talk show, K. was on there, and there was also something about the Brazilian rainforests – call RTL and see if you can obtain a video recording of it. ... Then I'm looking for documents from correspondence with the KfW Reconstruction Bank, that was about two or three years ago, they're about a new process, see if there's anything in the file. ... Then order 36 bottles of this wine and try to get

the price down a bit. ... Leave all the mail downstairs, I'll definitely be back in the office this evening.

And that was merely a short excerpt from the secretary's four-page transcript! In later years, Höing, together with a young colleague, tried to do something about Korf's tendency to overwork them. She wrote a terse memo to him:

Re: The question of untidiness in our office: The solution lies with you and you alone. Until you realize that the amount of work you give us is unreasonable, and as long as we have to do the most important things at the very last minute, without regard to normal working hours, i.e. no matter how exhausted we already are, as long as we have to deal with dictation tapes that aren't classified by responsibility or prioritized, which sometimes means a triple workload, we can't change anything. In my view, it's a miracle that more things don't go wrong, and if you think about all this calmly, you, too, will see that I'm right.

But whenever Höing felt completely dejected, when the boss had gone berserk or overstepped the bounds of even her resilience, the Korf effect kicked in. As she later recalled, still amazed by his attitude:

He could quite suddenly change gear and be radiantly charming again. I told him as much: 'It really gets me down, these vagaries of yours. You can be so incredibly nice sometimes, but as soon as you're back in the office, you become so horrid.' He laughed his head off.

At times, on the other hand, when Korf had a headache or a cold, "he seemed like a little boy who wanted to be stroked. I always gave him some kind of household remedy."

Korf's unwavering path was lined with no fewer than three milestones in 1979. Two of them were proud anniversaries, the third the greatest conceivable accolade for the former underdog.

The first reason for celebration occurred on 13 August, which was Willy Korf's fiftieth birthday. The guest list for the lavish party in Baden-Baden was like a *Who's Who* of high society: big names such as Beitz, Benteler, Burda, Friderichs, Galen, Oetker, Pöhl, Späth, Speer, and Stauffenberg were in attendance, as were the ambassadors of Tunisia and Saudi Arabia.

The most original gift, however, came from the secretary who had so often been put through the wringer by the birthday boy. Sometime beforehand, Renate Höing had undertaken to produce a comedy film, based on a jointly written script, featuring almost all 150 members of staff at head office making fun of themselves and the company. Secret filming on Moltkestrasse, which was carried out by a cameraman hired from broadcaster SWF, had to be scheduled when Korf took a short holiday. The film director held nightly meetings in the conference room. Each department contributed a scene suitably exaggerated for comic effect.

The canteen, for example, explained its new menu specially devised to prevent people from falling asleep in the office, featuring such tempting dishes as Arabian onions stewed in stress and served in a hectic rush with telephone salad. Or how about nervous onion sorbet cooked using direct reduction and accompanied by cold coffee? In a scene shot on the tarmac of Baden-Oos airport, two pilots from Korf-Transport sat in front of a toy model of a Korf corporate jet playing a game in which cards bearing Willy Korf's typical destinations were thrown down like trumps: "Moscow!" – "Madrid!" – "Abu Dhabi!" Engrossed in their novel card game, they failed to notice a real plane thundering over their heads on its approach to land. In the grand finale set in the foyer of company headquarters, a cleaning lady mopped the floor while singing "Happy Birthday, dear Willy" – whereupon the camera dollied back for a long shot as all the employees joined in. This unique film, capturing that characteristically 1970s mix of stiff formality and anarchic cheer, had the air of an amateur dramatics troupe performing in a corporate setting. And it was clearly overlooked when the Oscar nominations were made that year...

At one point during the making of this cinematic triumph, the only person not involved nearly caught wind of what was going on. "One evening, we'd finished editing the film and somebody from our team had already fetched a bottle of bubbly from Korf's office for a toast," Höing remembered. "At that moment, Bernhardt came out of his office. We only just managed to hide the bottle in time under someone's jacket."

Willy Korf was so thrilled with the movie when it was finally presented to him that he regularly showed it to business friends around a table with ten executive chairs, a television and a video recorder. This conference room wasn't in his head office, but on board his luxurious Falcon 50 corporate jet. We can only imagine what sort of impression the film must have left on his unsuspecting associates.

What the bizarre video did not show was the fact that a whole string of significant technical feats were being achieved behind the scenes in Korf's empire. A prime example of this was in furnace construction technology. In 1974, a freelance mechanical engineer by the name of Gerhard Fuchs had been granted a patent for a water-based cooling system for the electric arc furnace. Working with his own small firm near the BSW site in Kehl, he was already bound to Korf, twelve years his senior, by contracts for services: "We had a very close relationship, like father and son." The success of this patent led Korf to take a 50 per cent stake in Fuchs's business, which was renamed Korf & Fuchs Systemtechnik GmbH and equipped all Korf's plants with the new water-cooling system.

Previously, the interior of an electric arc furnace had been lined with refractory bricks, which had to be replaced frequently depending on the aggressiveness of the arc, causing downtime and production outages. Water as a coolant had been all but outlawed because if it got into the melt, it could trigger catastrophic oxyhydrogen reactions. But in the early 1970s, the Japanese used water cooling for the first time, although their cooling elements were located behind the refractory layer. In experiments conducted in Kehl and Hamburg, Fuchs and Korf managed to use water cooling elements of about one square metre in size above the level of the liquid melt *instead* of the refractory lining. This method was so revolutionary that it was later copied by many competitors. Korf's team of highly creative developers headed by engineer and metallurgist Hubert Knapp went on to augment this technology with water-cooled furnace lids and electrodes.

Another example of Korf's technical innovation was the project named Electric Furnace for the Year 2000. In the late 1970s, Korf put his researchers to work on this vision, among them Werner Marnette, who had been specially recruited from Aachen University and had done his doctorate on plasma metallurgy. "It was unbelievable how much attention Korf paid to his technical teams," Marnette said in admiration years later. "We were given the freedom to develop ideas and also implement them. We experimented day and night. Korf was the driving force. The atmosphere was amazing." The resulting improvements, together with the mother of all innovations, the Midrex process, were what slowly allowed Korf's name as a pioneer of new steel mill technology to filter through into authoritative scientific circles.

This reputation suited the ambitious entrepreneur very well, for he was hoping that academic recognition would make it easier for him to join the almost impenetrable club of the steel industry's major players. The best ticket to the top was an honorary doctorate from the renowned Aachen University. Using a series of intermediaries, Korf kept knocking discreetly but persistently. Again and again, he reminded people of his accomplishments. And in 1979, he found himself on the verge of achieving this academic goal.

For a long time, the undeclared pursuit of the title of doctor honoris causa didn't look promising for Willy Korf. In June 1977, two and a half years before the happy outcome, a source from Aachen University reported in a memo to Korf's Baden-Baden headquarters that the honorary doctorate procedure had been put on hold for the time being owing to problems with the university senate. For one thing, the student representatives were categorically against awarding an honorary doctorate to an industrialist, since they were "all capitalists" (this was still the 1970s of rebellious far-left student politics). Furthermore, the professors wanted a candidate who'd made a major contribution to academia – whereas Korf, who'd merely gone to commercial college and hadn't earned a degree, excelled precisely because his scientific knowledge had been honed in the real world.

Korf's industry experience counted for little, however, at a university of applied sciences, especially one which awarded very few honorary doctorates compared to other universities. Respected for its high standards, a title awarded by Aachen University therefore conferred an even higher distinction on its recipient. The outlook for Korf seemed bleak, although according to the source, the committees opposing his doctorate had let slip that the decision might be reconsidered the following year when the senate had been reappointed. And if no doctorate was awarded, well, there was also a chance of Willy Korf being made an honorary citizen or honorary senator instead.

The following year, 1978, also passed without Korf receiving higher honours. This may have been because many of the decision-making professors enjoyed close ties with the executive boards of large corporations. However, even the faculty members at Aachen University must have noticed by now that Willy Korf, an entrepreneur active on four continents, had almost reached the pinnacle of his economic success. Mini steel mills with licensed Midrex direct reduction plants seemed to be in operation or under construction everywhere: in West Germany, the USA and Canada, in the USSR, Venezuela, Argentina, Trinidad and Tobago, in the UK and Iran, Saudi Arabia, Qatar and Nigeria. This success was based more than almost any other on genuine innovation – one of the key achievements paving the way to an honorary doctorate. And this finally sank home at the university, where Korf clearly had a handful of admirers.

Among them was Professor Hermann Schenck, head of the

Research Centre for Technical-Economic Corporate Structures in the Steel Industries. In December 1978, Schenck explained to the senate why Willy Korf should be awarded an honorary doctorate. Being a true innovator, he was an exception at a time when "the steel industry was undoubtedly on the wane" because the euphoria of the previous years had led to overcapacity, while "daring, empathy with new technology, and unbridled joy over progress" had hardly "emerged with sufficient strength". To be sure, many engineers had sought ways to tackle the problem that coke might become far too expensive to keep traditional steel mills competitive. But the past year had shown that "of all the proposed methods, practically only the Midrex process fostered and nurtured by W. Korf has survived." Large German steel companies, on the other hand, had "resignedly given up on the further development of their own ideas and even acquired Midrex licences."

According to the professor, Willy Korf possessed an unusually high grasp of the extremely complex subject of metallurgy, something that came naturally to him and had been sharpened through intensive self-study. Schenck's praise of Korf went as far as to acknowledge the shortcomings among the educational elite – something rarely heard in the lofty circles of German higher education:

> Every conversation with him about metallurgical problems and their technical and economic impact makes it clear that his highly intuitive talent, coupled with single-minded enthusiasm, doesn't need academic consecration to achieve more engineering proficiency than many average graduates of technical sciences."

Or, expressed in simpler terms, Korf had a better grasp of industrial engineering than many alumni of the subject. After such an endorsement, only one more formal hurdle had to be cleared for the sake of compliance: Korf had never put his name to a scientific paper. Schenck's elegant solution:

> Mr Korf has mainly appeared in public with lectures and

interviews …; it is understandable that there has been no room for specific scientific considerations in his explanation of his plans for the technical reorganization of the steel industry, whereas his presentation of the main technical aspects is absolutely convincing."

Quod erat demonstrandum; Korf had already publicly shown that his scientific knowledge met the required standard, without having to publish a paper. Proof that Korf deserved an honorary degree had been delivered. After this plea by the respected doctoral supervisor Professor Schenck, no further obstacles stood in the way of an honorary doctorate for Willy Korf.

On 30 November 1979, the day which marked nothing less than the professional and social zenith in the life of the 50-year-old Willy Korf, Aachen University awarded him a coveted honorary doctorate at the behest of the Faculty of Mining and Metallurgy. Korf received the award "in recognition of his outstanding creative engineering achievements in the development and large-scale technical implementation of a novel process for iron extraction as well as the realization of the concept of mini steelworks." Every word spoken that day about Korf – the non-academic 'David' among the established professorial players, who had been shunned, criticized and ridiculed for so long – gave him the greatest possible satisfaction. And he savoured it to the full. Not that he let it show, as far as he could control his feelings – and he usually could, when it came to public appearances.

Even so, in his acceptance speech in the old senate meeting room of Aachen University, he couldn't resist toying with the image of the 'little guy' who was more agile than the big fish of the steel industry. Looking back on his early years, Korf spoke of his "technical layman's mind" and of "world-renowned companies … before which a small entrepreneur would normally be paralysed in awe." Or, at least, a *normal* small entrepreneur would be… And of course, David couldn't refrain from a sideswipe at the Goliaths, saying that in the German "steel monopoly" there was "little call for technical innovations since there was no competition, no cost or price incentives." Before David had stepped onto the industrial stage, "there had been no revolutionary changes in the basic production methods for a century."

At the reception that evening in the black and gold hall of the Steigenberger Quellenhof, a prestigious hotel in Aachen, after Henriot champagne had been served in the atrium, over veal tenderloin in puff pastry served with truffle duxelles and tarragon sauce, Korf passed from group to group and was graciously patted on the back by his famous and influential guests. Just how good this felt for Korf after he'd been disregarded for years is demonstrated by a folder containing more than a hundred letters of congratulations and commemorative telegrams, alphabetically indexed.

From among this collection, the most satisfying correspondence for the newly titled honorary doctor must have been the rather dutiful letters from the directors of his large competitors. Even though some of them prefaced their lines with a peevish "As I have gathered from the press ...", the way the Krupps, Klöckners, Thyssens and Hoeschs paid their respects was priceless to Korf. Nevertheless, the folder tells of more than just satisfaction. Korf wouldn't have been Korf if he hadn't been prepared to bury the hatchet and broach new, surprising collaborations with his old adversaries at the next available opportunity – for instance while out hunting together.

Korf's third outstanding event of 1979 was the tenth anniversary of one of his most successful ventures: Korf Engineering GmbH in Düsseldorf. The celebration was held in the ballroom of a large Düsseldorf hotel on 13 December (a fortnight after he'd been made an honorary doctor). Appearing in front of his staff and business partners, Korf reviewed the highlights of their time together. After his old US partner Midland Ross had pulled out, the former Korf-Midland-Ross-Engineering had become Korf Engineering in February 1972.

Instead of the Americans, Klöckner plants held interests in Korf's plant engineering company. But this honeymoon was also short-lived, for after just five years, in 1977, Klöckner left as well, to be replaced by Vöest-Alpine from the Austrian city of Linz.

The first operational challenge for Korf Engineering GmbH had been the construction of the steelworks in Hamburg in 1969, and later the French steelworks in Montereau. By the late 1970s, Korf Engineering was invited to bid for almost all steelworks contracts globally. The initial team of eight had grown into a force of almost 250 planners and engineers, building turnkey mini steel mills and Midrex plants all over the world, and exporting electric furnaces, continuous casting plants and rolling mills.

This growth underpinned Korf's transformation from a pure steel manufacturer to a consultant and steelworks builder, just as his plants had previously documented the change from merchant to producer. With orders on hand of around a billion marks, this company was very successful – in contrast to many of his other interests, which had been hit badly by the steel crisis. Korf summed up the *raison d'être* of his plant construction company to his audience as follows: "Our development had cost us dearly at times. Korf Engineering GmbH was an attempt to recover this money." But that wasn't all – for the company was his gateway to the world's steel markets, the next step of his journey.

Formative homeland: Iron-ore was mined in the Siegerland as early as the late Middle Ages

Willy Korf as a baby in 1929

The grandfather's agricultural trading company in Au an der Sieg in the fifties

Only child Willy Korf with his parents Grete and Arthur Korf, ca. 1933

Home of the grandfather Gustav Korf, who was one of the first car owners at the time

Grandfather Gustav and his second wife Frieda, the parents Grete and Arthur, Willy

Growing mobility: Willy Korf with his pre-war Mercedes V170,
ca. 1948

A matured 19 year old Korf after the takeover of his grandfather's company

Hungry for life: 28 year old Korf waterskiing on the river Rhine near Kehl

Intermezzo: Advertising brochure for his own plastic boat production in 1958

Aviation pioneer: The German "
Taxiflug" (1959-1963), which serviced amongst other places seaside resorts

The small family: Willy Korf, wife Brigitte,
daughters Astrid and Sylvia, ca. 1966

Headquarters of Korf Stahl AG, Baden-Baden, 1975 (today: Südwestrundfunk)

Global: Willy Korf as an international entrepreneur in 1975

Big political stage: Willy Korf with German Chancellor Willy Brandt, ca.1973...

...and at Rumaninan's Dictator Nicolae Ceausecu's state visit in 1973

(Almost) always on duty: with Federal
Minister of Economics Hans Friedrichs,
ca. 1976

Global player: Korf-airplane Falcon 20 (call-sign "D-CORF") in Rio de Janeiro

Companions: Lothar Spaeth, Prime Minister of Baden-Wuerttemberg...

... Chairman of the Board, lawyer Max Kreidels, ca. 1979

State visit of King Khalid of Saudi Arabia, German Chancellor Helmut Schmidt, Korf, 1980

Korf in the midst of Saudi dignitaries, on the right Count Otto
Lambsdorff, Federal Minister of Economics, 1980

Briefcase fanatic: A well sorted arsenal of briefcases accompanied Korf on every journey

Befor the crisis, ca.1980

Entrance-hall of the Korf-Headoffice

A lot in common: Lothar Spaeth main speaker at the "25 Years of Korf" jubilee,1980

A lot to show: Korf presenting a model of MIDREX 400 directreduction plant

Triumph! Korf in the middle of his social network. His daughter Sylvia on the left

Tragic! Prophetic portrait, 1989

"We were like brothers": Cousin Helmhold Schneider, ca 1985

CHAPTER 7

All the world's a stage

"Our ideal is to achieve continuous flight powered by free solar energy like a perpetual motion machine, with air refuelling for emergencies, coupled to an aerial, unmanned Midrex steel mill, so we can always land wherever the market is, and where no one's expecting us since there's no radar!"

Korf never shied away from foreign countries, cultures or languages following his first visit to America – and even less so after branching out into chamber pots in Nigeria. On the contrary, he loved to establish bridgeheads and undertake pioneering ventures abroad. Over the years, he'd picked up fluent English to the point where he could now discuss complex technical matters. This was unusual for Korf's generation, where polyglot industrialists were a rare breed. He was even seen on television standing in front of a model of a Midrex unit, surrounded by visitors, some dressed in Arab attire, as he explained the principle of direct reduction in a raspy, German accent: "Gentlemen, this is the Midrex 400 unit. Here you have the reformer, where natural gas is converted into hydrogen and carbon monoxide. This together gives the reduction gas ..."

Korf's knowledge of Russian was at the other end of the scale. But that didn't stop him from chumming up to the Soviet rulers.

After all, he owned both a Midrex licence that opened any door and a company that could solve any problem: Korf Engineering. Even so, Korf only joined this particular party somewhat late in the day.

In early 1972, a trade mission representing the German industrial sector went to Moscow to negotiate the construction of a huge Russian steelworks. The delegation was headed by Hans Birnbaum, CEO of Salzgitter AG, a nationalized steel company. At the Hanover Fair in April, Korf caught the deputy Soviet premier Vladimir Novikov in a confab with Birnbaum about the steel deal which they'd already recently discussed in Moscow. Korf promptly invited Novikov to Hamburg to show him his state-of-the-art Midrex mini steel mill. The Russian was impressed by what he saw – not least because the Soviet Union had vast quantities of natural gas ideal for any gas-fired reduction plants in the planned steelworks complex.

The following November, Birnbaum flew to Moscow on a company jet for the final talks, accompanied by Willy Korf. On 17 November, Salzgitter AG and the Korf Group signed an agreement to build a steel plant in Kursk with the Soviet trade organization Metallurg-Import. It was the largest industrial project to date involving collaboration between West Germany and the USSR. It was also Korf's most significant foreign venture outside his own plants.

Kursk, a historical trading centre on the River Seym, was the centre of a huge iron ore-mining area with an annual output of some 40 million tonnes. But to build the biggest and most advanced steelworks in the eastern hemisphere – and the first large steel plant based on the Midrex system – other German partners were needed: Krupp and Siemens. It hadn't taken much for Korf to personally persuade the Russians to adopt his technology, but he left it to his deputy Wolfgang Bernhardt to handle the intricate contract negotiations with the German consortium. Once again, Bernhardt found himself having to curb the enthusiasm of his boss, who was already getting carried away with dreams of expansion. As Bernhardt later explained:

This was another of those conflicts between Korf and me. He wanted to build half a dozen Midrex plants himself as part of a giant steel complex. I said: 'We can't – it's too risky for us.' 'Why?' he asked. I told him we could manage one or two plants, but that a project on that scale could only be accomplished by an experienced plant builder with a licence agreement.

Both Bernhardt and reason prevailed – to Korf Engineering's advantage, as it turned out. Lurgi GmbH, at that time considered the best plant construction company in the world, was granted a sub-licence by the Korf Group to build the Midrex plants – in return for a hefty fee, of course. Much of the commercial risk was thus shifted onto someone else's shoulders, as was so often the case with Korf's companies. Financing the costly steelworks, the subject of tough negotiations at the highest political level, exceeded all normal bounds.

Eventually, several years and several billion marks later, the German–Soviet project succumbed to an outdated gigantism. Most of those involved, including the unsuspecting German taxpayer, had to write off enormous losses. In fact, the only one to do well out of the whole deal was Korf. Time and again thereafter, he would be welcomed in the Kremlin like a state visitor and as a friend of the Soviet Union.

Korf also offered his advanced technology far more widely than the USSR, becoming a major supplier of industrial equipment globally. In spring 1973, he showed Romanian dictator Nicolae Ceaușescu around his steelworks in Hamburg during a state visit to West Germany. On this occasion, Korf's intended technology transfer to the East failed to materialize. Nevertheless, by 1980, the Midrex process was in use at a long list of steel mills around the world, while other steel plants had also been agreed or were already under construction, such as two Midrex units in Nigeria, four in the Soviet Union, three in Iran, and two in Hadeed in Saudi Arabia. All in all, actual or planned steel production employing the Midrex process totalled 17 million tonnes annually.

Although Korf was especially well known in the Arab world, however, this did not prevent him from doing business with Israel for a while. He discreetly ensured that, for example, a stake he owned in an Israeli plant didn't come to the attention of his Arab partners. To this end, the Israeli connection was simply placed under the auspices of KIH in order to keep it out of Korf-Stahl's annual reports. It was also useful that Korf had acquired a fistful of passports over time. For one thing, there were always a few lying around in consulates waiting to have visas stamped in them. And Korf was extremely careful to only take papers to Arab countries that didn't bear any Israeli entry stamps.

The Saudi steelworks in Al-Jubail was a magnificent result of Korf's Middle East diplomacy. The DEG German Investment Corporation and Korf-Stahl had each taken a 7 per cent share in a new company, the Saudi Arabian Iron and Steel Company in Hadeed. The majority shareholder was the state holding company SABIC. Their joint aim was to build the first steel plant in the country (including two Midrex units) producing 1 million tonnes of reinforcing steel and wire rod per year. In Jeddah, Korf also became a 40 per cent shareholder of a dilapidated rolling mill, which Korf Engineering intended to revamp.

Korf was never deterred by the fact that such partnerships drew him into cultures with their own particular way of doing things; with hindsight, perhaps he should have been more wary. His old friend Karl Wienand, who'd travelled extensively on behalf of the Social Democrats and the German Chancellor, was well versed in the customs and traditions of the Middle East. As such, he was able to talk Korf out of overly ambitious adventures, and step in to navigate through diplomatic impasses, when necessary.

Shortly before the end of Helmut Schmidt's government in 1982, Wienand and Korf travelled with the bosses of other German companies and banks into the desert to visit Libya's head of state, Muammar 'Colonel' Gaddafi, who, according to Berber tradition, used to welcome even his most important guests in a Bedouin tent. Planning was underway for a steelworks in the coastal city of Misurata, east of Tripoli, for which Korf was to deliver a Midrex plant. However, work on the foundations couldn't proceed because one Berber had settled there while passing through and seemed unwilling to budge for anything in the world.

The German delegation was whisked by helicopter to Gaddafi's improvised headquarters in the desert, which were flanked by two Leopard tanks he'd obviously acquired from German army surplus. Gaddafi's Bedouin tent was full of plastic furniture of the type sold at any garden centre. All the visitors could get out of Gaddafi was that nothing could be done about the single resident – a Berber was a Berber, and was allowed to claim any spot of Libyan soil that happened to suit him. So far, so bad.

At the same time, Karl Wienand also had another mission. He'd been asked by the Chancellor to talk Gaddafi politely but firmly out of a planned visit to Germany. Gaddafi had been invited by Liberal eccentric Jürgen W. Möllemann, president of the German–Arab Society, even though shortly beforehand, an exiled Libyan had evidently been assassinated by Gaddafi's secret service on Bonn's market square. Employing a good deal of flattery, Wienand informed the dictator that if he visited Germany, protests would be inevitable, which would be terribly undignified for such an important leader. This prospect swayed the vain revolutionary to abandon his plan.

At the end of this memorable desert trip, Wienand whispered to his friend Willy Korf that Gaddafi was obviously unpredictable, that the embargo policy against him was about to come to a head, and that Willy should stay out of the steel project. The whole Libyan affair (at least for Willy Korf) evaporated like a mirage in the desert.

Other international projects, however, were more successful. Being his own best salesman, Korf ceaselessly ploughed his way through the airspace of every continent (except Australia / Oceania). And being a passionate aviator, he was only too keen to take to the skies whenever the opportunity presented itself.

Thomas Starke, who joined *Badisches Tagblatt* (Korf's hometown newspaper) in 1981 as business editor, soon had his first 'airy' encounter with the local business hero when Korf offered to show him around the BSW steelworks in Kehl for an article, promising to escort him there personally from Baden-Baden. The young editor, expecting to be driven there, was astonished when Korf opted for a chartered helicopter instead. They reached the Rhine from the small airport in Baden-Oos in no time. Starke, who'd never flown in a helicopter before, was fascinated: "Despite the factory tour, we ended up talking more about aviation than steel that day!"

When Willy Korf finally acquired a Dassault Falcon 50 intercontinental trijet in 1980, allowing long-haul flights taking up to eight and a half hours (and hence direct trips to the east coast of the USA), he encountered a snag, for the runway at Baden-Oos airport was 200 metres (650 feet) too short for the aircraft. After a while, he decided to have it extended so that his corporate plane, with a take-off weight of almost 18 tonnes, could get airborne without breaking airport regulations (for the first few flights, it'd been a case of grit your teeth and up, up and away!).

By this time, Korf was no longer condemned to silence in the air. He could make telephone calls to the mainland via shortwave radio stations once they'd been arranged by his chief pilot, Anton Schulze. This worked best during a full moon over the Atlantic, but even then, only in intercom mode, the standard procedure in radio communication. Because unauthorized listeners could eavesdrop using shortwave receivers, Korf followed his pilot's advice not to discuss any confidential business.

The half-dozen briefcases full of documents that Korf took with him and systematically worked through on every flight were legendary. As Franz Burda once admitted to his travelling companion: "Next to you on the plane, I always felt downright lazy!" At the end of a holiday together in Barbados, there was still no mercy for Burda: "Even on the way from the hotel to the airport, [Korf] couldn't resist explaining the balance sheet of Georgetown Steel to me in great detail!"

Shortly before touchdown in Baden-Baden at around four in the morning, the control tower was notified by radio, and the runway lights were switched on especially for Korf. Back on solid ground, Korf and his companions often went straight to the only local nightspot that was still open – for breakfast. And after just two hours' sleep, Korf was back in the office by 7 a.m.

Time wasn't money for Korf. That would have been too mundane. Time was his unit of measurement for the transformation of creativity into success. In this more complex interpretation, time meant the time he had left to accomplish a task. This kind of efficiency is described in a poem by Christian Morgenstern. It's about a fictitious character who frequently appears in Morgenstern's poetry, and who coincidentally bears the name Herr Korf:

A novel clock has Korf designed
Where dual pairs of hands move round.
One pair is the usual kind,
The other pair is backward-bound.
When it shows two, it's also ten;
When it shows three, it's also nine;
So when he looks, a businessman
No longer is afraid of time.
For on this clockface Korf devised,
Where hands of Janus turn about,
The reason why it's highly prized
Is time just cancels itself out.

The real Korf, Willy himself, put it more succinctly: "When you have time, there are no limits." This quotation appeared in the issue of *Wirtschaftswoche* declaring him Manager of the Year 1973. It's one of those sentences that journalists love to reproduce verbatim because it allows them to pigeonhole the person coining it.

There were several reasons why Willy Korf and the press thrived off each other. Quickly learning how to play his public image as a David against the Goliaths of German steel, at the same time he grasped how to nurture his good relationship with the media – and continued doing so even when he himself might have been described as a Goliath (although he never was). He gave the press pack what they wanted: stories of a disruptive rebel who refused to be brought down by the big bullies of the steel industry – and in return, the reporters flattered him. He let the press photographers take high-contrast pictures of him alongside his attractive wife talking eye to eye with foreign leaders, Brigitte Korf lending German business a touch of glamour.

Nothing (except perhaps princesses and scandals) sells newspapers better than tales of the little guy standing up to his oppressor. Rarely did the media have to bend the truth so little for a top story as in the case of Willy Korf. And then there was Korf's great mission in civil society: what he saw as the enormous injustice of huge state handouts for inefficient giants like Thyssen, Krupp, Klöckner and Arbed-Saarstahl, while he went largely empty-handed. Journalists were happy to carry this message into the world on Korf's behalf, especially later when the steel crisis, fuelled by public subsidies, threatened to put an end to both his business activities and their inexhaustible source of stories.

The fact that he gave his planes registration numbers like D-CORF and D-BBWK (Baden-Baden Willy-Korf); that he liked to wear dark blue pinstripe suits ("not from a particularly expensive tailor," as someone cuttingly remarked in his early years); that by 1972 he already had a car phone in his Mercedes 350SL and used it to make calls as long-distance as New York – these were all things the media loved about him. And they also loved his inconsistencies.

On the one hand, Korf was every inch the consummate host, the last one to leave the party, and whose receptions and hunts were always good for a few printable anecdotes. For instance, there was the story about how he hosted one of his legendary parties in Baden-Baden to celebrate his sixtieth birthday and was joined by 150 carefully chosen guests, including journalists, bankers and local dignitaries – while not a single representative of big steel received an invite. On the other hand, as he confided to newspapers time and again, he was "bored to tears in the company of the jet set." And in 1973, with the 1968 movement of mass student protests still ever present in people's minds, he complained: "We have too much establishment, too much establishment everywhere. Something needs to change."

There were certain areas in which Korf fostered a real mystique and an air of inaccessibility. These included the precarious financial basis of his business activities, as well as his private life, outside the standard scenes from state receptions and meets 'n' greets. The large feature that *Capital* magazine produced on him in 1968 was let down by including almost nothing about Korf the man: "Only with palpable discomfort does he mention such customary details as the fact that he met his wife during a ship-naming ceremony at Stinnes." Korf was "a very matter-of-fact type … who was reluctant to reveal any private information," was all the reporter could say. In light of this, he shifted his view of Korf, no longer seeing an "ambitious, aggressive, self-sufficient entrepreneur … but for once as an insecure young man."

Accordingly, every personal detail about Willy Korf that the newspapers managed to get their hands on was reported as if it were of national significance: "8.15 a.m.: Time for Korf's regular deep dive – into his swimming pool!" shouted the headline of an article setting out his daily exercise routine in *Welt am Sonntag* in October 1980. The Sunday paper, which had especially close ties to Korf's empire, continued by divulging details about his breakfast: "Tea and crispbread."

Eight years earlier, the same paper had been vocal in its praise when Korf opened his steelworks in Hamburg: "He visits his factories by jet. They're the most modern in the world. Experts have compared his advances in steel to the revolution ushered in by the Wankel engine in the car industry." Although the author may simply have been mirroring the prevailing opinion at the time, the Wankel engine itself, first launched in 1964 in the NSU Spider, proved short-lived. Its excessive fuel consumption put an end to production of the smooth-running rotary engine used in the NSU Ro80 in 1977 – and indeed to the entire NSU brand, once it had been swallowed up the Volkswagen Group and merged with Audi. Was this bold journalistic analogy an inadvertent omen for Korf? In the whirl of headlines, and without the power of hindsight, this question was never asked – until the crisis hit home.

Just two years before his most difficult hour, Korf had a small collection of clippings from *Der Spiegel* reproduced for a glossy chronicle celebrating the twenty-fifth anniversary of the Korf Group. Naturally, only those snippets were shown in which tributes such as "After a seven-year price war with Korf, the big players grew weary" and "In Willy Korf's mini-company, revenue multiplies year after year" stood out. The collage also included a cartoon depicting Willy Korf as a pesky insect sitting on the bald head of a fat steel boss, who was vainly trying to finish Korf off by hitting himself on the head with a fly swat representing price cuts. That was much to Korf's liking, as were the pictures of him on the front covers of *Wirtschaftswoche* (in a leather armchair), *Industriemagazin* (holding a cigar), *Capital* (alongside the bosses of BASF, Ruhrkohle and Siemens) and even *Business Week* (proof of his Anglo-Saxon triumph).

Korf was so adept at managing the media that the fickle press hardly ever found a fly in his ointment, even in later years once he'd gone through the agony of defeat. One of the few exceptions occurred in June 1987 when *Capital* indirectly accused him of being careless with money. It also claimed he was careless with his newly formed group of companies, which it described as being anything but transparent and solidly financed, just like the old corporate group, adding that rough estimates on the back of an envelope often took the place of exact figures. But this criticism was a drop in the journalistic ocean. And even in this article, despite its suspicion, the magazine declared his innovative manufacturing technology to have good sales prospects under the right circumstances.

Korf's charm and his powers of persuasion worked wonders with the press. The media rarely forgive the mistakes of the heroes they love to build up and knock down. Yet Korf's record was almost unsullied, and he remained the likeable rebel he'd always been for the editors. Helmhold Schneider, his cousin, summed up Korf's sense of controlled spectacle in his short book about Willy Korf *A Life Dedicated to Steel*. Korf had known how important public relations were to him, wrote Schneider – and his PR strategy had paid off, for even during his personal crisis, it ensured he had "a positive, benevolent press until the end."

It's not that the media failed to notice how Korf shrewdly exploited all possible sources of state aid or generally outsourced the financial risks of his business ventures. But they let him get away with it so that they could continue to be enchanted by his dynamic charisma. This is clearly illustrated by the example of Norddeutsche Ferrowerke, yet another of Korf's international co-productions.

Taking a 25.1 per cent stake in this new plant producing sponge iron in Emden on Germany's north-eastern border in 1976, he managed to persuade Norway's state-owned iron ore company Sydvaranger to acquire the remaining 74.9 per cent. Two Midrex plants were to go onstream in 1979 and produce around 2 million tonnes of sponge iron a year – initially not for Korf's own steelworks, but only to be sold to third parties. The gas needed for the direct reduction plants was to be supplied from the Ekofisk field in the Norwegian sector of the North Sea. With northern Germany plagued by unemployment, during the negotiations over the 400 million mark plant, Korf blatantly tried to pressurize the German government, especially Hans Friderichs, the Liberal minister of economic affairs. As one newspaper wrote at the time: "Needless to say, Korf collected tens of millions in state subsidies from national and regional government for the plant in Emden."

The Norwegians had only got involved in the first place because the regional gas monopolists, first and foremost Ruhrgas AG, had colluded to sell natural gas to Korf for an exorbitant price. Originally, the steel giant Hoesch had wanted to join Korf on this project, but was scared off by the aggressive gas cartel. Not even Friderichs, normally quite sympathetic to Korf, could help him this time, for despite being a minister, he dared not challenge the influential Ruhrgas.

It just so happened that Sydvaranger was planning to build a direct reduction plant anyway, albeit on the southwest Norwegian peninsula of Stavanger. Korf got in touch with the company's bosses and persuaded them to move their plans to Emden. Thanks to its privileged access to the Ekofisk gas fields, Sydvaranger was able to supply fuel for the Midrex plants much more cheaply. Construction began in 1978, and the production of high-quality sponge iron commenced in 1981. Nevertheless, the joint venture went into administration as quickly as July 1982. The price of gas had risen so drastically on the world markets that sponge iron produced in this way could no longer be sold profitably. This was the first time since Korf's Nigerian adventure, so many years earlier, that one of his assets underwent full-blown bankruptcy.

Prior to this shock and the following stage in the great decline of the global steel industry, Korf's companies enjoyed a short phase of relative prosperity. On one of his many trips abroad, Willy Korf and his deputy Wolfgang Bernhardt visited a trade show in the USA in 1979. They were astonished to find that Korf-Stahl's booth was positioned alongside that of an old acquaintance, Horst Weitzmann, now head of Germany for a US engineering company. This was the very same Weitzmann who, when working for Thyssen, had been asked to deal with the awkward patent lawsuits brought by Ludwig von Bogdandy, the inventor of Purofer.

It was at this time that Korf was seeking a replacement for Peter Kehl, the original CEO of his Hamburg steelworks, who wasn't up to the pressure. Acting on impulse, he told Weitzmann that he needed a new number one at HSW. Weitzmann asked: "What's up with Kehl?" – referring to the boss. But Korf mistook Weitzmann's question as an enquiry about the same post at Badische Stahlwerke, his steel mill in the town of Kehl. "Well, that's also a possibility," he promptly replied. And it was in this curious fashion that Horst Weitzmann joined BSW as a director in December 1979, being promoted to CEO three months later.

At that time, the situation at BSW was far from ideal, and it was barely making a profit. "It looked like the Foreign Legion!" exclaimed Horst Weitzmann. The majority of the workforce were Turks, followed by Yugoslavs, unskilled workers from Alsace, and agricultural labourers from the Hanau region. There was a myriad of department heads defending their fiefdoms to the hilt. BSW's structure was totally at odds with the doctrine of the mini steel mill, which was all about relatively flat hierarchies and far fewer areas of responsibility. Weitzmann also noted how cluttered the plant was: "The stocks were piled up to the third floor," he observed, joking that anyone falling out of a fourth floor window would be completely safe, since they would land on the huge quantities of material.

Weitzmann's friend, Klaus Didillon, by now one of Korf's closest aides, had in the meantime been promoted to director of technology. Together, Weitzmann and Didillon sparked a kind of cultural revolution in Kehl. "Korf and Bernhardt gave us free rein to turn this ship around," Weitzmann recalled. "We reorganized the firm from top to bottom." By collaborating with a successful mini steel plant in Japan, they managed to introduce efficient management methods that almost doubled per capita output. Middle management was replaced, and the workforce was reduced to a better trained, more dedicated core, instead of the previous army of semi-skilled workers. Weitzmann won over the works council to his point of view by taking two representatives with him on his trips to Japan: "Because we have a different culture from East Asia, I didn't want them to emulate the Japanese, merely empathize with them." Success ensued, and in 1981 "real money was earned" in Kehl. As CEO of BSW, bound only by instructions from the parent company Korf-Stahl, Weitzmann was now in position for the most dramatic phase in Willy Korf's industrial career.

Korf, meanwhile, was increasingly preoccupied with the causes of the global steel crisis. Of course, it wasn't lost on him that it had mainly been brought about by the soaring prices for crude oil and natural gas since the 1973 oil crisis. This had hit all types of steelworks hard, including his electric arc furnaces as well as the outdated Siemens-Martin furnaces. Because the latter took four to eight hours for a single smelt, they urgently needed to be made more efficient, especially with energy going up in price all the time.

In his Brazilian plant in Pains, which had gradually become his second technology centre alongside Kehl, Korf had his metallurgist Dalton Nosé patent a new process in 1980 designed to solve the problems of steelworks equipped with Siemens-Martin furnaces. It comprised blowing oxygen into the melt from the bottom of the furnace, slashing the tap-to-tap time by half. This process was sold all over the world from Brazil, even though it wasn't suitable for modern electric arc furnaces. Not without a touch of vanity, Korf named this process Korf Oxy Refining Fuel – or KORF for short.

He reserved the biggest media hype for the KR Process. KR stood (in German) for coal reduction, a term that basically said it all, for Korf was increasingly relying on coal rather than coke or gas. Trials had been conducted in Germany since 1977, and the KR Process was unveiled to an international audience of business, media and political representatives on Friday 27 August 1982, in a dedicated test facility at the mini mill in Kehl. This was a joint venture by BSW (51 per cent) and Vöest-Alpine. Once again, Korf had managed to have nearly half the 30 million marks he'd invested in developing this "groundbreaking technology" reimbursed by German research minister Andreas von Bülow.

The main advantages of the KR Process were that it performed direct reduction without furnace, ran on ordinary power plant coal instead of coke or gas, and produced molten pig iron instead of cold sponge iron in its fluidized bed coal gasifier. By freeing up steel production from the high-priced trio of electricity, coke and gas, Korf was absolutely convinced that this was the advent of a promising new technology.

Whenever Korf took to the big public stage on such occasions, he couldn't help but conduct steel industry policy at the same time. The launch of the KR Process was no exception: he railed fiercely against European industrial policy in the most serious crisis to hit the steel sector since the war, proclaiming: "The main reason for this crisis is the European Economic Community, where certain countries refuse to understand that unprofitable overcapacity must simply be shut down." Instead, the governments of Belgium, France, Italy and the UK had spent a total equivalent to 10 billion marks in subsidies on their largely nationalized steel corporations in 1981 alone, simply to prop up tens of thousands of unsustainable jobs and to secure votes.

Since 1976, there had been a powerful lobby in Brussels known as the European Steel Association, or EUROFER. It brought together the major players in the industry with the aim of wringing a corporate-friendly policy out of EEC bureaucrats and negotiating advantageous production quotas for all its members – and its success was undeniable. Smaller, independent entrepreneurs like Korf were barred from EUROFER, something he found intolerable. In 1981, Korf, who'd done more than anyone else to promote mini steel mills, became one of the co-founders of the rival European Independent Steelworks Association (EISA), also based in Brussels. This was where the operators of smaller steelworks with electric arc furnaces – the 'Davids' – joined forces in their efforts to influence Europe's legislators and subsidy planners, who tended to support the Goliaths. However, EISA's impact in Brussels was modest.

Whatever the reason, it certainly wasn't due to any lack of

will on Korf's part to influence those in power. Despite not having grown up with the polished language of diplomacy, the speed of his business expansion was matched by his dexterity at making political contacts. This is verified by a file preserving his correspondence with top politicians and officials from all the main parties in the Bundestag, Germany's national parliament. Many of the names can be traced over a period lasting several years as formal contacts evolved into close acquaintances.

Politicians were fascinated by Willy Korf's unusual combination of boundless creativity and non-conformist manner alongside his discipline and ability to get things done. The sharp business expertise he demonstrated was equally captivating. When Hans Friderichs was the country's minister of economic affairs, at the end of an emergency meeting held one evening, he asked the two steel industrialists present to draw up a written assessment of what had been discussed. "When, gentlemen", he urged shortly before midnight, "can you submit a position paper?"

"That's something we need to talk about," replied one of them, stalling for time.

"Tomorrow at noon," said Korf – and he was as good as his word. He never waffled, and straight-talkers like him were popular with politicians. Korf, who never joined any political party, took the view that a businessperson should theoretically be able to get along with – and hopefully influence – all the main political parties. But if there was one party he preferred over the others, it was – unsurprisingly for an industrialist in the 1970s – the FDP, the Liberals. After all, they advocated a market that was as free as possible, along with the leanest possible state, views which were the closest to Willy Korf's own attitudes to politics and business. There was a certain tragic irony in this, as would become apparent when his business operations later collapsed into administration.

However, Korf undoubtedly put feelers out into every political camp early on. And using his fine antennae, he could sense which individuals in those parties were destined for greater things. Shortly afterwards, that person would receive the obligatory telegram from Baden-Baden on taking office, followed by a series of letters with an increasingly personal touch, sometimes even in Korf's almost illegible handwriting. Invitations to dinner at his residence in Baden-Baden ensued; lavish books and other small gifts were sent. These were all stepping stones enabling a political friendship, once established, to evolve.

"I was delighted to meet you again at the trade show in Hanover and discuss South Carolina with you," went a typical letter from 1977, addressed to Ernst Albrecht, the Christian Democrat premier of Lower Saxony. Korf had already received political backing from Albrecht during the rebar war when he'd been a European civil servant in Brussels. Enclosed with the letter, as if by chance, was a book about the Georgetown rice plantations: "Our American steel company in Georgetown has taken out a five-year lease on the Greenfield Plantation owned by the Duke family, and has built a guest house in the French colonial style at Litchfield Plantation. Should you ever visit South Carolina again in the near future, we'd be delighted to welcome you there as our guest." The guestbook of the small hotel, where pianists at the grand piano in the evenings evoked the atmosphere of a time long gone with the wind, has been preserved. Its pages are full of famous names from the realms of West German business, politics and showbiz.

The historic atmosphere across the Atlantic wasn't the only thing that Willy Korf had to offer Germany's legislature and executive. There was also, for instance, his aviation service with its fleet of luxury jets. While this was perhaps excessive for a steel manufacturer who remained relatively small – at least on a global scale – it was ideal for politicians in a hurry with long-distance travel requirements. This was particularly the case for those journeys which, for whatever reason, couldn't be funded by their party or the taxpayer. Besides, the flexibility of Korf-Transport's pilots in terms of destinations and times was unparalleled. One of the beneficiaries of this service wrote the following letter of appreciation:

Dear Mr Korf,

Rather than wait until we next meet, I would like to take this opportunity to thank you most sincerely for the precious help and support you have given me by allowing me to make use of your aircraft. Without this kind assistance, it would barely be possible for me to manage my many obligations.

It was signed with the very best regards by Walther Leisler Kiep, who in 1976 was Lower Saxony's minister of finance. Just to be on the safe side, the letter was marked "Personal and confidential". Korf's aviation service also delivered the favour of flying Kiep from Hamburg to Munich and then home to Hanover on 11 May. On several occasions, Korf had invited the minister to borrow one of his planes "if ever he were in need."

Such small kindnesses were bestowed upon political friendships at other times, too, not just in the 1970s. But they were something of a headache for Korf's secretaries in Baden-Baden, where internal resources were tied up by these diplomatic gestures. In an internal memo dated 14 October 1976, for example, Korf's secretary Renate Höing enquired about how "the costs (pilot's expenses, landing fees, etc.) for the minister's flights on our aircraft" were to be covered. After receiving instructions, eleven days later she reported back as follows: "I have informed Kiep's personal assistant Ms Haberlandt that the flights up to and including 2 October are considered part of our election support and do not have to be paid for. All flights from 3 October (election day) onwards will now be invoiced." Assuming that such secretive practices were once commonplace among industrial corporations in Germany (and possibly still are), it is remarkable how much political parties receive in election funding from the state.

In the increasingly difficult situation that the European steel industry found itself in the second half of the 1970s, Korf's penchant for private diplomacy also resulted in some half-baked initiatives which he had to be talked out of by his more down-to-earth colleagues on the board.

On 8 September 1978, for instance, Korf wrote to Klaus von Dohnanyi, the secretary of state in the German foreign office: "I would hereby like to repeat my suggestion to invite the leaders of the German steel industry, which now consists of only eight companies, to a round table discussion so that everyone – uninfluenced by vested interests – can express their opinion on the current situation." Dohnanyi promptly agreed, suggested four possible dates, and offered to invite everybody. But when a copy of his offer reached Korf's deputy Wolfgang Bernhardt, he immediately objected, writing to Korf in a memo: "I don't think such a meeting would be advisable at the moment." He explained that Dohnanyi wasn't the right person to host the steel summit, since certain people at the Ministry of Economic Affairs and Finance might feel snubbed. This was something to be avoided, wrote Bernhardt, especially given the ambivalence regarding Dohnanyi even within his own party, the Social Democrats. Korf made his excuses and abandoned preparations for the meeting. Once again, Bernhardt had brought the impulsive Korf back down to earth at the last moment. Korf now had to tap his network in some other way.

Profitable cooperation between politics and business was often tricky in the first place. Not all the mutual favours that businesspeople and politicians wished to grant each other could come about as their engagement diaries were too full. Not even the hunting invitation – that elitist, yet highly efficient, way of cultivating contacts – always worked. "On Friday 17 December and Saturday 18 December 1976, we will be hosting a hunt for red deer and wild boar," wrote the organizer of a state hunt to Willy Korf on 27 October 1976. But despite this opportunity for a "substantial dinner combined with some merry drinking", Korf had to turn it down:

> This year, I have to decline your kind invitation to hunt, as I have already agreed to attend Mr Flick's hunt on 17 December, and will be holding a closed meeting with Dr Bernhardt and Mr Kreifels, chairman of our supervisory

board, on 18 December. Nevertheless, I hope that we can see each other in person again at some point, because we certainly have a lot to discuss.

Perhaps the wording "I have to decline" was a little brash, since Helmut Kohl, the premier of Rhineland-Palatinate, probably wasn't used to receiving refusals! But Willy Korf had, by this point, climbed so far up the social ladder that he couldn't help occasionally rebuffing future Chancellors who possessed long memories. And years later, as head of state, it was Kohl's opportunity to consider a request from Korf.

In May 1989, Korf's office wrote to Horst Teltschik, by that time chancellery minister in the third cabinet of Helmut Kohl's seemingly endless reign: "Assuming the Chancellor will be accompanied by gentlemen from the business community on his upcoming trip to Poland, Dr Korf would also like to join him." Almost six months later, white smoke rose from the Chancellor's office at the eleventh hour: "I would be delighted if you could be part of my delegation to Warsaw on 9 and 10 November 1989." Signed with a giant squiggle: H. Kohl.

One of the politicians particularly courted by Willy Korf was of course the premier of his own region of Baden-Württemberg: Lothar Späth from the Christian Democrats. Späth was to become a key figure in the ups and downs of Korf's businesses, and not just in the local region. When it came to the crunch, however, he carried out this role quite differently from how Korf had long imagined. At first, while things were still going well for the pair of them, the beginnings of a wonderful political friendship could be observed: dozens of letters, increasingly personal in tone, have been preserved, and many more were written. This correspondence began early on and continued throughout Späth's rapid ascent in Baden-Württemberg and his political party in south-west Germany.

Even so, Späth's first experience with Korf had been anything but pleasant. In 1970, having been a member of the regional parliament for barely two years, Späth was promoted to its finance committee. The region was governed by a grand coalition, and Hans-Otto Schwarz of the Social Democrats was the minister of economic affairs. During a routine discussion concerning some minor aid for the young Korf, Lothar Späth felt the need to interrupt the collective approval by audaciously questioning whether this support was financially justifiable. He was quickly brought down to size twice. First, Schwarz put him down in the committee, even accusing Späth, without any reason, of having "publicized" the matter. And shortly afterwards, Späth received a terse letter from Korf, whom he'd never met, condemning him for not having a clue about business. After that, they didn't hear from each other for years.

But in the mid-1970s, according to Späth, he received a call from Korf's new deputy Wolfgang Bernhardt, whom he'd known for some time. Apparently, Bernhardt told him that he'd stopped working for Flick's manager Eberhard von Brauchitsch in Düsseldorf in order to join the steel producer Willy Korf ("a very interesting businessman, by the way"), and asked Späth whether he would like to meet Korf in Baden-Baden, seeing as they were already in the same part of the world. Bernhardt later claimed that he didn't arrange this introduction and only knew Späth in passing at the time. However it came about, the meeting between Korf and Späth took place, they looked each other in the eye, and their unfortunate first contact by post was soon forgotten. After that, Späth and Korf both continued their steep career trajectories. Following that first meeting, Korf, with his unerring nose for up-and-comers, was certain that staying in touch with Späth would be promising. And he resolved to work his way into Späth's favour.

On 13 February 1978, when Willy Korf sent a letter to Lothar Späth congratulating him on his appointment as regional interior minister, it was rather formal. Only seven months later, with Späth now having been elected minister-president, Korf was bold enough to invite him to visit one of his companies in Baden-Württemberg. Späth thanked him in a standard reply, but made the effort to add a few handwritten lines: "I, too, look forward to meeting you in the near future." On 29 October 1980, Späth delivered the keynote speech at the celebrations marking the twenty-fifth anniversary of Korf's first company, describing the "greatly respected Mr Korf" as "prudent and far-sighted" in an address which Korf assured him a year later had "left the audience extraordinarily impressed."

In 1981, it was Späth's turn to thank Korf "for the opportunity to accompany you to the USA and the hospitality enjoyed there." Korf had treated him to the usual celebrity programme: a transatlantic flight on the company Falcon, a tour of Georgetown Steel, an overnight stay in the guest house. (Späth had no inkling that years later, when he resigned as minister-president of Baden-Württemberg, his all-expenses-paid trip with Korf would be investigated by a parliamentary committee of enquiry.) In return, he sent Korf a set of silver corks, which Korf promised to reserve for bottles with exceptional contents.

What was the purpose of all this flattery and blandishment? These subtle tools of long-term strategy weren't designed for immediate effect. Being a shrewd businessman, it wasn't so much silver corks that Korf was hoping for from the people he met and wrote to (of whom Späth was simply one of the more important ones), but financial support for his companies. Another of his tactics was private invitations. "I was a guest at his house on Kaiser-Wilhelm-Strasse two or three times," recalled Lothar Späth. "Such invitations were more like a state reception than a casual meeting: his hospitality was very generous, and there were illustrious guests there. But after five minutes, every conversation turned to business. If you were invited to the Korfs, it wasn't just to have a beer and play cards."

There was intent behind every letter, every contact, every personal word. Back in 1977, when Späth wasn't yet a minister and the steel industry had been in decline worldwide for two years, Korf wrote to Rudolf Eberle, the regional minister of economic affairs: "An important decision that we desperately need concerns the electricity prices charged by the state-owned utility Badenwerk AG. We are still paying too much for our electricity in Kehl compared to our competitors." Two years later, Korf was able to take this long-term problem suffered by his Kehl plants to Lothar Späth when he was minister-president, even sending a telegram for reasons of urgency: "REQUEST DISCUSS WHOLE PROBLEM INFORMALLY IN PRIVATE." And in 1980, Korf invoked the risk of highly subsidized steel competition from neighbouring European countries to Späth: "All the more important for us are the research subsidies from the German Ministry of Research and Technology, which are intended to maintain our competitiveness through measures to improve efficiency and save energy." Of course, in the same letter Korf also thanked Späth "sincerely for your birthday wishes" – it wouldn't do to forget to show gratitude. As Benjamin Franklin's saying goes, little strokes fell great oaks – and in this regard, Korf was a master lumberjack.

CHAPTER 8

La dolce vita

"You simply can't bear to be hemmed in or constrained in any way!"

"I couldn't imagine ever retiring as an entrepreneur," Willy Korf told *Welt am Sonntag* when he was 50. Many others shared the same view of Korf as a tireless all-rounder: "Your life is all about your business, and your business is all about your life – so much so that the two are inextricably intertwined and fill up every hour of every day." The way in which Max Kreifels, chairman of the supervisory board, equated Willy Korf the man with Willy Korf the businessman in a speech celebrating his fiftieth birthday makes him sound like an ascetic without any private interests. Yet nothing could be further from the truth. Even if most of the virtues and characteristics ascribed to Korf – diligence, willpower, assertiveness, courage, discipline, technical expertise, perceptiveness, creativity – doubtless referred to a professional context, Willy Korf the husband, family man and friend shouldn't be left out of the equation.

Nevertheless, Kreifels was right to the extent that these aspects couldn't be removed from the way Korf was perceived as a businessman. How did he live out his longing for freedom and recognition on a private level? What sort of constraints did he impose on those close to him? It is also interesting to examine what the usual trappings of success may have meant to him – as he managed the inevitable tensions between grand gestures and informality, extravagance and frugality, egoism and selflessness.

There was his villa: a white, detached house in the historicist style, built at the end of the nineteenth century, with a garden 6,000 square metres (1½ acres) in size on Kaiser-Wilhelm-Strasse in Baden-Baden, the millionaires' neighbourhood. The previous resident had been a lignite magnate with a fleet of horse-drawn carriages. How could a young outsider like Willy Korf, unknown in this fashionable spa town, possibly acquire a property like this in the early 1960s? At first, having just become an industrialist in Kehl, Korf inhabited a tiny, rented flat. But estate agents sometimes have a sixth sense about wealth. One told Kurt Walker, a Liberal town councillor in Baden-Baden and also an architect, that a very moneyed man was seeking an upmarket residence. Attention quickly turned to the house on Kaiser-Wilhelm-Strasse, which Walker's father had once done some architectural work on.

Kurt Walker agreed to do the same for the new owner, Korf. He installed a large underground indoor swimming pool with a sauna, and added a garage as well as accommodation for a caretaker. One room was converted into a library, complete with precious wood panelling removed from scrapped ships in Hamburg. His friendship with Korf began at this time, said Walker. "I also got to know his mother, whom I befriended because she was the same age as my own. I often joined Willy when he visited her. He had put her up with a landlady on Winterhalterstrasse in a house directly below his villa, also in the historicist style, where he maintained personal offices on two floors." When his beloved mother died in late 1979, it hit Korf very hard, although he refused to let it show on the outside.

Korf soon found his place in society in Baden-Baden, again with the help of his new friend Kurt Walker, who was well connected in the town. It was he who introduced Korf to Franz and Aenne Burda and their three sons, as Walker had built the company headquarters in Offenburg for Franz Burda senior. From then on, Korf was increasingly mentioned in the same breath as the publishing dynasty, too.

At one of the gatherings of Baden's high society, the Korfs were introduced to construction magnate Christine Esswein from Karlsruhe. Widowed at a young age, she had taken over as boss of Füssler GmbH & Co. KG. It turned out that she and the Korfs shared a taste for an extroverted lifestyle. Soon they were travelling together, for instance flying to New York along with the Burdas. Not surprisingly, the Füssler company built Korf's first steelworks in Kehl – and several more besides.

Reciprocal invitations to each other's private villas became more frequent. The Korfs and their new acquaintances liked to drive to nearby Alsace for dinner. They also enjoyed going on holiday to the south of France. The Korfs liked staying at the Eden-Roc Hotel owned by the Oetker family in Cap d'Antibes near Cannes, where Henry Kissinger and Rita Hayworth had also stayed. "People had a lot of fun relaxing and having a good time," said Daniela Esswein-Hardieck, Christine Esswein's daughter, describing the leisure time of this industrialist set in the 1970s. "That style no longer exists today. You either hide your money away from envious people, or you try and avoid the nouveau riche who still flaunt it." Such scruples weren't yet widespread in the 1970s.

Whenever Korf was in Baden-Baden (and he spent about half his time there), he cultivated certain habits that he cherished. Tennis in summer, not golf; a few lengths in his own swimming pool every morning. "Every Saturday, we'd hang out in the sauna together," said Walker. "He'd call and say something like: 'Hey, I've just got back from the Shah of Iran. Come over tonight – I've brought back a huge tin of red caviar!' Then we'd sit there in the evening and shovel down caviar." Korf had sold the Shah a mini steelworks, a project which brought him into the turmoil of the Islamic Revolution in 1979.

Around this time, Kurt Walker drew up the plans for a chalet in Gstaad, Switzerland, home to a number of international film stars. The country house cost Willy Korf about US$1.5 million – at the time a sum even more exorbitant than it would be today.

Korf sometimes flew to Gstaad every week. And he was very generous when it came to letting other people use his chalet. As Dalton Nosé, Korf's Brazilian development engineer, recalled:

> On one occasion I told him I was going to look for a school in Europe where my daughters could learn German, and then go skiing in France afterwards. 'No!' shouted Korf. 'Forget France. Switzerland is much better! I insist you stay in my chalet in Gstaad!' And for three years in a row, I spent my skiing holidays in his Swiss chalet.

No one could accuse Korf of being miserly towards close colleagues, friends and relatives. Once, the journalist Thomas Starke from *Badisches Tagblatt* bumped into Korf when they were both doing a spot of Christmas shopping at Peter Liebmann's well-known antique store in Baden-Baden. Starke chose two engravings for his mother worth about 50 marks, while Korf "bought half the shop": a sterling silver dinner service costing perhaps 20,000 marks alone, antique vases, a 200-year-old English side table. "He must have spent 100,000 marks," estimated Starke, who would like to have found out whom the gifts were intended for.

Korf was one of those people who could honestly say that they weren't interested in money – it was just always there somehow. It's similar to the way in which islanders hardly notice the sound of the sea. "No matter where we were," said Walker, "he would always say: 'Send me the invoice.' He never paid cash, everything was charged to his account." This was backed up by Korf's elder daughter Astrid Korf Wolman: "He had a lavish lifestyle, and was generous to a fault to his friends and employees."

Korf's family perceived life in the villa, with its domestic staff and frequent receptions attended by prominent guests, quite differently from visitors and envious outsiders. Dieter Spethmann, the former boss of Thyssen, described his impression in a strikingly taciturn manner: "I first met Korf in his house in Baden-Baden, where he had invited my wife and me. Everything was very lavish: the location, the size, the furnishings, the staff. We didn't live like that." No doubt his views were shared by many of Korf's competitors and business partners. For Korf's daughter Astrid, on the other hand:

> [He] was never pushy, he never put himself above other people. Compared to many others with the same status, he was rather modest. We had domestic staff at home, too, but we ran a very informal household. We children went to normal schools. We had normal friends, and no one ever checked their social background. I felt my father was very natural, including in the way he dressed.

But there was also the public-private Korf, a persona of many facets. There was the dapper gentleman, with his trademark dark blue double-breasted pinstripe suits and white pocket handkerchief, who confessed to the press: "In this respect I'm rather vain" (*Welt am Sonntag*). There was the man who loved antiques "whenever they give him a clear impression of the era when they were made. Starting from historical situations, he tries to anticipate future ones" (*Die Welt*). There was the man who liked to smoke Havana cigars on social occasions, prompting Franz Burda junior to give him a small piece of advice on his fiftieth birthday: "You got into the habit of smoking cigars in order to get noticed after your father's death, when you drove to the stock exchange in Cologne with his friends. But there's no longer any need for that." Then there was the art collector who, together with his wife, acquired Impressionist and Modernist works. And, of course, there was the hunter who, in autumn and winter, shot birds and small game with his colleagues, as the journalists well knew. But they also knew the real reason for such open-air gatherings (as Korf himself had explained on more than one occasion): "There are some conversations you can have in the open air that would be less pleasant in a stuffy office."

The bosses of Germany's steel corporations, normally rather solitary predators, met up for this purpose, sometimes joined by prominent politicians, on Korf's hunting ground in the Rhine Valley between Kehl and Offenburg. They started off with a few drinks and jokes at each other's expense. At 9 a.m., the hunt began with a blast on the hunting horn by a long-serving sales manager. Then Korf himself, as the owner of the preserve, gave a short briefing, in which he mainly laid down the rules about what could be shot and what not. At noon there was a rustic stew; at dusk the hunt was called off, after which there was a big feast at which the hunt master announced the game killed, the hunting king was crowned, and many a humorous speech was given. On one occasion, Walter Scheel, who'd been the German president from 1974 until 1979, accidentally shot an owl, having probably mistaken it for partridge. The other hunters had discreetly tried to make it disappear, but then one of the beaters hurriedly called out for all to hear: "Your owl, Mr President!" Declared king of the hunt, Scheel predictably had to endure a certain amount of ridicule that evening.

The hunting feast was regularly attended by someone who hadn't worn a hunting outfit or held a gun during the shoot: Korf's deputy, Wolfgang Bernhardt. It was at this time that talk turned to tangible interests, politics and business. Bernhardt normally kept his private life separate from that of Korf, since they already spent a large part of their days together. And in a small town like Baden-Baden, gossip would have spread quickly, especially among the staff at head office. In addition, Bernhardt's private network was still stronger in Düsseldorf where, in addition to his many close friends, he also owned a house.

There was, however, another reason why the two men usually led separate 'night lives': Bernhardt simply needed more sleep than Korf. The latter was able to last out so long at social gatherings that his crony Franz Burda once said to him: "You have stamina, you and I can both hang around all night. There's nothing better than going home at sunrise. At the break of day, your Brigitte always says: 'Come on, Willy, let's go home.'"

Korf's aptitude for nocturnal activity had previously been described by the tribal chief in his colourful robes, who had always accompanied Korf at receptions and other festivities during his Nigerian ventures: Chief Ben Oluwole, the former director of WASCO. Even at that glorious time in the early

1970s, he had this to say about the man from the cold, remote north: "Korf is fortunately similar to Africans, for he also enjoys partying the night away. ... He has not only a head, but also a heart and, in addition, a sense of honour and dignity. Most Europeans I know aren't like him."

However, Korf's reputation for generosity didn't mean that he counted many people among his close friends. He had business associates, to be sure, political friends, partners, allies, even the occasional drinking buddy, and probably thousands of acquaintances. But there were only very few real friends with whom he could discuss private matters, mull over problems, and share his innermost feelings. That might be a little surprising, for Korf was clearly not a suspicious person; if anything, he was too unsuspecting. And this despite the fact that he'd come to know his industry as a shark tank during the rebar wars, price wars, and internal wars when his industrial partners had suddenly deserted him. But he didn't take this personally.

Korf always assumed that the people he worked with had only the best intentions and abilities – until he was proven wrong. Even then, he didn't necessarily break with someone once they'd met his approval, but simply blanked out what didn't fit into his benevolent image of them. Korf treated politicians in the same way, too, even if they were truly powerful and influential. There was a disarming naivety about Korf, who – despite some warnings from his advisers – never asked by what intrigues and unscrupulousness someone might have risen to their influential position. After all, he didn't ask such questions of himself: they simply didn't occur to him.

Accordingly, it was perhaps only to be expected that a few 'friends' of the Korf family would cause bitter disappointments in challenging times, even humiliations. All too soon, when the going got tough, some well-known person or other would prefer to be no longer associated with Korf or his family (despite having been proud to be seen with him in the past). Another might no longer be willing to assert the influence which hitherto had been to their mutual advantage, while some were simply afraid that unsightly stories from times when they had perhaps been a little too close might come to light.

Nonetheless, Willy Korf had a few good, genuine friends. One of them was the architect Kurt Walker. Then there was his friendship with Edgar Georg dating back to their teenage years. And Karl Wienand, that cunning old trooper from the Social Democrats, whose character was a little too opaque for the liking of some Korf family members, was a friend – even if he did tend to make deals with Korf behind the scenes. In a strict, almost fatherly way, of course, Max Kreifels was friends with Korf, who conversely almost regarded Gerhard Fuchs, the young engineer, entrepreneur and business partner as his own son. Then there was Aenne, the grande dame of the Burda dynasty.

These friendships were cultivated attentively by Korf: he never forgot to phone on birthdays, and he was regularly in touch just to see how they were. Moreover, he stood by his friends in their hour of need. The fact that the global businessman who worked sixteen-hour days found the time for such minor matters was due to his practical knowledge of modern management theory, which he had picked up early on in the USA.

Korf practised a form of 'networking' in which he created the major connections personally. Having done so, he then left it to others to build on the nodes he had established, strengthening the network from many decentralized locations, so that in the end the whole system all came together in his hands again. His instrument for fine-tuning the architecture of these networks was the telephone – a device to which he seemed to have become virtually attached.

This was also the solution to the riddle of why the man with the overflowing schedule was often in a hurry, but almost never in a rush. Instead, he could be seen playing tennis on the private court on Winterhalterstrasse on many weekends. Kurt Walker, his frequent match partner, marvelled at Korf's constitution: "He was a mediocre but ambitious player. His pace of life should have given him a heart attack. True, he had a few health problems, for example with his urinary tract. But there was nothing wrong with his heart, which was as healthy as a horse."

Korf not only made time for regular tennis matches. He also found an astonishing number of weekends to be with his family. If he was travelling internationally, he called home every day. If he was at home, he loved to gather his wife and daughters around him (although whether they always enjoyed having to join him for afternoon coffee at 4 p.m. is another matter...). Korf could be quite draconian at home. One time, after a heated argument, he impulsively cancelled the company jet, which had been scheduled to fly his elder daughter Astrid and her friend Xenia to Harvard – because they'd pilfered a bottle of champagne from the wine cellar.

But then there was also the other Willy Korf, the generous, boyish charmer, whom his wife affectionately called "my little frog" because of his fondness for spending hours lying in the bath. This Willy Korf couldn't refuse his Brigitte her glamorous haute couture, his daughter Astrid their flights abroad together, and certainly nothing to his youngest child, Sylvia, the "chaotic one" of the family. The 'baby' remained the apple of his eye, even when she destroyed flowerbeds while playing in the garden or later wrote off a car. She also bore a greater resemblance to her father thanks to her impetuous temperament, whereas Astrid was more diplomatic and stood out as a mediator, and sometimes accompanied her father on his business trips. But Korf, who kept business and family strictly apart, almost never spoke to Astrid about business matters. What he did impart to her was his sense of optimism in his entrepreneurial attitude that the glass is always half full, rather than half empty.

Many details about the Korfs' family life are divulged by a humorous birthday newspaper made by Astrid and her friend Xenia for Willy Korf's sixtieth birthday. The A3 sheet filled on both sides with satirical stories and funny anecdotes bore the masthead of local newspaper *Badisches Tagblatt* – and no wonder, for the paper was published by Xenia's family. It was handed out to the guests at the big party, which was completely different from that held ten years earlier when Korf turned 50. Whereas at that time, the guest list mainly comprised prominent, influential people, this time a third of the gathering consisted of friends of his now grown-up offspring, while representatives of the world of steel were completely absent. On other occasions, too, such as holidays, Korf liked to mix young and old when putting groups together, and often included his children's friends.

Perhaps it was due to the semi-private nature of the party that the special birthday edition of *Badisches Tagblatt* also contained some humorous yet delicate revelations about Willy Korf: that he was a "horrible snorer", and that "deep down he was an underpants fetishist" (housekeeper Christl Esch had to lay them out for him "like soldiers on parade"). But the funniest item was a photo showing the birthday boy on holiday on the beach in Sylt, dressed only in his birthday suit. Naturally, with Korf being the boss of a prominent corporation, the party was also attended by a handful of high dignitaries, too. Fortunately, the revealing, mischievous birthday newspaper didn't provoke a scandal. Evidently, those present had long ceased to be surprised by the candid nature of the Korfs!

The guests were particularly moved by a short poem recited by the 22-year-old Sylvia, who was wearing a white, rhinestone-studded dress:

> Dear Daddy!
> Many, many years ago,
> Just 60 years, not one day more,
> You got up to say hello
> And find out what life had in store.
> You've learned a lot about mankind
> And seen so much with your own eyes.
> You may be old, but not in years,
> You're stylish, confident and wise.
> You've given much in your career

And piles of gifts for you abound.
Happy Birthday, Daddy dear,
How glad we are that you're around!

On the videotape of the party, the poem is met with huge cheers – perhaps because the heartfelt, sincere simplicity of this words accurately reflected Korf's own essence.

Sharing life with the founder of Korf-Stahl meant not only wealth for the other members of the family, but also taking a back seat in equal measure. For they had to share life with his business, as was painfully noticeable on occasion.

Kurt Walker remembered joining the Korfs on a family holiday to the island of Sylt in the 1970s. Both the architect and the industrialist had holiday homes there and, naturally, they'd flown there on one of Korf's planes. "We were sitting on the beach on a giant sandcastle, and Korf was talking incessantly on one of those early radio telephones, which were huge at the time." Because of his obsession for phone calls, on that holiday, too, he usually arrived late at the restaurant where they'd arranged to meet.

Korf's wife Brigitte was especially used to waiting in vain. For example, when the trio of Korf, Kreifels and Bernhardt met up in Baden-Baden to discuss the fate of the company, Brigitte would sometimes call in the middle of the meeting to remind her husband to come home. Korf typically assured her that he'd be there in five minutes, before hanging up. Kreifels once asked him in astonishment: "Wasn't that a barefaced lie? You know that's impossible!" "But she knows", Korf replied with a disarming smile, "what I mean by five minutes."

Brigitte Korf was tolerant of her husband's idiosyncrasies and high-handedness in all sorts of ways – otherwise, it would have been impossible for two such extroverted and sometimes extravagant people to live together. What Korf loved about her was precisely her way of not conforming to mediocre norms. Anything but a housewife, Brigitte Korf loved attending official and social functions on the biggest of stages; at balls, at least as many flashbulbs popped around her as her husband. The Korfs were generally regarded as belonging to high society. In 1980, when the Korf Group celebrated its twenty-fifth anniversary, the couple stood on the top landing of the staircase of the Baden-Baden assembly rooms and greeted the hundreds of invited guests, who all made their way up the stairs to deliver their congratulations.

In their first few years together, Brigitte had often joined her successful husband on trips abroad. However, she had to overcome her deep-seated fear of flying each time. Speaking at a corporate function, Korf's pal Franz Burda made light of this situation: "Because you had your briefcases, Willy, it was usually my job to calm Brigitte down on the flight. Once, after flying together from Georgetown to New York on an ancient crate, you got off happily as soon as we landed. I, on the other hand, had a bruised arm because Brigitte had been gripping it so tightly!" During such panic attacks, Burda added, Brigitte had even torn his shirt on more than one occasion!

At Korf's fiftieth birthday party, too, Burda couldn't resist providing a few insights into the Korfs' family structure which were met with, at best, dutiful amusement:

> No one knows better than Brigitte that it's often not that easy living with Willy. From childhood, Willy screamed "Mama!" at the top of his voice whenever he wanted something. On hearing his shout, his mother would drop everything and rush over to him in case something serious had happened. But all he wanted was a glass of fizzy water! This was especially the case when he was ill in bed: "Mum, fetch me this and that!" That, my dear Brigitte, hasn't changed to this day. Whenever you describe how taxing it is when Willy's at home, all your friends know exactly what you mean!

But Korf wasn't one to stay cooped up at home on the sofa for long. Outside, there was plenty of new territory just waiting to be conquered. The media didn't fail to notice that there were other women eager to get to know this ambitious entrepreneur, who was surrounded by so many stories and an undeniable aura.

As early as 1971, the writer Uta von Witzleben tried to describe in *Die Zeit* what made him so special. On the sidelines of a party, she noted:

> Women who talk about him and want to be introduced to him wonder what that certain something is that makes him so attractive. A jealous man would probably reply: "If he didn't have the name, the success, the money, no one would look twice at him!" That's a moot point. He himself … very much gives his guests an impression combining adventure, romance, iron will, outstanding ability, and discipline.

This mixture was irresistible to some. For the entrepreneur, however, no temptation, no matter how great, could seriously divert him from his path. As Korf's cousin Helmhold Schneider put it: "He always found attractive women entertaining and was keen to talk to them. He was no Adonis, but he had charisma. But he wasn't a bon vivant. His business appointments were ultimately more important to him."

However far he travelled, Willy Korf always made his way back home.

CHAPTER 9

Capital

"Flight paths, flight schedules, flight safety, flight experience mean a lot to us, but they aren't everything."

The sweet life of Willy Korf the bon viveur was expensive, yet the bitter life of Korf the hard-working businessman was even costlier. Despite all the crises afflicting the steel industry, however, Korf's supply of money seemed inexhaustible – financing new steelworks, developments and business interests, not to mention aircraft. Understandably, people often wondered where all this money came from. But whenever they tried to investigate the secretive realm of his accounting, they usually found more questions than answers.

It wasn't surprising that Korf, a lover of modern painting, had a work of financial art on display in his Baden-Baden headquarters: 'One Thousand Mark Puzzle' by Canadian artist Robin Page. Naturally, a TV documentary about Korf in 1981 couldn't resist a shot of this oversized banknote cut up like a jigsaw puzzle and rearranged. "Does this refer to Korf's business in any way?" asked the narrator. "Well, Korf has always solved his financial puzzles so far!"

It was probably just an off-the-cuff remark; without an all-access pass, the filmmaker couldn't have known that behind the scenes, the financial reality of the Korf Group always looked a little different. If the accounts were a jigsaw, then a few pieces seemed to be missing.

This was clearly not due to an unwillingness on Korf's part to consider how to make money grow. "I'm particularly fascinated by financial constructs. I enjoy financing new projects," he told the paper that made him Manager of the Year 1973. And in this article singing his praises, the author noted: "His great advantage is being both an amateur technician and a financial expert."

Before Carl-Theodor Meinecke was appointed his financial director in 1972, Korf always placed himself in charge of money matters. But not even someone like Willy Korf could be that versatile: a visionary, a technical innovator, boss and organizer, networker and pioneer – as well as a true financial expert, ideally with the conservative nature of an accountant. Given the increasingly complex structure of his many nested business interests on several continents, he was no doubt aware of this need, which is why he eventually created the post of financial director. However, whoever was responsible for money matters at Korf-Stahl would find it difficult to get the boss to listen.

At first, Korf's banking network was fairly straightforward. In the 1960s, his principal bank was Bank für Gemeinwirtschaft, which held a 50 per cent stake in Korf's steelworks in Kehl via its subsidiary, Investitions- und Handelsbank in Frankfurt. Korf refused (or at least, he told the press that he flatly refused) to work with the other big banks. He was afraid of their interference, he said, and didn't want "to become reliant on them and end up being bought out one day on behalf of big steel."

This risk may or may not have existed. It might simply have been the case that none of the traditional big banks would touch Korf with a bargepole – especially since they maintained good relations with his equally traditional large competitors. This stand-off between Korf and some of the most renowned banks persisted throughout his life. For the time being, he was content to work with a handful of smaller, regional, 'second-tier' banks.

But in the mid-1970s, with Korf's annual turnover easily exceeding a billion marks, two new, invigorating factors came into the equation. The first was Dresdner Bank: one of the 'big banks' hitherto so reviled by Korf. It was its boss himself, Jürgen Ponto, who loosened the purse strings in 1976 (a year before he was murdered by members of the Red Army Faction) after meeting Korf personally.

Once again, Korf's charisma had done the trick, as Manfred Meier-Preschany (M.P.), then head of credit at Dresdner Bank, reported: "Ponto came in one day and said he'd met Korf and been impressed by him. He'd promised to lend him 10 million marks on condition that we could have someone on the Korf Group's supervisory board. That someone was apparently me!" Meier-Preschany, something of a rough diamond who was simply known to everyone in the steel industry as 'M.P.', immediately agreed.

Shortly afterwards, the banker met the well-rehearsed triumvirate of Korf, Kreifels and Bernhardt. Korf was rather reticent; Kreifels did most of the talking. There was a method to this: the lawyer's excellent reputation, his meticulousness, and his dedication to Korf's business activities (which came across despite his solemness) didn't fail to make an impact on Dresdner Bank's emissary. Furthermore, M.P. couldn't help noticing the chemistry between Kreifels and Korf. He got the impression that the businessman took heed of the lawyer, who was, of course, the head of his supervisory board.

Well-regarded teams, like Korf's 'triumvirate', can greatly simplify decision-making procedures in the world of business, especially where huge sums – often tens of millions – are at stake. According to an insider from those days, whenever an application for a large loan was received, only two things really mattered: Who chaired the supervisory board? And who was the auditor? If both names sounded good to the bank's ears, the money was more or less already on its way. "As long as the head of the supervisory board said the CEO was creditworthy, the issue was settled," said M.P.

There was no need (or any great inclination) for due diligence beforehand, especially if the firm seemed ambitious enough. What counted was personality. And whether a loan applicant had what it took to guide their factories into the future was simply extrapolated from the success of their previous projects. Really, it was all done by rule of thumb. Even as far as innovative ventures were concerned, the bank took the view that there wasn't that much in the way of new projects in industry – nearly everything had already been done somewhere else before.

Despite all this, after taking a closer look at Korf's assets and liabilities, Dresdner Bank initially had significant misgivings. In particular, there were doubts about Korf's Achilles' heel: the equity ratio. Basically, all his businesses were undercapitalized, and that was putting it mildly. Meier-Preschany decided to confront Willy Korf: "At our first proper meeting, I said to Korf and his team: 'You appear to be walking on very thin ice!' To which Kreifels replied: 'You're absolutely right!'"

Time and again in the subsequent years of this partnership, there were moments when M.P. demanded action to improve the equity ratio: "I, like others, didn't fail to issue urgent reminders to consolidate the situation." That was the modest version. Some bankers also told Korf and his team in no uncertain terms that they regarded his negligent fondness for borrowed liquidity discourteous: "Stop chasing the dream with other people's money!"

Even with lenders' good will, leaps of faith, and willingness to take risks, a financial partnership with Korf was always like sitting on a powder keg. To those who were aware of the financial ins and outs in Korf-Stahl, the sword of Damocles always seemed to be hovering over the company: "No one in the group knows every single detail of Korf's financing skills. Few close associates are sure that Korf's company isn't just one big bubble," wrote one journalist in 1980 who, unusually, refused to give him wholehearted support.

Korf, for his part, did everything he could to dispel the concerns of his lenders, especially his new main backer Dresdner Bank, in his tried and tested manner: in 1976, having only just made his acquaintance, he invited Meier-Preschany to the USA to show him his American plants – and, of course, his impressive colonial-style guest house. Once again, this effort didn't fail to have the desired impact. After his return, M.P. wrote to Korf on 25 October:

> As far as I was able to ascertain in the short time available, I have no hesitation in telling you that I am impressed by your Team America. Assuming this management also has the necessary financial basis, then I have no anxiety regarding the American part of your group.

Unfortunately, this period of confidence didn't last long. The internal report by an analyst dated 1 February 1977 submitted to Meier-Preschany, now a member of Korf's supervisory board, used alarmist language. It dealt with 1975 and 1976, the beginning of the crisis in the steel industry, which also dragged Korf into its vortex. The group had suffered "considerable drops in turnover", while Korf-Stahl's losses of 34 million marks had been shouldered by Korf's private holding company KIH. The group's annual losses had only been kept below 10 million marks because additional losses had been absorbed by external partners, mainly Klöckner.

The report also drew attention to a litany of black holes in Korf's balance sheet, on which not even Dresdner Bank could shed any light. For example, there was talk of "withdrawals amounting to 24 million marks, the use of which is not known to us in detail" as well as of "equity ratios that are no longer satisfactory" – namely an equity ratio that was a lousy 10.2 per cent of the adjusted balance sheet total. "The reported net debt of 680 million marks, almost as much as annual turnover, gives cause for concern ... Korf is thus in a much worse position than most of his comparable competitors."

There was more besides: "... questions are still unanswered

..." – "... receivables whose recoverability cannot be assessed by us since we do not have access to the debtors' balance sheets ..." – "It's also unclear ..." – "Under these circumstances, it remains doubtful whether we can consider this item to still be fully recoverable." – "... we urgently need to improve the information we currently have." – "So far, we have not received any planning data whatsoever for 1977." – "We have received neither balance sheets for the Brazilian holding companies nor detailed information on how the projects mentioned are financed." And as far as America was concerned, "equity ratios at Korf Industries Inc. have deteriorated alarmingly." In response, the branch of Dresdner Bank in New York now only gave Korf credit with reservation until the equity ratios were improved.

Dresdner Bank, which had been so supportive of Korf, was largely in the dark about its dealings with him and their impact. Its auditor concluded that the bank must demand:

> a switch from expansion to consolidation within the Korf Group. Even then, it is uncertain whether this will be enough for the Korf Group to strengthen its own resources within a reasonable period of time to the extent necessary. Under certain circumstances, further strengthening the shareholder base will be unavoidable, whereby the incoming financial resources must of course be used exclusively to consolidate the existing undertakings, not to fund new projects.

Despite these danger signals, Dresdner Bank remained loyal to Willy Korf, for better or for worse. And so, on 11 January 1978, Korf thanked his financial backer and controller Meier-Preschany in writing: "for what you did for our group of companies in 1977, both as a member of the supervisory board and as a banker." Sadly, he couldn't thank him with a bonus, for the Korf Group was still in the red.

The second significant increase in Korf's financial scope was attributable to another display of his brilliant skills as a diplomat and salesman. In sober understatement, his company history *25 Years of Korf* noted:

The German and American Korf Group achieved a significant improvement in its capital structure in 1975 and 1976 when the Sheikdom of Kuwait joined the shareholders. In the course of substantial capital increases, the Kuwaiti Ministry of Finance provided 30 per cent of the new share capital in first Korf-Stahl and later also Korf Industries, Inc.

Something reported so briefly was, in fact, one of the milestones in Korf's corporate history. Korf himself, and no one else, had pushed open the door to Kuwait's finance ministry. Of course, by now word had spread in the Middle East that his Midrex plants were ideal for the region because of the abundance of natural gas there, and many state-owned Arab investment companies wanted to become involved in the technology. In the case of Kuwait, it wasn't the investment itself that was unusual; after all, Iran had also acquired a stake in Krupp. What was unusual was the fact that an oil-rich Arab state had chosen to invest in an unlisted group of companies.

For a long time, the July 1975 sale of 30 per cent in the German Korf Group to the Kuwaitis was kept under wraps. Korf concealed this deal from the public – and from the German competition regulator – for a good three years. It wasn't until August 1978 that he admitted the merger, for which he should have sought approval from the antitrust authority in Berlin. The motive for keeping this deal secret was that Korf was involved in negotiations for a major contract in Israel, and was afraid that the Israelis might walk away if they discovered that Kuwait held a substantial stake in his business.

Assuming this was the real reason, it was another example of how cautious Germans had to be in the Middle East if they aspired to do business with Arabs on the one hand and Israelis on the other. When Korf finally disclosed the identity of his new partner, he tried hard to give the impression that the Kuwaitis' influence on the running of his companies was minimal, despite holding almost a third of the voting rights. Korf sought to downplay the issue and put a positive spin on the partial loss of his freedom by stating on television:

> The Kuwaitis' involvement in our company is a purely financial participation without any business interest. The Kuwaitis invest their money internationally in companies and seem to have taken a shine to us – partly because we're active in developing countries, in Arab countries, and now play a major role in the steel industry there.

In the meantime, the Kuwaitis had installed observers in Korf's companies, along with regular channels of communication. In the USA, where they'd acquired 30 per cent of the voting rights, Kuwaiti representatives sat on the board of directors. And although the Kuwaiti Ministry of Finance didn't have anyone on the supervisory board in Germany, Korf and Bernhardt themselves regularly flew to Kuwait to report personally to Mohammed al-Attiki, the finance minister. Admittedly, his ministry didn't directly influence Korf's business activities. But from then on, hardly anything could be done without the approval of the Kuwaitis, who analysed Korf's figures meticulously.

Despite the control Korf was forced to relinquish, some might say he was lucky to have made the deal when he did. As the crisis in the steel industry rapidly deepened with each passing year of the 1970s, his figures would have become less and less attractive to any Arab investor's strict financial controllers.

For the time being, though, the capital increase flowing in from the land of inexhaustible oil wells allowed Korf to soar to new heights. At a time when the whole steel industry was already in the doldrums, it enabled him to found Norddeutsche Ferrowerke in Emden (although Korf limited his investment to just 25 per cent) and to lay the foundations for his projects in Saudi Arabia: the steelworks in Al-Jubail, the 7 per cent stake in SABIC, and the 40 per cent stake in the rolling mill in Jeddah, which had been built by the state oil company Petromin. Of course, Korf could have used the money for consolidation and crisis prevention. But that wasn't his style at all.

Korf being Korf, his method of financing new projects had its own unique pattern, as long-time financial expert Manfred

Berner ascertained. For instance, in Al-Jubail, Korf held a minority stake in the new steelworks, which included two Midrex plants and a continuous casting plant. The capital, which had to be raised externally despite the financial injection from Kuwait, was actually supposed to be recouped from the profits made by Korf Engineering, which was involved in building the steelworks. "However, we used those profits to cover other losses, so we didn't accumulate any capital at all," Berner explained. "But now we had this stake that still had to be financed." In accounting terms, this was done via supply volumes and bills of exchange (promissory notes for future payment) issued for them:

> There were financial intermediaries who had these bills of exchange discounted at numerous banks on quite favourable terms. We had countless banks. I couldn't understand why they didn't get suspicious when they saw in the monthly credit statements that new ones had been added while others had disappeared. These weren't permanent business relationships. They were spread out among so many banks because we couldn't get such large volumes of bills of exchange discounted at our main banks – after all, they were all on the supervisory board!

On one occasion, legal proceedings were brought against the Korf Group on suspicion of bill fraud through bill renewal, but the public prosecutor's office could not prove it. Every month, there were new supply transactions that weren't paid for exclusively with bills of exchange, but partly in cash. This rather more tangible cash component appeared to satisfy some financial controllers, temporarily at least.

In addition, there was another, supposedly reassuring factor: at a time when countries with petrodollars were investing liberally, Korf – who built industrial plants and had a form of technology that was in demand all over the world – had full order books. Whenever contracts were signed, a down payment of perhaps 35 per cent of the total amount was due. This made for impressive cash surpluses in the short term, because not much was built in the first few months. Korf used these advance payments to plug gaps elsewhere in his empire. Furthermore, he financed 60 per cent of his loan interest with bills of exchange from the steel business, an unprecedented approach in the industry. "As long as everyone made a profit in the process, he could carry on with his investment activity," Berner said years later. "But the whole system was doomed to disaster as soon as anyone made a loss."

This unconventional system of relying on bills of exchange for financing was another nail in the coffin for the Hamburg steelworks. Although products were officially sold and raw materials purchased by Korf's holding company KIH, from 1975 onwards this was unofficially the responsibility of Hellmut Schulte-Derne, a member of the executive board of Korf-Stahl. Almost everything that was important for HSW, such as the electricity price charged by power utility Hamburger Elektrizitätswerke, was decided outside the meetings of the executive board and the supervisory board of Korf-Stahl. In the end, only Kreifels had to give his blessing.

Schulte-Derne had sole purchasing rights for all raw materials, ore, scrap and additives. While formally holding no legal position at all at KIH, he decided production quantities and sales channels, while Klöckner with its 49 per cent shareholding had allowed itself to be reduced to a silent partner. "Klöckner had no rights at all," confirmed Schulte-Derne. "I don't know why they put up with that, even though they were doing really badly at the time." Korf received payment for supplies after 30 days, but the Hamburg steelworks were paid with 90-day bills of exchange. "Everything that made a profit in Hamburg was skimmed off by KIH," said Schulte-Derne – and the entire process took place at Klöckner's expense.

This practice stretched the unequal partnership past the point of no return. Long-time Klöckner boss Herbert Gienow rebuked Korf for decades afterwards: "For him, sales were just a means of siphoning off liquidity, because steel is paid for in advance.

But instead of using this liquidity to pay us, we received bills of exchange, all of which subsequently bounced."

Behind this conflict were two completely opposing philosophies. It's certainly true that production and sales were separated at Klöckner, as in Korf's group of companies. But for Klöckner, sales weren't only a mainstay – they also represented the origins of the group, which had emerged from Peter Klöckner's trading company Klöckner & Co. and only later created a supply base with its own production – in exact contrast to Korf-Stahl, which had developed from a steel plant. And this meant a fundamentally different mentality, said Gienow: "Whereas at Klöckner, sales gave a valuable boost to production when times were hard, at Korf liquidity was siphoned off in difficult periods. We might have been partners at HSW, but the bills of exchange we got from him sometimes weren't worth the paper they were printed on."

Some of Klöckner's executives even thought Korf was playing a double game: "He didn't let this joint venture make any money, yet made profits on the same market with his BSW," said one of them. "That was his skill. When there were any lucrative wire mesh deals to be had, he steered them to Kehl, and he sent export trade to Hamburg. That's how he socialized the losses."

Yet Gienow never confronted Korf at a time when it might still have made a difference. Didn't he have any evidence of his partner's suspected tactics? Was he ignoring them? Did he prefer to simply avoid the uncomfortable and hard-to-pin-down Korf? "The shareholding structure would have allowed Klöckner to take a look at the books at any time and rectify matters," claimed Meier-Preschany. "Why didn't Gienow do anything about the problems he'd spotted at HSW? Was he so spectacularly successful at Klöckner? I can't remember."

It was inevitable that Korf and Gienow would one day meet again – and they did so at the International Iron and Steel Institute, one of the elite circles of large manufacturers. Although Korf wasn't a member, he nevertheless visited it to promote his technologies and proposals to an influential audience. Gienow refused to shake Korf's hand – a belated, helpless expression of a failed partnership, which all in all cost Klöckner many millions of marks.

The rotten apples in the Korf Group started to turn increasingly bad as early as the mid-1970s. The first serious complaint from the Kuwaiti partner on the US side of the Korf empire led to little more than a reshuffle. Korf Industries' performance had been consistently poor for a while, and so local boss Wolfgang Jansen, who embodied Korf's pioneering and go-getting spirit, had to be fired. He was replaced by Roger Regelbrugge who, with a good dose of optimism, could be described as a potential consolidator. Even this step was long resisted by the loyal Korf, and Kreifels and Bernhardt had to exert gentle pressure on him to make him agree.

Regelbrugge wasn't just an aloof accountant. A young employee who'd just joined Korf's US arm first met Regelbrugge while the latter was getting ready for a business trip. Despite the difference in rank, they chatted a bit about the upcoming journey when the boss suddenly had an idea: "Hey, you're not married, are you? You've got a passport. Why don't you come with me?" The young employee, who happily accepted the invitation, was hugely impressed by this spontaneity.

Beyond the symbolic replacement of a possibly negligent chief executive, the overdue revolt of the preservationists in Korf's empire failed to materialize. No one, neither Korf himself, nor the chair of his supervisory board, nor his lenders reacted to the quiet or even not-so-quiet rumblings inside and outside the Korf Group. "Korf knew what was going on," said Berner. "But anyone who told him would be quickly rebuffed. Korf was always in forward gear. He never included the question of consolidation in his calculations about new investments."

Because he believed wholeheartedly in his strategy, he always managed to persuade sceptical partners to be patient. Korf gave the banks private collateral without hesitation when they asked for it – for example, in the form of mortgages on his beautiful white villa. Even his trusted advisor Bert Pfluger, although more knowledgeable than most about Korf's accounts, was unable to restrain him: "I certainly sometimes urged increased caution. As an auditor, of course I'd have to say that all those admonishers were right. And I might have had to resign if I'd been advising him as an auditor. But I wasn't his auditor. That's a job that never appealed to me."

Korf convincingly countered his critics by pointing out how petty their concerns were. Hadn't he proved many times over that his industrial group was almost predestined for growth? "Willy Korf was a man who had his eye on his earnings rather than his assets," said Pfluger. "If he'd taken an interest in balance sheet theory, he'd doubtless have preferred Schmalenbach's dynamic balance sheet." Perhaps it wasn't a good omen that Eugen Schmalenbach, a professor of business management at the University of Cologne, had learned vividly what insolvency meant when his father's hardware company had gone to the wall.

Much has been said about Korf and his own personal philosophy. His friend and partner Gerhard Fuchs, with whom he'd joined forces in Korf & Fuchs Systemtechnik, pronounced: "If there were ten items on the agenda and two of them were positive, Korf wouldn't talk about the other eight." Another of these bons mots was that a company with revenue of 30 million marks and 3 million in profit wasn't as interesting to Korf as one running at a loss but with revenue of 300 million. "He was someone who took high risks – and often underestimated them," said his financial director Meinecke. The world – and probably Korf himself – was also dazzled by his fascinating ability to ingratiate himself with some of the most important people around. He succeeded particularly well in this during the Social–Liberal coalition, with the inconspicuous yet crafty Karl Wienand as an invaluable aide behind the scenes (even after the end of Wienand's political career following a series of scandals). Meinecke illustrated Wienand's role with a typical example of the politician's support to Korf:

> Once I phoned Karl Wienand when Manfred Lahnstein was
> finance minister in Helmut Schmidt's cabinet because we
> needed an appointment at the ministry. Wienand said: "I'll
> introduce you to Lahnstein right away. If I tell him you're
> coming, he'll have to make time for you." That was Karl
> Wienand. He knew something about everyone and had
> everyone in his pocket.

But being carried by a network of relationships and popular
support was deceptive. Times were about to change, and not
just in a political sense. "Korf's weakness was his merciless
optimism," said Heidelberg business lawyer Jobst Wellensiek,
who was soon to play an important role in Korf's world – a
transformed, drastically reduced world with no way out.

In retrospect, according to Wellensiek, this fateful reversal
was already on the cards on the eve of the 1980s: "Korf didn't
have sufficient controlling in place, or if he did, he ignored it."
Wellensiek claimed that Korf only really had liquidity twice in
his business career, namely "when he sold the production of
structural steel mesh to Klöckner, and when he brought the
Kuwaitis on board."

Platow-Brief, one of the oldest and most influential German-
language publications containing business information and
economic analysis, first revealed the state of Korf's liquidity at
the end of 1981, just as the steel crisis was about to enter
its eighth year. It listed Korf's two main lenders as Dresdner
Bank and Bank für Gemeinwirtschaft, along with Bayerische
Hypothekenbank, Badische Kommunale Landesbank (BaKoLa),
the state banks of Hesse and Hamburg, and Berliner Bank.
According to *Platow-Brief,* the debts owed by Korf's KIH to these
seven banks, as well as legions of smaller banks, totalled 423
million marks in December 1981, while the liabilities of Korf-
Stahl amounted to 128 million marks. With more than half
a billion marks of debt, Korf's credit lines were completely
exhausted. Any further deterioration was bound to lead to
insolvency, no matter how inventive the accounting.

CHAPTER 10

Into the abyss

"We fly by sight and by instruments. And although we do observation flights and good-weather flights, we get our kicks from flying blind, low-level flights and nosedives!"

The ensuing tempest brought a deluge that washed away what little solid ground remained beneath Korf's feet. The devastating flood of subsidies paid out by the governments of Western Europe to prop up ailing, outdated steel conglomerates that were partly or even fully state-owned, had swelled to billions upon billions since the crisis began in 1975. Entire industries had become far too expensive for the world market following decades of neglected rationalization, but no government could afford to put thousands, even tens of thousands of voters out of work; no politicians were willing to sacrifice the big, old influential names of the steel industry to competitors from neighbouring countries. And the corporations, whose persistent lobbying via EUROFER in Brussels was now bearing fruit, had made themselves comfortable, safe in the knowledge that change was unlikely. "The 70 per cent of European steelmakers that are reliant on their governments have stopped thinking and acting like independent companies," Korf publicly complained. "They've begun to regard themselves more as a kind of employment agency."

As had happened in the disastrous days of the rolled steel

syndicates, albeit on a much larger scale, the world of steel had turned upside down. Since 1978, the USA had imposed punitive tariffs to defend its steel industry against cheap imports from the European Economic Community; Europe, in turn, had introduced a quota system in 1980 that fixed production quantities and prices almost like a planned economy. In Belgium, Luxembourg, France, the UK and Italy in particular, the steel market had effectively ceased to function. Instead, every tonne of semi-finished products was being increasingly subsidized to keep it saleable on the world markets and within the EEC.

Subsidized foreign steel also flooded West Germany, benefiting steel corporations across the border. But the state handouts didn't reach smaller, family-run companies like those owned by Korf, which had neither the big names nor the large workforce required to qualify for public subsidies. In 1982, Korf 'only' employed just over 3,000 people domestically; the fact that he had well over 10,000 employees worldwide counted for nothing politically. Korf's main competitor (and the closest to his operation in Kehl) was the Arbed-Saarstahl Group in Saarland, which provided work for almost 18,000 people in West Germany alone, despite being registered in Luxembourg.

It didn't matter that little Korf, producing 2.7 million tonnes of crude steel every year, had worked his way up to a respectable thirty-fifth place among the world's leading steelmakers – because Arbed-Saarstahl was well ahead of him, up in eighth place, with almost 10 million tonnes. Nor did the admiration of the US business magazine *Fortune* mean a great deal, even when it ranked the "German maverick" 393rd in its Fortune 500 Company List; Korf was left out of official ratings because shares in his company weren't freely tradable. Ultimately, his global turnover of 2.8 billion marks was no use either: Korf didn't receive a pfennig in subsidies, while Arbed benefited from financial support in abundance. Korf explained to *Welt am Sonntag* how this affected the balance of power:

We struggle for every mark in cost savings per tonne, and our technicians are constantly coming up with new ideas. In the last few years, for example, we've considerably reduced electricity and electrode consumption, shortened the smelting time, laid off staff, and applied new processes to significantly boost productivity. All these efforts have enabled us to cut our production costs by maybe 40 to 50 marks per tonne, but we simply can't compensate for the advantage our competitors get from subsidies, which amounts to 260 marks per tonne. For anyone who works for me, that must make their blood boil.

West German taxpayers' billions being paid out to Arbed was bitterly ironic, for it was West Germany that had nobly resisted the European disease dubbed 'subsidy-itis', which violated the spirit and the letter of the European Coal and Steel Community Treaty. And Prussian civil servants normally take their treaties very seriously.

Others were less troubled by the legal situation – first and foremost Romano Prodi (the future President of the European Commission) when he was appointed head of the Italian Steel Industry Association. Klöckner's boss Herbert Gienow could already see disaster looming "because Prodi was a professor of insolvency law." The European Coal and Steel Community Treaty was naive in that it only banned cases of direct, open subsidies by the state. The Italians responded by simply carving up their steel industry into assets and liabilities. The debts remained with the government, while the miraculously deleveraged tangible assets were transferred to the private sector, which could now operate free of all burdens, had effectively been gifted with new steel plants, and didn't even have to pay any interest or depreciation on them.

In less imaginative West Germany, on the other hand, even the likes of Krupp, Klöckner and Thyssen were largely left out in the cold. As Gienow said: "For years, the German steel industry put up with the fact that all its European rivals were subsidized by their governments to the tune of 25 per cent of their sales." That amount was estimated by some to add up to about 80 billion marks in taxpayers' money. Only Arbed-Saarstahl, because of Saarland's historically unique position, received concessions worth 3 or 4 billion marks from Bonn over the years and was thus able to offer steel at knock-down prices while working in the neighbourhood of Korf's far more economical production.

On 10 September 1982, Korf and his BSW steel mill in Kehl committed a symbolic act of resistance against an aspect of the subsidy policy that in his view was tantamount to unfair discrimination: he sued the Social–Liberal government – with which he'd been on such good terms – at Cologne administrative court over its subsidies for coking coal. Of course, it wasn't the socialists who had invented these subsidies.

German hard coal, unsustainably expensive by international standards, had been subsidized in the form of coke since the end of the 1950s in order to make it much cheaper for domestic steel producers, as a way of supporting the coal and steel industries. However, this didn't benefit the entire steel industry, but only the traditional steelworks of large corporations that still used traditional, coke-fired blast furnaces. The smaller, more modern electric steelworks like BSW, which were independent of coke, didn't receive any comparable aid.

Korf was backed up in his legal challenge by Otto Bachof, a prominent professor of public law at the University of Tübingen, who concluded that Korf could invoke the principle of equality before the law. When Korf threw down the gauntlet to the government, obviously he'd finally stopped believing in political fairness and goodwill. In the final phase of the Social Democrats' and Liberals' coalition, he found it impossible to get anything done in Bonn. He realized the wheels of justice turned very slowly, but he had no idea that even his own interest in the proceedings would be ground down by the events that soon followed.

In the meantime, Korf had become a prominent advocate of economic liberalism, and could never resist offering his support for the American free market ideal when speaking to the press:

> If it wasn't for subsidies, restructuring would have come about naturally, just like in the USA. If your factory no longer makes any money, either you go bankrupt or you do something else. If the national and regional government had promoted Saarland as an area for new types of industry a decade ago, if they'd promised loans to retrain steel workers and for certain investments, the 10,000 to 12,000 jobs at stake at Arbed-Saarstahl could have been saved for about a third of the money that's used every year to subsidize a dying steel giant.

Otfried Forssman, who was in charge of Korf's French activities at the time, perfectly understood Korf's almost missionary zeal expressed in countless interviews:

> He was right that this was destroying us. We couldn't compete with the united taxpayers of Europe when it came to cheap reinforcing steel. The British, the Belgians, the French all undercut us. Sometimes we wondered when they would stop, where their pain threshold was. Our problem was that whereas the old, established steel locations with their thousands of jobs could use social blackmail, we couldn't. It wasn't fair. But the world isn't a fair place.

It wasn't fair either that Korf had to cope with the loss of three of his closest colleagues and advisers within the space of twenty months during this most threatening phase for his business. This sombre period began without warning on Monday 2 February 1981. On this snowy day, Korf, Bernhardt and the lawyer Otfried Lieberknecht were waiting outside the Düsseldorf office of Max Kreifels, chairman of the supervisory board. They'd been waiting for Kreifels for a long time, which didn't bode well; normally, Kreifels was extremely punctual. What they didn't realize was that he'd been involved in a fatal road accident.

Unusually, Kreifels had decided to drive to the meeting alone. The snow ploughs had cleared the motorway, leaving snow piled up along the crash barrier. According to the subsequent police reconstruction, while travelling along a straight stretch of road in the afternoon twilight, Kreifels' heavy car suddenly sped off the carriageway, as if it had mounted a ramp of snow, and crashed into the pillar of a motorway bridge scheduled for demolition. Max Kreifels was killed instantly.

At the funeral service in Düsseldorf five days later, Korf told the mourners that he was shocked to the core when the police notified Kreifels' law firm of what had happened. "Minutes of paralysis and horror followed," he said. "We simply couldn't believe that Max Kreifels would never return to his office where we'd met so often over the years." He continued: "It was an hour or so before the first of us who'd heard the news regained their composure and could start thinking clearly again." In his address, Korf paid tribute to his companion of seventeen years as "both confessor and counsellor".

Wolfgang Bernhardt, Korf's deputy, took it upon himself to speak to the staff in Baden-Baden on 9 February about Max Kreifels, in his dual role of company lawyer and chair of the supervisory board: "The death of this man, this perpetual mover and shaker, still seems unreal." At the end of his eulogy, Bernhardt invited everyone to join him in intercessory prayer, and concluded with an appeal: "Let us honour Max Kreifels by working hard to continue building the Korf Group."

But whatever the effect of his exhortation, events took a different course. Franz Burda remembered Willy Korf telling him a long time after: "If Kreifels had still been alive, none of this would have happened."

It was as if a curse had befallen the company. At the beginning of April 1982, Klaus Didillon, the most talented of Korf's engineers, and who had successfully restructured BSW, crashed head-on into an oncoming car while out his motorbike on a country road near Korf-Stahl's headquarters. His sudden death tore another gaping hole in Korf's plans: Didillon had been on the verge of becoming the chief technical officer of Korf-Stahl, having already briefly been BSW's chief executive before being promoted to head office. In technical matters, he was regarded as

Korf's right-hand man, and he was held in such high esteem in Kehl that the workforce would have done anything for him.

On one occasion, Didillon had visited an electric steel plant in Japan whose production with just two furnaces was more efficient than BSW was achieving with three comparable ones. All it took was an intercontinental phone call to Kehl, and by the time Didillon returned, the middle furnace had been shut down and more resourceful Japanese logistics introduced. This was another man who, always loyal to Korf, would probably have averted what was about to happen in Kehl.

But the loss of extraordinary talent and vitality wasn't over yet. On 30 September 1982, Korf's deputy Wolfgang Bernhardt resigned. The only faint consolation was that his decision to quit had not been completely out of the blue. Over the previous six months, serious differences had emerged between Bernhardt and Korf over the right strategy for the company in this extremely difficult period. Was this because the affable 'triumvirate' with Kreifels had been shattered? Kreifels' replacement, Johannes C. Welbergen, who was previously head of Shell in Germany and the new chairman of the supervisory board at Korf-Stahl, had not been able to fill the gap left by the lawyer's untimely death. As Bernhardt explained much later: "With Kreifels gone, it became far harder for me to keep Korf down to earth. It had been much easier with Kreifels to help me."

Of course, Bernhardt continued to voice his misgivings to Korf, warning for example that the lawsuit he himself had brought over coking coal subsidies might not succeed. None of this leaked out to the media or even the supervisory board. But as time went on, Bernhardt found it harder and harder to get through to Korf. Furthermore, Bernhardt refused to be reassured by the fact that Korf had always found ways and means to get through his difficulties.

Korf, for his part, maintained his relentless optimism. His glass was half full, Bernhardt's at least half empty. After sharing a bottle of Riesling or two with Karl Wienand at the latter's home, Korf often complained about that "killjoy" Bernhardt:

"If we spent the whole time consolidating, we'd never get anywhere."

While Bernhardt and Korf were growing further apart, a tense meeting of the supervisory board was hosted by Dresdner Bank in Frankfurt. Bernhardt made it known that he disagreed with the chief executive on important issues:

> The members of the supervisory board began delving into the tension between Korf and me. They wanted to know my opinion since we clearly disagreed. And that was the only time I walked out on a meeting. I didn't want to let them drive a wedge between us.

It didn't feel like the right place for Bernhardt to speak freely, even though a company director was supposed to be accountable to the financial partners and lenders gathered there. His personal loyalty prevailed. But in view of the strained financial situation, he couldn't go on much longer like this:

> It got to the point where Korf and I realized a choice had to be made between A and B: they couldn't both be right. I finally said to myself that the company was called Korf, not Bernhardt, and so it was the number two who had to go. A firm can't carry on with its boss going one way and his deputy trying to go another.

Bernhardt officially left the executive board at the end of September, agreeing to stay on "in an advisory capacity" until his second five-year contract expired nine months later on 30 June 1983. Korf, whose personal relationship with his deputy was still intact, even tried to persuade Bernhardt to retain managerial authority despite his imminent departure; Bernhardt felt this proposal was unrealistic and declined. Even so, he kept his office next door to Korf's at headquarters, so that at first the rest of the staff didn't notice anything was amiss. The executives were only informed by Korf on 20 October in a brief memo, which announced that he and Carl-Theodor Meinecke (the financial director) would assume Bernhardt's responsibilities on the board for the time being. In fact, this memo was so uninformative that the very next day, Bernhardt followed it up with a three-page statement addressed to senior management.

In his unmistakable style, Bernhardt wrote: "I won't be leaving until mid-1983. You'll still have to put up with me for a while, albeit with a different status than before. If I ever 'bossed you about' in the past, I won't be doing that anymore." Korf's 'minister of the interior' announced that he would continue "to support and encourage the staff as I have always done to the best of my knowledge until I finally depart." And he concluded on a gentle note of caution for the competition: "Our many opponents, our rivals and our other 'friends' shouldn't rejoice too soon. My willingness to fight if necessary remains unbroken. My warning to everyone, no matter where they happen to come from, is: Look before you leap!"

With this statement circulating like wildfire throughout the company and even finding its way onto the company's bulletin boards, it's odd that the media didn't catch wind of Bernhardt's planned exit until almost a month later. When it did make the papers, it was even reported by the business press in America. Odder still is that Korf's sales director Hellmut Schulte-Derne and his technical director Heinz Schmidberger only learned of Bernhardt's departure from the media during a trip to the USA. On their return, they confronted Korf: Why hadn't they been informed? What on earth was going on? Nothing, Korf replied; as far as he was concerned, the matter was over, and the reasons were purely private.

The impression made by Korf was reminiscent of the silent loneliness of the great Roman emperors in their final stages (if we are to believe Hollywood's accounts, at least). Statements issued by Korf's company had become increasingly monosyllabic and defiant, especially when reporters enquired about the reasons for the losses and the gloomy economic situation in the steel industry. To Willy Korf, negative developments were simply inconceivable.

As for the strategic defensive into which the sales of Midrex plants had been plunged across the world by the rising price of natural gas: "Despite the energy crisis and higher gas prices, there will still be a large market for Midrex," Korf predicted as late as 1979. What about the permanent crisis at his mechanical engineering company Mohr & Federhaff, which simply couldn't get back on its feet? "We're a little more in tune with making steel than we are with mechanical engineering," Bernhardt told *Süddeutsche Zeitung* in 1980. But in 1982, when the steel crisis reached its nadir, the arguments for carrying on as before gradually ran out. The direct reduction plant in Emden? Closed and in liquidation. The mini steelworks in Montereau near Paris? Fifty per cent was acquired by Sacilor, practically placing it in French state ownership, according to the British *Metal Bulletin*.

Things started spiralling downward faster and faster. In autumn 1982, the final warning signs began stacking up. Several of these ill-fated developments were completely beyond Korf's control. On 1 October, Helmut Kohl was voted in as Chancellor, taking the place of Helmut Schmidt, in what was nothing less than a political watershed. To make matters worse, the well-established network that Korf had assembled in the Social–Liberal coalition disintegrated.

As the freshly elected government tried to find its feet, the severe problems of the steel industry were far from top of the new cabinet's agenda. Inexperienced ministers were too busy working out what they were supposed to be doing, practising statesmanlike poses, and heaving removal boxes into their predecessors' vacated offices. Moreover, with the government strapped for cash, the catchphrase 'steel subsidies' was considered an inherited anathema rather than a tried and tested policy tool. Korf, when the time came, found himself running up against walls of rejection and beginners' ignorance among the recently replaced state secretaries and ministers.

Meanwhile, the bad news from the USA piled up thick and fast. US steel production had almost collapsed under the onslaught of subsidized cheap steel from the nationalized industries of

Western Europe and Brazil. The global economic crisis hit the paragon of capitalism hard. Korf Industries, despite having made a slight profit of 2 million dollars in 1981 while the rest of the US steel industry was already suffering slumps of around 35 per cent, was now also finished. And the productivity of Korf's plants in South Carolina and Texas wasn't nearly as good as reported in the press: "The plants were running lousily. Except when there was a big order for a Midrex plant, the order books were empty," remembered Horst Weitzmann, who as CEO of BSW in Kehl had just moved up to the board of Korf-Stahl at the time.

In the end, instead of the hoped-for 80-million-dollar profit, Korf's American operations incurred a loss of about 100 million dollars in 1982. Korf, with his holding company in Charlotte, could hardly get any credit at all in the USA – and the little he could muster came with extortionate interest rates. His attempts to persuade the Kuwaitis to increase their 30 per cent stake in Korf Industries also fell on stony ground. Internal equity, which according to the auditors' report had reached 27 per cent of the balance sheet total at the beginning of 1982, had been melted away by the losses like snow under the midday sun. And now this calamitous data from the USA flew across the Atlantic and burst unchecked onto KIH's balance sheet – with devastating force.

As late as December 1982, Korf's German banks were still planning to grant Korf a syndicated loan of 20 million marks to maintain the US business. "This tells you how persuasive Korf was for the supervisory board, even at that time," said his financial expert Manfred Derner. But it was to be Korf's last success as a great communicator. The banks had realized that even once-powerful conglomerates like Arbed-Saarstahl were financially ruined and only surviving thanks to the government's billion-dollar support package. What would stop Korf from going bankrupt, especially without the benefit of the state safety net? "A lot of the small banks that had been happy to do business with us suddenly got the jitters," Korf would later recall. "Within four weeks, we lost credit lines totalling about 50 million marks."

A last-ditch attempt to avert the looming insolvency of KIH as the top-level holding company and parent organisation of Korf's American activities was mounted three days before New Year's Eve – at the highest political echelon. At 6 p.m. on 28 December, Helmut Kohl, the new head of government, sat down with four gentlemen in his equally new office in Bonn. On his left were the two state secretaries, Waldemar Schreckenberger and Dieter von Würzen, on his right Willy Korf and his new supervisory board chairman, Johannes Welbergen. Since Korf had already been warned that neither guarantees nor subsidies could be expected from Kohl in the short term, he took a different tack.

Korf proposed that KIH's interests in the Brazilian mini-steel plant in Pains and the Saudi Arabian steel company in Hadeed – worth a total of 65 million marks according to Korf's calculations – be temporarily 'parked' with two state-owned institutions: the DEG German Investment Corporation and the KfW Reconstruction Bank (DEG already owned equal shareholdings in both steelworks, equivalent to Korf's own shares). This would have freed up enough liquidity for KIH to survive the first half of 1983, allowing Korf time to apply for funding from the German government. The proposal also had a certain charm for the new Chancellor, since it was an opportunity to present himself as a discreet crisis manager without risking any additional cash from state coffers for the time being.

However, to bridge the turn of the year, an initial tranche of 16 million marks had to be released on New Year's Eve, by means of a guarantee from DEG, in return for a deposit of shares in Pains. Could this be done in time? Around 11 a.m. on 29 December, less than a full day after the meeting in the chancellery, Schreckenberger called Korf to announce the reprieve: the plan would go ahead as discussed, and he'd already issued instructions to DEG through state secretary Volkmar Köhler from the development aid ministry. Immediately,

Korf phoned Lothar Späth, the minister-president of Baden-Württemberg, in Badgastein, where he was on holiday. Späth had held out the prospect of a 40-million-mark guarantee for BSW from the regional government if Bonn agreed to provide matching aid. For a few hours, salvation seemed within reach.

However, just one day later, on 30 December, disaster struck when the executive board of DEG declined to issue the 16-million-mark guarantee of which Korf had already seemed so sure. Walter Scheel, the ex-president of Germany and now chairman of DEG's supervisory board, unexpectedly turned up at the meeting and refused to approve the guarantee without written instructions from the development aid minister, Jürgen Warnke of the Christian Socialists. But Warnke was on holiday and couldn't be reached for days. DEG's board insisted that such transactions were not in the organization's remit without Warnke's approval. And without a guarantee from DEG, there could be no guarantee from the regional government. That meant no liquidity for Korf, and hence no way for his business to continue.

The chain of salvation made up of Kohl, Schreckenberger and Köhler had broken down when it got to Walter Scheel – the man once mocked for shooting an owl at Korf's hunting party; the man whom Korf had flown all the way to Brazil and back in his company jet in order to show off his projects; the man who'd been a prominent member of Thyssen's supervisory board. Is it any wonder that Korf's team began indulging in conspiracy theories as the dominoes of the painstakingly assembled rescue plan began to topple? "It's a scandal what they did to me in Bonn!" Korf still raged much later. "They just exploited me as a young celebrity to bring in foreign orders!" Bizarrely, when asked years later, the former president couldn't recall the dramatic events of 1982, or anything about his acquaintance with Korf.

Meanwhile, in the crucial days leading up to New Year's Eve, it was apparently business as usual at Korf's headquarters in Baden-Baden. "We didn't notice anything different, not even from the correspondence," said Korf's secretary Renate Höing. "We were just slaving away as usual. Korf would never have told us we weren't doing well. He was so optimistic and there was never any talk of the company going downhill." Privately, too, as a family man, he tried not to let on, and that wouldn't change in the aftermath. "He was certainly under stress," said Astrid Korf Wolman, "but we didn't experience any drama. He gave the impression that that was how it was, and that we now had to make the best of it."

While he was still in charge, the indefatigable Willy Korf relentlessly tried to find a way out of the financial crisis. Franz Burda recalled Korf approaching him and his brothers for a 10-million-mark loan: "I said no. We could have given it to him, but we didn't want to. We knew his business was a bottomless pit."

Lothar Späth, the regional premier who was apparently so close to Korf, was similarly besieged by him: "He kept begging me to help." And indeed, Späth had a keen interest in at least keeping BSW alive in Kehl with its many jobs. If the holding company KIH went to the wall, he was afraid that the insolvency would become infectious, with knock-on effects throughout the region. However, Späth saw little financial leeway apart from the vague possibility of a guarantee – but only if similar aid was forthcoming from Bonn: "Korf asked us to prop him up for just three more days, after which the cheques would start arriving from Brazil. I told my team: We're a public authority, we can't get mixed up in any business that isn't crystal clear."

Even so, there was a rescue proposal based on an idea by its CEO, Horst Weitzmann. The European Community's quota system meant BSW was forbidden from increasing its profit margin by producing in line with demand or capacity. Therefore, in addition to Korf's holding Neckar Drahtwerke GmbH in Ebersbach, Weitzmann suggested affiliating other manufacturing companies in the region to the steelworks in order to create more added value, for demand by subsidiaries was not subject to the quota limitations. As the crisis continued, separate negotiations were therefore held between

Späth's ministry of economic affairs and the boss of BSW, while Korf kept searching for comprehensive but increasingly unlikely solutions for his entire group of companies.

As part of this quest, Korf and his team rushed to Hamburg several times to discuss with the mayor, Klaus von Dohnanyi, the possibility of concerted action with Baden-Württemberg – an attempt that was ultimately fruitless. In the meantime, Weitzmann and Späth appeared to be getting close to an agreement. But with AEG-Telefunken's recent petition for insolvency having almost cost Späth his job, he was still very wary, telling Weitzmann: "Look, it'll take an awful lot of cash to rescue Korf. Let's consider the jobs in Baden-Württemberg separately. I can see your proposal is viable. If you can execute it and leave the rest of the group to go its own way, I'll help you." Späth was also afraid that BSW would go bankrupt if drastic action wasn't taken soon: "We thought that was the board's responsibility, not Willy Korf's." Nevertheless, both Späth and Weitzmann insisted that Korf had always been informed of the alternative rescue plan.

The hands of Korf's watch ticked mercilessly and inexorably towards twelve. On 6 January 1983, he drew up a petition for composition proceedings for his top-level holding company KIH to stave off bankruptcy, and filed it the following morning with the district court in Baden-Baden. On the recommendation of his lawyers, he proposed that Heidelberg business lawyer Jobst Wellensiek (who was unknown to him personally) be appointed as the administrator. Korf hoped that this step would at least insulate his factories and technology companies from the wave of insolvency about to crash in from the USA. At this time, KIH's official press release still stated that Korf-Stahl and its subsidiaries such as BSW and HSW "weren't affected" by composition proceedings. Although this may have been formally correct, the substance of Korf's announcements was rapidly crumbling away.

But anyone who thought that the humiliating trip to court

had damaged Korf's sovereignty or his engaging charisma was wrong. On the very day the petition was filed, an emergency meeting was held in Düsseldorf for the scrap dealers who'd supplied Korf's KIH with his indispensable raw material and were now waiting to get paid. Years later, Horst Weitzmann was still astonished by the scene that had unfolded:

> Korf sat there in the middle like a prince on the widest chair, smoking the fattest Havanas. And the spokesman for the scrap dealers, who really ought to have been furious with him, stood in front of him like a subordinate and delivered a eulogy, stating that all those gathered there owed it to Korf that scrap had become such an important commodity, adding that now, after many years, the first bills of exchange had unfortunately bounced. They were all his creditors, yet they paid homage to him!

And they promised to continue delivering scrap to Hamburg and Kehl – as long as the banks stuck by Korf.

But assurances like this were dwindling swiftly. Almost every day brought new, dramatic turbulence. On 7 January, Horst Weitzmann resigned from the executive board of Korf-Stahl, having joined only a short time before. There were two reasons for his departure. One was the board's powerlessness: "Whenever it came to the crunch, Korf acted like the company's walking general meeting. Being the majority shareholder, he took decisions on his own. When I realized that the man I liked was losing touch with reality, I was torn." In addition, it seemed that Welbergen, the new chairman of the supervisory board, was intent on organizing a coup. He'd taken Weitzmann aside and into his confidence, saying:

> Korf has completely lost touch with reality. Steel production is finished, but I can still make something out of the engineering division. I'm ready to take over as CEO, you're already on the board, so let's start a technology group together. Spethmann from Thyssen will buy HSW, close it down, and then he'll get the EEC production quotas from HSW. Krackow from Arbed-Saarstahl will buy the steel plant

in Kehl.

However, Weitzmann, who felt deeply attached to the steelworks that he'd managed to turn around single-handedly, demurred; he'd long since forged plans of his own. Weitzmann was sure that insolvency was now also rolling inexorably towards Korf-Stahl and hence his Kehl plant – but was convinced that the regional premier backed his rescue plan. As Lothar Späth concluded: "He can only have assumed that the regional government would have to take care of the firm, regardless of whether it went bankrupt."

The final factor prompting Weitzmann to make his decisive move was delivered by the 'steel moderators'. Back on 16 November, Otto Graf Lambsdorff, Germany's new minister of economic affairs, had revealed his plan to the leaders of the German steel industry (including Korf) to ask three prominent experts for proposals to defend German industry against other countries' subsidy offensive: Alfred Herrhausen from the board of Deutsche Bank, Marcus Bierich, a director at Allianz and previously at Mannesmann AG, and Günter Vogelsang, who had previously been a director at Krupp. Korf and the other industrialists had agreed, and after a few weeks of exploratory talks, the three moderators put their recommendations for strategic mergers between the players into a report – which remains unpublished to this day.

It was rumoured that under the moderators' plan, the BSW steelworks in Kehl was to join Arbed-Saarstahl – of all companies – which couldn't be allowed to go bankrupt due to all the subsidies it received. The truth of the matter was that in talks with the moderators, Korf had welcomed the idea of a joint sales syndicate for BSW, Arbed-Saarstahl, Lechstahlwerke and Maxhütte to cover southern Germany. According to Korf's records, all those attending the meeting with the moderators agreed that mergers weren't an option in the short term. Nevertheless, Arbed had been mentioned as a new partner. "That was when I lost my composure and declared we were too good to be sacrificed!" recounted Weitzmann. At that time, about 1,000 people were employed by BSW in Kehl.

On Sunday 9 January 1983, a real-life business drama played out in Kehl, with the lead roles taken by Weitzmann and Korf – in opposing camps. On that morning, Willy Korf was still sure that he'd managed to persuade his seven main creditor banks to largely waive their claims and inject new liquidity into Korf-Stahl, whose survival was ultimately in the banks' own interest. He thought his technology companies Korf & Fuchs Systemtechnik, Korf Engineering and Midrex Corporation, which were still profitable, were a secure bargaining chip. And he also believed that he'd convinced no fewer than twenty-five banks to keep their credit lines open for at least another week, enabling him to pay the staff's wages on the following Monday. He was confident that the necessary foundations had been laid to restructure Korf-Stahl.

What happened next was meticulously recorded by Korf in a confidential internal memo dated 13 January 1983. Evidently, he believed that his rights had been grossly violated, and he intended to enforce them in court.

Perhaps Korf had a hunch that Sunday morning, an instinct that made him pick up the phone around ten o'clock and call Weitzmann at home. His wife answered and told him that her husband was in the office. When Korf phoned Kehl five minutes later, several men were obviously gathered around Weitzmann's desk.

"What's the reason for this meeting?" demanded Korf.

"We intend to file for composition tomorrow morning," replied Weitzmann.

"What on earth for?" Korf retorted.

"We can't pay any wages tomorrow because the banks have stopped their credit lines."

Korf exploded. Furious, he reminded Weitzmann of the standstill agreement reached with the banks guaranteeing that wages would continue to be paid. He added that according to the tax group agreement, a petition for composition couldn't be filed without the approval of Korf-Stahl. He stressed that the agreement of the chairman of BSW's supervisory board would also be required; that person was Korf, and he would never give his consent as long as the banks still stood by him.

Korf could no longer contain himself. His secretary Renate Höing, who was almost always on duty for Korf, including that Sunday morning, remembered what happened: "I went to his home, knocked on the door, opened it, and saw him screaming down the phone at someone." Korf then slammed down the receiver and alerted a legal advisor. According to company records, shortly afterwards Weitzmann spoke to this Munich lawyer and promised not to take any action without first informing Korf.

At about 1 p.m., Korf tried phoning Weitzmann at his house once more. Again, he only reached his wife, who told him that her husband wouldn't be home until later that afternoon. By 3 p.m., he still hadn't arrived. At 5 p.m., all his now distraught wife could tell Korf was that her husband had "called from an unknown place to tell her he wouldn't be coming home that day. Moreover, he wouldn't tell her where he could be reached either, so that his problems wouldn't affect her." Korf's phone calls also revealingly went unanswered at the home of another BSW executive. It then dawned on him "that something monstrous must be going on behind the scenes."

Dismayed, he drafted a letter to Weitzmann instructing him not to file "any petitions for insolvency" without his consent, warning him that if he refused, "on behalf of Korf-Stahl and its shareholders, I will hold you personally liable for any harm caused as a result." Around 11.30 p.m., this letter was delivered to the Weitzmanns by a courier – who handed it to Mrs Weitzmann because, as expected, the boss of BSW was not at home.

The following day, Monday 10 January, was pay day in Kehl. Korf's legal adviser Karl Grüter arrived at Kehl district court at about 7.30 a.m. in order to personally hand a copy of this letter to the judge and thus thwart any attempt to file for composition that day. He was too late. Weitzmann, joined by someone else from the board of BSW, had already been there on Sunday afternoon and filed the petition for composition proceedings with the out-of-hours judge. Hans Ringwald, a lawyer from Stuttgart, had already been appointed as a provisional administrator. Korf was speechless when Grüter told him what had happened.

The company was also speechless for a day without its head or an authorized press officer. Media enquiries arrived in Renate Höing's office thick and fast, yet Korf, the crisis manager, couldn't be reached. "We had about a thousand phone calls from domestic and foreign journalists. The phone didn't stop ringing. We just took messages for him the whole day. He wasn't there at all."

In the meantime, Korf was giving Weitzmann a dressing-down. When Weitzmann arrived at his office first thing on Monday morning, Korf had already taken over his desk. Beside him was a letter of resignation he'd brought with him for Weitzmann to sign. But the matter wasn't as simple as it seemed to Korf. Weitzmann couldn't be accused of having ignored the instructions of both BSW's parent company and the chairman of its supervisory board (basically one and the same person) when he'd filed the petition. He was convinced that he'd acted correctly and legally.

Years later, Weitzmann maintained that he was right to have filed for the proceedings: "Chief executives of limited companies have to comply with the Stock Corporation Act. And this law says that if one of the two criteria for filing a petition for composition is met, then that's what has to be done. And in this case, both criteria had been satisfied." The two criteria were over-indebtedness and insolvency, and in Weitzmann's view, they both applied to BSW, given the tax group and profit transfer agreements with Korf-Stahl. In 1982, the plant, like all the others, had made a huge loss which Korf-Stahl was unable to offset. And BSW had had no chance to build up assets in the previous lucrative years, for everything had been used to cover the losses of the parent companies.

Although Meier-Preschany from Dresdner Bank branded the way in which Weitzmann had filed for composition "ungentlemanly", Weitzmann thought the buck stopped with Korf : "Korf should take the blame for his constant high risks. That's not responsible corporate management, tackling new investments while knowing full well that the whole business is in terrible trouble. I had to act. I felt obliged to the people in the company who trusted me."

It would have been tricky for Korf simply to fire Weitzmann. Suddenly able to produce to the administrator promises by the regional bank and other banks to grant loans amounting to double-digit millions, the workers' representatives on BSW's supervisory board were completely on Weitzmann's side. And his internal influence carried considerable weight.

Realizing that there was nothing he could do, once again Korf showed another, fascinating side of his nature that had already come to light when he'd been abandoned overnight by his US partner Midland Ross in 1972. In a flash, he came to terms with the situation, let his anger dissipate, and tried to find the best possible solution. As Weitzmann said: "All of a sudden, Korf was totally calm. He didn't shout. The group had got into a terrible state for both internal and external reasons. We asked ourselves what could still be salvaged."

At an extraordinary works meeting at BSW on Tuesday 11 January, Korf and Weitzmann backed each other up and spoke shoulder to shoulder with the administrator and the regional ministry of economic affairs. They all placed the blame for insolvency squarely on the ruinous subsidy policy rather than problems of their own making. Beleaguered as he was, Korf must have been flattered by a banner held aloft by some of the staff which welcomed him and alluded to the rumours of a merger with Arbed-Saarstahl: "BSW needs Korf, not Krackow!"

The administrators, Wellensiek and Ringwald, promised to do what they could to ensure that BSW would get what it needed to survive – namely, additional manufacturing plants for more added value – with the aid of regional economic policy. Hans Ringwald, a close acquaintance of Lothar Späth, had been chosen by Weitzmann for the challenging post of administrator at BSW on the recommendation of the economic affairs ministry. "There were only two top administrators in Baden-Württemberg. One was regarded as a foil fencer, the other as a bull," said Weitzmann. "In our situation, I wanted the bull."

It had been this 'bull', Ringwald, who'd advised Weitzmann to petition for composition since both criteria had been met. He'd also indicated to Weitzmann that if he focused on the jobs in the region, he'd get Späth's support. "With his strong Swabian [a region of south-west Germany] accent and his bald patch, people thought Ringwald could do no wrong," said Otfried Lieberknecht, Max Kreifels' partner, and praised him as one colleague to another. "He was doubly and triply sly. He wasn't just a bull. Ringwald was also capable of subtle action." For a while, the administrator even became a co-owner of BSW.

But what about the minister-president, the regional premier? Assessments of Lothar Späth's role in those days and months vary greatly. While Weitzmann and Wellensiek attested that he was primarily concerned with regional interests and jobs, Korf's partner Gerhard Fuchs said he complained bitterly to him about what he called "Späth's betrayal": "He told me how close they were, that they'd almost reached a deal. He couldn't believe that the knives were out behind his back." Of all people, the politician and the entrepreneur with such similar personalities – both creative, visionary, enthusiastic – turned out to be on opposite sides when crisis struck. Korf's financial director Carl-Theodor Meinecke ironically observed: "We always said that if Korf had been a Swabian, things would have turned out differently." Later on, Späth (who was indeed Swabian) took a rather detached view of his treatment of Korf:

> I could have granted him some unlawful concessions because he was my friend. He might even have expected that. Our relationship wasn't a love affair; we simply respected each

other in our roles. Sure, I was happy to help him with contacts and connections. But I definitely had a similar relationship with twenty other businesspeople in Baden-Württemberg.

It was a temporary relationship of convenience, nothing more.

Interestingly, confronted with accusations of complicity in Korf's decline, Späth later implicated another politician. In 1987, he found himself opposite Otto Graf Lambsdorff in a debate hosted by the weekly *Die Zeit*. He proceeded to take Lambsdorff to task:

> The German government was largely responsible for Korf's bankruptcy by subsidizing Arbed-Saarstahl and the other steel companies. It ruined 'little' Korf. It's absurd that Lambsdorff, who countersigned the subsidy for Arbed-Saarstahl, criticized the premier of Baden-Württemberg for not believing in the free market – a man who was forced to watch the only steelworks in Baden-Württemberg go bankrupt!

For Korf, the week of reckoning that had begun with "Bloody Sunday of Kehl" (to quote Gerhard Fuchs) wasn't yet over. On Friday 14 January, despite all his resistance, the insolvency engulfed his holding company, and Korf-Stahl also had to file for composition proceedings. Only Wolfgang Bernhardt, his former deputy and still his adviser, joined Korf on the evening of that fateful day, their personal ties outweighing their professional divergences.

The media, however, with no insight into the inner workings of the group, was still surprised by the force with which the crisis overwhelmed Korf and dragged down one bastion of his empire after another. Journalist Thomas Starke from *Badisches Tagblatt* was in attendance when Korf finally revealed the true state of affairs at a press conference: "Afterwards, Korf said to me that it had been one of the most difficult hours of his life." To cap it all, Mohr & Federhaff, Korf's continuously struggling mechanical engineering arm, was also insolvent.

The next domino to fall was in Hamburg. On Thursday 13 January, Korf had written in a confidential memorandum "that the Hamburg steelworks should definitely leave Korf-Stahl in some form or other" to help finance the minimum quota of 35 per cent of creditors' claims, which had to be met if composition was to be successful for KIH. Inwardly, therefore, Korf had already bidden farewell to his unloved joint venture with Klöckner. At any rate, the relationship was beyond repair. Max Kreifels, chairman of Korf's supervisory board, who had a distaste for lawyers, auditors and people from Hamburg, noted that Gienow, Klöckner's chief executive, was all three.

At the press conference held to announce the insolvency of Korf-Stahl, Korf had publicly announced that the situation at HSW with its full order books was "completely safe", and that he intended to part with the plant in an "orderly manner". But on 20 January, the majority shareholder Korf filed for composition for HSW, too – two days before payday. This time, the administrator was Gerd Weiland, a lawyer from Hamburg and also a Social Democrat politician. He chaired the budget committee of Hamburg's parliament, which had subsidized and guaranteed Korf's joint venture so intensely over the years, thanks to the Social Democrats' majority in the senate.

The 49 per cent shareholding in HSW, which was held by the regional bank Hamburgische Landesbank via the investment company Ferrokontor, now cost Klöckner – not to mention the city of Hamburg – dearly yet again. Because Gerd Weiland couldn't obtain anything from Korf-Stahl or KIH (which were themselves protected from their creditors) due to a lack of assets, to satisfy the creditors' claims he had to collect the outstanding amounts from Klöckner and its regional bankers. Weiland's highly unusual demand that the sums owing to the creditors be paid in full was approved.

Accordingly, all the debts were paid as if HSW had never been insolvent; they were predominantly settled by the regional bank in Hamburg because Klöckner and the government of Hamburg eventually allowed HSW to go bankrupt after all. "The loss of HSW cost us around 30 million marks at the time, which was a lot of money in the 1980s when Klöckner was already doing badly," said Herbert Gienow. Most of the 800 jobs in Hamburg were saved, at least, even though the still ultra-modern plant was run for years by first the administrator, and then a series of supposed and actual investors.

Not long after the wave of petitions for composition, Korf-Stahl began receiving rather unwelcome post on a daily basis. The composition proceedings had triggered a flood of financial claims, most of which were sent by registered mail and directly addressed to the executive board. The letters essentially consisted of clauses and rows of digits, and were signed "Yours respectfully": "... therefore, in accordance with clause 17 of our general terms and conditions, parallel loans I and II are hereby called in and must be repaid immediately ..." – "... due to the deterioration of your financial situation, we are no longer able to maintain the aforementioned lines of credit ..." – "... we request that you repay the current drawdown of 13,986,801.79 marks ..." – "Hamburger Stahlwerke GmbH owes us the sum of 14,838,395.95 marks as of 21 January 1983 ..." Such letters kept arriving for months.

There were also outstanding invoices from even the smallest tradespeople sent by their solicitors: "Maintenance fee for alarm system: 49.72 marks". And then there were invoices at the other end of the scale, such as from a large subcontractor in Gelsenkirchen, which had been paid with bills of exchange that had, regrettably, bounced: "... our claim in the amount of 14,794,413.90 marks is made up as follows ..." The demands were apocalyptic; the creditors would never even come close to being satisfied. "We've never known money or fear," had been the motto of Carl-Theodor Meinecke, the financial director now working for the administrator.

There was no longer any future for Korf-Stahl. Like its parent company KIH, it went into administration after failed composition, owing to its lack of assets. Almost 140 people lost their jobs at head office in Baden-Baden; the smart new building on Moltkestrasse, which had only been leased, was taken over by broadcaster Südwestfunk as its new television centre. And Korf lost not only his two German steelworks but also his French steel mill in Montereau (to the partner Sacilor), along with his shareholdings in the technological jewels of his crown, Korf & Fuchs Systemtechnik (Fuchs bought it back) and Korf Engineering (which his partner Vöest acquired).

In addition, he lost his 51 per cent share in the coal reduction process, which was also swallowed up by the Austrian Vöest, and the world rights to the Midrex process, which were bought by Kobe Steel, the fifth-largest Japanese steel group. Under pressure from the German insolvency proceedings, the American Midrex Corporation was forced to sell Korf, including Georgetown Steel and the US holding company Korf Industries, far below market value. The Kuwaitis, unwilling to pump any more money into Georgetown Steel during Korf's reign, substantially stepped up their share from 30 to 51 per cent. And Georgetown Texas Steel in Beaumont, Texas, went to the US conglomerate Cargill Inc., which already operated a string of mini steel mills. Perhaps the bitterest humiliation of all was that Korf's stately Falcon trijet – with its conference room and on-board video screen – went into service with the Dutch Philips Group.

All in all, the collapse of the Korf Group caused a loss of about half a billion marks and was, at the time, one of the biggest bankruptcies in German industrial history. Nonetheless, most of the 10,000-plus jobs in Willy Korf's steelworks worldwide were saved for the time being. The efficient plants and their unique technology quickly attracted wealthy buyers.

Media commentators were quick to present their analyses of what appeared – on the face of it, at least – to be Korf's demise. The vast majority of them placed the blame on the unfair subsidy policy that had distorted the free market. "Let's not kid ourselves: every market is distorted in some way," said banker Meier-Preschany, putting the whole affair into perspective. He understood Korf's schemes better than most, and although he warned Korf, he had also continued to play the game with him for a long time. In the end, he had to write off a 30-million-mark loan with the biggest provision for bad debt in his career at Dresdner Bank: "What ultimately caused Korf to fail? Distorted competition, a wafer-thin capital base, too many ideas that were started and weren't finished for all sorts of reasons. All this contributed to his bankruptcy. But in the end, he failed because of himself."

Two years after Korf's bankruptcy, the rise and fall of Willy Korf was summed up by an anonymous Frankfurt banker quoted in *The Wall Street Journal:* "The problem with Mr Korf is that he never belonged to the club."

CHAPTER 11

Risen from ruins

"Before others spot us on the ground, we're ready to take off again."

Baden-Baden's steel industry captain was suddenly a fallen tycoon with a faded aura of infallibility and an empire in ruins. His popularity plummeted almost overnight. As Daniela Esswein-Hardieck recalled: "Many people in society, especially politicians, dropped Korf like a hot potato. Insolvency was a ghastly experience for him as he'd always enjoyed showing off his accomplishments." After his financial collapse, Korf and his glamorous wife, previously so ubiquitous in high society, kept a low profile for a time. "The press couldn't get near him," said business editor Thomas Starke from *Badisches Tagblatt*. That might have been true for the local paper, but it didn't stop journalists from the national media.

"Insolvency proceedings are a dreadful business. The corporation has been shattered," Willy Korf lamented to *Welt am Sonntag* in August 1983. However, the atmosphere of this interview, which took place on a hot summer's evening at Hotel Rebenhof near Baden-Baden, was anything but sombre. Korf turned up "punctually, dressed in an open-necked white shirt, and in a breezy mood." There was no sign that he'd only just landed that morning from New York, the reporter marvelled: "Back on solid ground again, he immediately got down to work, even though the end of his career had seemed a foregone conclusion in January." Korf was clearly still going strong – and those who didn't agree would soon change their minds.

For the first few months after his presumed 'end', Korf led an unusually quiet existence – by his standards, at any rate. Discussing this period about a year later, he said: "When you've been put through the mill of insolvency through no fault of your own, when you have to start all over again, you proceed cautiously without seeking publicity."

Whenever he spoke, it was usually to the exclusion of the media, albeit with the same winning effect that had always opened doors and opportunities for him in the past. This applied for example to his many meetings with banks, which by now had become a full-time occupation for Korf. The way in which he beguiled the banks with generous collateral to avert private bankruptcy, despite all the difficulties in which he found himself, was described by his adviser Bert Pfluger as Korf's "magician's art". Normally, in his situation, "the bailiffs would have been called in. This didn't happen because only the limited companies went bankrupt, whereas his factories continued to exist. He managed to stay in his villa. Despite everything, he always had a smile on his face. That was a gift." On the other hand, Pfluger had nothing to say about the personal financial advice he'd given Korf. While he and his family kept their elegant residence on Kaiser-Wilhelm-Strasse, the chalet in the Swiss mountains changed hands, eventually being acquired by a member of the large Flick family.

In his interview with *Welt am Sonntag* at the Hotel Rebenhof, the reporter also wanted to know whether Willy Korf considered himself rich or poor. Was he satisfied or dissatisfied? Successful? This final question was an outright provocation, but Korf neatly sidestepped the trap and refused to reveal the figures the journalist had his eye on:

> Definitely not successful. Insolvency can't be described as a success. A businessman never knows whether he's rich or poor. And as to whether I'm satisfied, let me tell you, I'm not at all satisfied. There are so many good things that I started and built up, and which have now suddenly been acquired by

other people. Some of them are putting these things to good use; others are neglecting them.

There was certainly some good coming out of the Brazilian holding, which the administrator Jobst Wellensiek had sold to "a group of people close to Korf" headed by Willy Korf's man in Brazil, Ralph Weber, and Korf's cousin Helmhold Schneider. Consequently, his mini steelworks in Pains and his Brazilian technology base were out of reach of the competition, and remained in Korf's direct sphere of influence. The contract of sale even gave him a buy-back option.

In Saudi Arabia, Korf's stake in the brand new Midrex steel plant in Al-Jubail was sold for about 45 per cent of its nominal value – not bad, bearing in mind Korf's weak position in the negotiations as a debtor down on his luck. Wellensiek, Korf and Meinecke had repeatedly travelled to Saudi Arabia for this purpose, but once again the decisive factor had been Korf's empathy with the princes in the royal family. "As a result, Korf managed to push the price up by at least 2 or 3 per cent," said Wellensiek. "In fact, he was held in high regard by most people."

Curiously, the insolvency dividend of Korf-Stahl also improved somewhat. Shares in Korf-Stahl, which were still traded to a limited extent in the over-the-counter market of the Frankfurt Stock Exchange, boomed during the company's bankruptcy like never before as a bizarre object of speculative investment. This at least somewhat increased the meagre dividend paid out to the non-preferential creditors. But all in all, this distribution was still only 13.3 per cent in the case of Korf-Stahl, and as low as 5.4 per cent for KIH. With the latter's debts totalling nearly 340 million marks, it was a drop in the ocean.

Anything that could be turned into cash was sold. On behalf of Wellensiek, the administrator, Korf's former financial director Meinecke even disposed of the insolvent mechanical engineering company Mohr & Federhaff. As part of the Wibau Group, the company became part of IBH, the international construction machinery holding company owned by the Mainzbased investor Horst-Dieter Esch. Pumping up his conglomerate with frequent acquisitions, Esch had already incorporated other traditional names such as Hanomag from Hanover. But in November 1983, Esch also went bankrupt with his entire holding company, a process which had major legal repercussions; Mohr & Federhaff's bad run of fortune clearly hadn't ended.

A similar fate befell the Korf Group's other mechanical engineering company, IBAG in Neustadt, which had been ailing for some time. Before the collapse of Korf-Stahl AG, Korf's friend and partner Fuchs had even tried to restructure the company, and had partly succeeded: "At the time of the bankruptcy, our goal was within sight," said Fuchs. "Unfortunately, I still had some 9 million marks' worth of bills of exchange from Korf in the safe. That broke our back. I'd been working for almost two years and, despite gaining a wealth of experience, had nothing to show for it."

Almost everything that remained of Korf's nested empire with dozens of companies and holdings was now gathered under the umbrella of the company of his first plant, BSW in Kehl, where Korf still chaired the supervisory board. After Horst Weitzmann's high-handed declaration of insolvency, 90 per cent of the shares in BSW had been pledged to banks (10 per cent had long been held by the Swiss family-owned company Moos Stahl AG). In return, the banks had undertaken to sell this capital to new owners, in agreement with the government of Baden-Württemberg. Naturally, Korf wanted to be among those new owners.

BSW now held the unspectacular remnants of Korf's once far-reaching group, including Neckar Drahtwerke, Besta Betonstahl, parts of Kaiser-Omnia Bau-Systeme from Frankfurt, and Isar Baustahl. It was a modest, if somewhat random, collection of entities. But because the glass of professional optimist Willy Korf was always half full, the outcome meant one thing: he had not been completely brought to ground. And neither had his original plant in Kehl.

Nevertheless, Korf found it anything but satisfactory that Horst Weitzmann was still BSW's CEO, and that the whole operation was co-managed by the administrator Ringwald and the banks. Therefore, before 1983 (the year of Korf-Stahl's bankruptcy) was over, Korf had already laid the corporate foundations for his comeback.

He founded a new limited partnership called Korf KG – in Baden-Baden, of course, in his second villa on Winterhalterstrasse, where he'd always maintained personal offices on two floors. After his rise and fall, this was to be the starting point for his resurrection; Korf wasn't a man to stay down. "If you're born a businessman and have spent your whole life working, you can't just stop," he pugnaciously told reporters. And he also gave one of them a tantalising hint of his future intentions: "After treatment in an oxygen tent" he was now already "in altitude training".

Korf had chosen the corporate form of a limited partnership because he'd always preferred general partnerships, he still wasn't afraid of personal liability, and simply because he had to move fast. He made himself a general partner of Korf KG and his grown-up daughter Astrid a limited partner. To begin with, only a dozen or so employees were working in the building on Winterhalterstrasse, including a few familiar names: Renate Höing was his secretary again; Manfred Berner initially still handled liquidation tasks for the administrator Jobst Wellensiek, before being appointed the financial director. And there was someone else from those halcyon days who was in close touch with Winterhalterstrasse, perhaps even more eagerly than before: Karl Wienand. Now a management consultant based in Italy, his mission for Korf was to use his discreet connections to get banks, financial backers and political supporters back on board. Achieving this seemingly impossible mission wouldn't be cheap, but who else was up to the job?

Parallel to Korf KG, it was the long-standing 'apple of Korf's eye', Korf-Transport GmbH in Kehl, that crystallized as the second nucleus of his new group. Despite Weitzmann, banks and administrators, Korf still enjoyed extensive autonomy there. In 1984, he brought the industrial engineer Peter Koch, a veteran of his business adventures, back to Germany and to the company as director of finance. Koch had worked for Korf since 1973 – in Baden-Baden, Amsterdam, and finally in Sheffield at the engineering and construction company Ashlow Ltd. This company, which had belonged to the Korf Group, was sold to British Ropes.

Korf-Transport, on the other hand, was Korf's last remaining profitable gem. With a fleet of around twenty semi-trailer trucks, it functioned as a freight carrier – for example between BSW and Isar Baustahl – and as a haulage company delivering cargo for external clients. It was also intended to provide the logistics required to network Korf's new global empire by land, sea and air.

Korf himself still staked his claim to leadership as one of three managing directors of Korf-Transport. And though he rarely intervened in its day-to-day business, he wanted to be kept abreast of the situation at his favourite company at all times. "Once, Korf called me from Brazil, well aware that it was two in the morning here," said Peter Koch. "He'd probably already had a few glasses of something and was bragging how profitable Korf-Transport was. Now he wanted last year's figures from me to prove it. Since he'd woken me up in the middle of the night, I was stuttering a bit. Korf shouted: 'If you called me at two in the morning, I'd be able to tell you the figures at once!'"

While the 'bounce-back' Korf was already working out what form a future Korf-Stahl Group would take (other than being a global entity, of course), the drama surrounding his original steel mill BSW wasn't over yet for him. Convinced that he'd be an owner of BSW one day and back in the driving seat, he lurked in the background, waiting to regain what he viewed as his natural rights.

For the time being, however, as chair of the supervisory board, he complied with the plan of Weitzmann, the

Baden-Württemberg government, and the two administrators Wellensiek and Ringwald to underpin the plant with medium-sized manufacturing companies. His friend and partner Gerhard Fuchs explained Korf's uncharacteristic submissiveness as follows: "The only chance Korf had to find a solution was if he was prepared to make all the concessions required of him, as this was the only way to cling on. That wasn't his usual style, but what else could he do?"

And so, for a brief period, there was now a new trio in Kehl – Weitzmann the chief executive, Ringwald the administrator, and Korf the chairman of the supervisory board – who answered reporters' questions together and even aroused wistful memories of the successful team made up of Korf, Kreifels and Bernhardt. As *Die Zeit* wrote: "At least at BSW, his talents are now supported by what he has always lacked: a Swabian treasurer, the administrator Hans Ringwald." The article omitted the most important difference between the two teams: Korf, Bernhardt and Kreifels had pulled together out of conviction and passion, without a power struggle smouldering backstage.

The unequal triumvirate pursued two goals in order to exploit the considerable potential of the mini steelworks in Kehl to the full and make the new BSW Group viable in the beleaguered steel industry. Firstly, a desperate attempt had to be made to put a stop to the glaring subsidy advantage still enjoyed by its overpowering neighbour, Arbed-Saarstahl. Secondly, BSW needed to be able to manufacture as much steel as it could, without being hamstrung by quotas allocated by EEC bureaucrats. "We've already reached a settlement with BSW's creditors, which was asking a lot," Korf explained. "Now we want to have a chance to fulfil this settlement by producing so much that we can start making a profit instead of a loss."

There were ways and means to achieve both strategic aims; whether they were completely legitimate was something the three wily protagonists left others to decide. They elected, more or less, to undermine the quota limitations imposed by Article

58 of the Coal and Steel Community Treaty. After all, 80 per cent of the wire rod they were now producing was for their own use, wasn't it? Nevertheless, to be on the safe side, an application for quota exemption was officially filed in Brussels, and Ringwald as well as Korf and Weitzmann used all the channels of negotiation at their disposal to haggle over definitions and quantities with EEC officials as if they were market traders.

The clearer it became that BSW was producing at full steam during these protracted negotiations – as if it were already officially allowed to do so – the greater the risk that the plant would fall foul of the EEC and its strict quota rules. Draconian fines were imposed on offenders who broke quotas, serious enough that they would put the end to BSW. Ringwald brazenly used this as an argument in Brussels for *not* penalizing BSW's deliberate quota overruns. His tack was: If you fine us to the full extent allowed, we'll go bankrupt and everyone will be put out of work – which won't exactly endear us to the region. Even Lothar Späth, the regional premier, supported this reasoning vis-à-vis the Eurocrats. And in the end, a blind eye was indeed turned for BSW. With the highly efficient plant working at maximum capacity and the company raking in the profits with impunity, sales reached record levels.

Simultaneously, BSW's management team made a new attempt to achieve their other strategic aim. The West German government was sued again, this time represented by Kohl's 'watershed' cabinet. The proceedings before Cologne administrative court, under case number 1 K 4032/83, concerned the petition dated 5 August 1983 for "injunctive relief against the subsidization of Arbed-Saarstahl GmbH and the granting of compensation for the previous subsidization by means of payments to the plaintiff [BSW] as well." BSW was again represented by Otfried Lieberknecht from Kreifels' law firm in Düsseldorf. Officially, Korf had nothing to do with the lawsuit, for he was purely a member of the supervisory board. Meanwhile, Hans Ringwald, the administrator, had already guessed that such delicate proceedings could drag on for a long time, observing that, "Like the church, the judiciary works in centuries."

Ringwald was proved right. The new government, although still inexperienced in office, showed professional reflexes: "We regard the lawsuit with composure," its spokesperson declared with emphatic boredom. He knew why: years would be spent playing for time. The centre-right government, which was dishing out subsidies to Saarstahl just as liberally as its Social–Liberal predecessor, delayed the release of certain files as long as possible, eventually only submitting them under duress – and even then with important pages missing.

For seven long years, the court in Cologne didn't schedule a single hearing. And when it finally deigned to do so, it based the value of the dispute on the size of the subsidies, which had amounted to almost 3 billion marks. This would have meant BSW having to pay out hundreds of millions of marks if the case had gone to trial, and so it withdrew the lawsuit in 1991. In any case, the court had already implied that it would not declare the subsidies unlawful. Cologne was even closer to Bonn than it looked on the map.

The only consolation for BSW, which had spent a small fortune on legal fees and procedural costs, was that the disputed steel subsidies had since become superfluous.

The cohesion in the fragile triumvirate of Weitzmann, Ringwald and Korf rapidly dissipated. Unsurprisingly, in view of their previous history and the precarious balance of power, serious tension arose between BSW's regents and their supervisory board chairman, who, misjudging his position, acted as the one calling the shots. As long as the bankrupt Korf-Stahl AG was still officially BSW's major shareholder, and the shares were merely pledged to the banks, his position as chairman of the supervisory board seemed incontestable. However, this proved not to be true.

In an unexpected coup in 1984, the administrator, with the support of the banks, forced Korf-Stahl to sell its pledged shares in BSW to Neckar Drahtwerke, a firm with healthy order books and high liquidity; bizarrely, the subsidiary now held the shares in its parent company BSW. The background to this was the banks' concern that they themselves, as the de facto owners of BSW, would also have to pay its debts. Consequently, the banks were happy to offload this obligation by selling the stock to Neckar Drahtwerke. The legality of this bold construct was debatable, even among experts, and was addressed in a series of articles. What was certain was that Korf's influence on the place where his career as a steel producer had begun was weaker than ever.

Ramifications soon followed. In a letter to Eberhard Leibing, one of Lothar Späth's ministerial directors, Korf complained bitterly on 14 May 1984 "that Messrs Weitzmann and Ringwald have now declared all-out war by proposing to convene a general meeting of BSW at which both Mr Georg and I are to be voted off the supervisory board." Edgar Georg, a friend of Korf's since his youth, had been appointed to the supervisory board after the insolvency, where he saw himself as the guardian of Korf's interests.

Korf immediately instructed his Stuttgart lawyer, Hans Thümmel, to intervene with Weitzmann, the boss of BSW. Thümmel had already acted as emissary and mediator to ease the increasingly tense relationship between Weitzmann and Ringwald, on one side, and Korf on the other. Thümmel now wrote to BSW's executive board, imploring them to refrain from "publicly disparaging" Korf by removing him from the supervisory board. The wrangling continued behind the scenes for a while, but at the end of July, Korf was finally defenestrated. While Edgar Georg was spared, Korf was no longer chairman or even a member of the supervisory board. His remaining foot in the company door had been squeezed out. "Don't defer unpleasant business" is still one of Weitzmann's management principles today.

What made Weitzmann, the now established boss of BSW, commit yet another act of apparent cruelty towards the factory's founder? As with previous events, a number of factors that had been building up for months came together.

First of all, there was Korf-Transport. It was 51 per cent owned by Korf KG, but for strategic reasons BSW had taken over the remaining 49 per cent. The way in which Korf used the liquidity of this flourishing transport company and its subsidiaries soon raised eyebrows, and finally led to clashes between the partners. Secondly, Weitzmann perceived Korf as an ambitious entrepreneur who hadn't yet got his feet back on the ground despite his financial predicament. "I didn't want to get rid of him at first," said Weitzmann, but Korf didn't seem to understand what was viable. "For example, he went to China with Chancellor Kohl and returned with a declaration of intent for a steelworks for a billion dollars, which he'd signed 'Chairman of Badische Stahlwerke'. He seemed to have lost touch with reality – and Ringwald agreed with me." On another occasion:

> Korf came up to me and said: "I've seen a Beechcraft King Air going cheap. Can't we buy it?" Ringwald had only just disposed of the four Korf-Stahl planes. Or suddenly an invoice arrived: "We request payment of … for charter flights by the chairman of your supervisory board." They were charging us a six-figure sum, while we were counting every hammer and nail here in the plant!

Korf's erstwhile financial director, Carl-Theodor Meinecke, shared this bitter impression: "I always wanted to write a book about losing reality. Korf would have definitely featured in it."

At some point, the regional chancellery in Baden-Württemberg decided to allocate Korf a substantial share in BSW (which was now doing well again) when its ownership structure was rearranged, in order to make it easier for him to have a fresh start. But the confusion in Kehl made not only the regional government but also the banks edgy. Weitzmann described the situation thus:

> We had to win over a whole new banking environment. HeLaBa, Dresdner Bank and BfG had been Korf's banks. Deutsche Bank and Commerzbank, on the other hand, hadn't

given him a second glance. They and the credit insurers chorused: "If Korf's involved again, we're out."

Lothar Späth, too, eventually dropped the idea of handing Willy Korf a stake in his old steelworks. The only assistance the premier gave Korf was to act as a mediator in Korf's dispute with Weitzmann and Ringwald over the ownership of Korf-Transport. His efforts certainly paid off for Korf, who received the company back in full, plus a guarantee from BSW to retain Korf-Transport as its freight haulier for a certain period.

However, this cargo contract was terminated in 1985: Korf and Weitzmann fell out over invoicing so badly that their relationship, which had gone through far more lows than highs, finally collapsed. BSW set up its own transport company, paid the agreed settlement, and continued its commercial development with Horst Weitzmann at the tiller. Korf lost all contact with his Kehl roots. But that didn't stop him from working undeterred on his comeback.

One of those sentences quoted by *Die Zeit* in 1985 – after a string of company insolvencies, disappointments, conflicts, dismissals and injustices that would have made a lesser businessman throw in the towel – was especially characteristic of Willy Korf: "I'm absolutely livid about everything that's happened – but it's no use now. I prefer to look to the future." He was true to his optimistic words of two years earlier, when he announced mid-crisis that: "Despite everything, I intend to continue working in steel and related technology. There are plenty of opportunities for me there, including abroad." In the back of his mind was a technological development on which he'd pinned his hopes. For having lost control of the Midrex and KR processes, a new metallurgical breakthrough emerged: EOF.

EOF stood for Energy Optimizing Furnace. Like so many other Korf developments, this new smelting process was based on a patent by his top man in Brazil, Ralph Weber. Trials had been underway in Pains near Divinópolis since 1978, and in 1985 Korf marketed the process as ready for series production.

An EOF could replace both electric arc furnaces and the old Siemens-Martin furnaces used in scrap-based steel production. It was fuelled by coking coal and oxygen. This seemed promising to Korf in times when electricity had become so expensive.

The furnace earned its name because the oxygen injected through a submerged lance into the molten metal most of the carbon monoxide present to form carbon dioxide, while the residual heat of the exhaust gas could be used to preheat the scrap economically. Moreover, whereas the Midrex process only produced a preliminary product, namely sponge iron, which was then melted down in an electric furnace, the EOF enabled a continuous process without any intermediate steps. Because of the EOF's favourable energy consumption and low capital expenditure, Korf calculated that a 400,000-tonne steel plant in the USA could save between 25 and 30 US dollars per tonne of steel.

Korf proceeded to travel the world promoting this new invention like a one-man advertising agency. He listed the advantages of the EOF into every microphone presented to him: "energy-saving, low consumption of materials, easy to handle, environmentally friendly, an inexpensive investment. ... With our new furnace, anyone can produce steel more cheaply. We don't want to keep our know-how to ourselves." After all, Korf had by no means given up his plant business, despite the loss of his flourishing technology company. Whereas previously he would have marketed this new development via Korf Engineering, he now personally invited even his rivals among the global steel producers to profit from his technology. "Selling furnaces to the competition also puts money in the till."

There was even a place where Willy Korf could bring this technology to life. A place where he could be a businessman again and produce steel, outside West Germany, outside the closed world of European subsidies that had treated him so badly. This place was, of course, in America. Wallingford, Connecticut, was small and inconspicuous, like everywhere else Korf had pitched his tents as a pioneer in the USA. In this town about 120 kilometres (75 miles) north-east of New York, a small steelworks with French operators known as Yale Steel Co. had gone bankrupt in 1979. The site, including the buildings and machinery, were in the care of the state development corporation when Willy Korf arrived, once again the pioneer. During the talks, which began right away, Korf discovered that "Americans always give an entrepreneur a second chance, even when he's already had to give up." And the land of opportunity was about to gift Korf another chance to put down roots and grow.

"When I took a look at the firm, I quickly realized why things hadn't worked out," he told the weekly newspaper *Die Zeit*. "From the outside, they looked like modern industrial units, but inside it was a museum. They'd imported ancient junk from France," such as a rolling mill from 1920 and an induction furnace from 1932. It was the perfect challenge for visionaries and technological pathfinders.

Korf and his "European partners" (whom he didn't want to name) founded the Connecticut Steel Corporation without further ado and appointed as president Daniel W. Schlett, who'd played a part in Korf's first American adventure. Korf resolved to invest 50 million dollars to clear out the steelworks, get it up and running with a rolling mill and continuous caster by the summer of 1986, and create more than 300 jobs. He declared Connecticut Steel to be the demonstration plant for his new EOF miracle furnace: "Here in Wallingford, we're not that far off the beaten track. Anyone who wants to see how we make steel is welcome to come by anytime." True, the capital largely came from the group of companies owned by steelmaker Walter von Moos, a reliable Swiss industrialist whom Korf had known for decades. But the reporters didn't need to know that. It was enough for them to see that Korf finally had something tangible to show.

He'd also invented a new term that was destined to be used all over the world: 'micro steel mill' – a new category of plant even smaller than mini steelworks and equipped with EOFs that were to raise the bar in terms of both efficiency and flexibility. Connecticut Steel was the prototype of such a plant, designed for an annual production of just 200,000 tonnes.

Back at the HQ of his old holding company in Charlotte, North Carolina, Willy Korf founded Korf Steeltec Inc. in order to have an engineering foothold in North America again. The dynamic combination of EOF and micro steel mill was to become the new company's first bestseller. There were even plans to market this type of micro steel mill in the USA as a 'Kor-Mill', a name that never caught on – perhaps because it contained too much Korf and not enough steel.

The man who had lent his name to so many innovations was once again firing on all cylinders. "He was someone who always bounced back, and that's why I loved him," said an observer who was familiar with both Korf and how things were done in America. "In the USA, bankruptcy doesn't matter; they just say that someone's had bad luck. But in Germany, you're stigmatized." There was no question of that in Korf's America, the country of his dreams. "Korf is a very energetic, innovative guy," was the verdict of industry expert George McManus from the trade journal *Iron Age Magazine* – two years *after* Korf-Stahl's insolvency.

In the USA, he was still able to mesmerize business partners and employees precisely because of his bounce-back mentality. "When Korf starts something, it's bound to turn out well," believed Daniel 'Dan' Schlett, who'd allowed himself to be wooed away from a top job at Otto Wolff to rejoin his old employer. One reason for this was Korf's optimism – still as intoxicating as ever – which he translated into age-old American promises: "There's a 100 million tonne market here in the USA. Anyone can sell steel. But you have to be smart enough with your share of it to make money."

Even the 200,000-tonne plant in Pains, Brazil, where inventor Ralph Weber had devised the patented technology of the EOF, now passed as a micro steel plant under the new classification.

According to the strategy of the resurgent Korf, wherever there was a conurbation of a million people – be it in China, Mexico, Saudi Arabia or Venezuela – there was enough scrap to make it an attractive site for one of his micro steel mills. This was particularly true since the micro mills didn't need expensive electricity.

"The micro steel mill serves smaller customers in a more scattered market," explained Korf. "You can minimize the risk of cheap imports. Why not earn a profit of 60 dollars per tonne on 200,000 tonnes per year instead of 20 dollars with an annual output of 600,000 tonnes? It means less capital input and a smaller workforce." *Die Zeit* was impressed by the man who was back in the saddle just two years after being at rock bottom: "Willy Korf, now in his mid-fifties, isn't the kind of person to sit down in the corner and sulk. He prefers to roll up his sleeves and climb back into the ring. And he might well succeed."

Accordingly, Korf KG's headquarters on Winterhalterstrasse in Baden-Baden was a hive of activity, just like in the good old days, before its original head office had moved to the new building on Moltkestrasse. At first there were only ten employees whom Willy Korf had gathered together in his 'second villa' near the family residence. But he was already steering the ship again with the air of a man who controlled a world empire.

Korf received reporters holding a Jamaican cigar in his mouth, jacket draped over the back of his chair, while his chauffeur ferried his legendary dark blue pinstripe suits between his Mercedes and his office. The study with its parquet floor and English period furniture was dominated by an open fireplace. The only visible scar of the past stood on the mantelpiece. Between family photos and a Chippendale clock, there was a motto in a glass frame that had been presented to Korf by Jürgen Krackow, the former boss of Arbed-Saarstahl, and which didn't quite fit the dignified atmosphere: "The more days that pass," it read, "the higher the number of people who can kiss my ass."

In the spirit of this motto, Korf enjoyed showing up wherever he was least expected to give the steel industry a few surprises and something to talk about. In early 1985, for example, he was hired as a consultant by his old business partners in Saudi Arabia, the Saudi Basic Industries Corporation (SABIC), who appreciated his expertise and efficiency. His previous 7.5 per cent share in the steelworks in Hadeed had fallen to SABIC in 1984. But this plant had broken even in its very first year of production with an output of 800,000 tonnes. Anyone who'd once been instrumental in designing something like this remained in demand even after insolvency, as Korf was only too happy to confirm to the press: "Since I'm so well known throughout the world of steel, many people ask me for advice."

It wasn't this consultancy job that really got the journalists excited, however, but a much more spectacular expert assignment, spiced up with high-level politics and an old rivalry. It began with indiscretions that initially gave rise to wild rumours, and finally forced the ministry of economic affairs in Saarland to issue an astonishing press release on 2 July 1985: "The government of Saarland has asked a team of experts led by Dr Willy Korf to advise it on the restructuring and rescue of Arbed-Saarstahl GmbH. ... Their visit has been agreed with the management of Arbed-Saarstahl; it will start on 9 July and last between one and four days."

The person behind this coup was none other than Oskar Lafontaine, the Social Democrat state premier. Straightaway, the media speculated that Korf – with political backing – was about to take over the highly subsidized, terminally ill steel giant, which had once even failed to support its own subsidiaries. This impressively demonstrated the faith that certain people still had in the largely penniless Korf. There was even talk of selling the conglomerate, which had debts of 1.2 billion marks, to Korf for the symbolic price of a mark. Willy Korf did little to nip these rumours in the bud. He told a radio reporter from SWF that a takeover of Arbed-Saarstahl was completely absurd "at the moment". But when pressed, he added cryptically: "Once we've completed our report, there may well be some interest on our part."

At that time, there were already two reports on Arbed by well-known management consulting firms, namely Roland Berger and McKinsey, which of course recommended drastic staff reductions and cost-cutting. Presumably, Lafontaine simply wanted to gain time by appointing a third expert to remind the West German government in Bonn how it could help solve the problem of Arbed – to be precise, by reducing the company's debt, which prevented it from being sold. Manfred Meier-Preschany from Dresdner Bank explained why he chose Korf, who himself had once failed as a steel producer, with a neat parable: "It was like the story of the Lufthansa pilot who ditched his plane in the water off France for lack of fuel. One might have expected him to be fired immediately. But he was kept on. The deputy CEO at the time told me: 'He certainly won't forget to refuel in future!'"

So Korf, of all people – with his Icarus reputation – was now to be shown the books, the boardroom drawers, and the innermost secrets of his once hated competitor. The man whose BSW steelworks had taken legal action against the subsidies paid out to Arbed-Saarstahl was now supposed to show the steel giant within a few days how to put its house in order.

Emmanuel Tesch and the rest of the supervisory board at Arbed-Saarstahl were distinctly unimpressed. But the management had received instructions from on high in the political world to give the unpopular inspector access. On 9 July, Korf and five of his experts entered the headquarters of Arbed-Saarstahl in Völklingen punctually at ten o'clock. Oskar Lafontaine himself had threatened the executive board that if they didn't let them in, the regional subsidies for Arbed would be revoked: "You won't get a single mark until Korf's been there."

"When Korf returned from Arbed, he was fuming," recalled his secretary Renate Höing. "There were certain aspects it seemed they didn't want to show him. He was shocked at how he'd been treated." On 14 August, Korf nevertheless handed in his report on Saarstahl to the regional government. In it, he'd come to the unexpected conclusion that the company could well be turned around into something "healthy". After all, the more than 3 billion marks in subsidies that had been pumped into Saarland's biggest employer had been used to make some investments in its future viability.

Despite his recommendation, Korf didn't become the new boss of Arbed-Saarstahl – he simply didn't have the resources to take over. When Arbed withdrew from the group in 1986, it was renamed Saarstahl Völklingen GmbH. The company dragged itself through the next three years until its insolvency in 1989 – an event that spawned Saarstahl AG, which still exists today.

Even though Willy Korf didn't get anything worthwhile from of the Arbed-Saarstahl episode (he never even received a fee for his report), it did rekindle the media's interest in him. "I would have needed three secretaries", he recounted afterwards, "just to turn away all the press enquiries!" All this was perhaps a bit too much commotion for Korf KG's small staff on Winterhalterstrasse, who had largely been recruited from Korf-Transport. Peter Koch, the financial director of Korf-Transport, experienced Korf's resurgence first-hand: "Korf drew few consequences from the bankruptcy. He still refused to delegate much. That was his nature: to build up something once again and proudly show it to the world. We were a close-knit little group there, even when the business grew in size. Later on, we were joined by three more excellent engineers, all of whom were based on Winterhalterstrasse. We often hung around late at night, on the phone to the USA."

Korf's creative, careless financial conduct of old also made a reappearance: "His financial expert Manfred Berner kept giving him verbal slaps on the wrist. But Korf would just say: 'Just leave it, we'll find a way to work it out.'" This was confirmed by Berner himself: "Korf hadn't changed a bit. He had persistent development euphoria; he was confident things would pick up again. And there was a lot that could be done with our technology."

Since Korf no longer had any production facilities in Europe, however, his previous system of finance based on bills of exchange – a method both tempting and calamitous, which had led to his downfall once before – was no longer workable. In addition, because Willy Korf now focused more on his engineering services than his own production plants, the revived Korf Group needed much less equity. But even this smaller amount was not available, because the domestic banks weren't prepared to give Korf the time of day. There was nothing for it: a new, affluent partner had to be found.

Once again, but for the last time, Korf found this partner at a fateful meeting of two soulmates – on this occasion in his own house. It was in 1985, at one of those business receptions that used to be attended by top politicians, but not anymore. Nevertheless, it was still a lavish, prestigious affair, as if nothing had changed. Among the assembled guests that evening was the chief executive of Frankfurter Metallgesellschaft (known by its initials MG), Karl Gustav Ratjen. He had brought with him his young colleague on the board and future successor, Heinz Schimmelbusch from Austria. The latter later remembered "how champagne was served and one of the men declared cynically 'There's always enough of *that* kind of liquidity in this house!'"

Schimmelbusch was aware of Korf's strained finances. Lurgi GmbH, West Germany's largest plant engineering company and a subsidiary of the MG Group, had been a Midrex licensee for a long time. It competed with the engineering division of Vöest-Alpine, which had since absorbed the old Korf Engineering. Schimmelbusch was therefore well aware of Korf Engineering's potential for innovation and expansion, but was still interested in joining forces with Korf to generate synergy in commodity trading. MG was active in the global scrap and iron ore trade, especially in Brazil, where Korf also had plenty of experience. There were clearly enough overlaps for a promising partnership.

Heinz Schimmelbusch, a Jesuit student with a doctorate in

political science, had a well-earned reputation as one of the most dynamic managers in the metal industry. An expansionist and restless spirit like Korf, similarly ambitious and willing to take risks, Schimmelbusch was also perpetually in search of new goals, ever better figures and greater achievements. And it would only be another four years before he reached the top of the powerful Frankfurt conglomerate in 1989, taking charge of its hundreds of subsidiaries worldwide.

Following this, an unprecedented series of acquisitions would soon begin, taking the group to its limits and right into the midst of perilous oil futures deals. The highly speculative transactions by its Manager of the Year 1991 (*Top Business*) would eventually cost MG its entire liquidity and almost its very existence; they also cost Schimmelbusch his job in December 1993, the supervisory board virtually chasing him out of the door.

But, in the mid-1980s, those events were still a long way off. For a while, therefore, Schimmelbusch and Korf – soon to become close friends – would travel side by side in their journeys.

CHAPTER 12

Thin air

"We know what our destination is, even if we're not sure how or even whether we'll arrive."

The two new friends, Heinz Schimmelbusch and Willy Korf, quickly forged a series of partnerships that enabled plenty of fresh cash to be injected into Korf's business. For example, MG took a stake in the micro steel mill with its promising EOF in the Brazilian municipality of Pains. The goal was to roll out this technology in Russia, China, and anywhere else where ample cheap coal coupled with an unstable electricity supply gave it the advantage over the electric arc furnace.

Schimmelbusch and Korf travelled on business together across Brazil, the USA and Poland, among other destinations. Schimmelbusch soon became aware that Korf, a gifted salesman, required not only a bigger organization, but also a certain degree of supervision. Korf needed someone to keep him down to earth, a role that in the past had fallen to the likes of Wolfgang Bernhardt and Max Kreifels. As Schimmelbusch later explained: "My aim was always to place him and his activities within an organizational structure which still allowed him to pursue his entrepreneurial side and his ideas. Lurgi was a suitable choice as there were certain managers there he could work well with."

However, Schimmelbusch struggled to set his plan in motion. "It wasn't always easy going," he said. "Korf was difficult for a bureaucracy to handle." Nevertheless, in October 1986, after substantial teething troubles, Korf Lurgi Stahl Engineering GmbH was established with Albrecht Kroeker from Lurgi as its commercial director. The purpose of this joint venture was to offer EOFs – as well as turnkey mini and micro steel mills – worldwide. Meanwhile, Korf's tiny engineering company in Charlotte, North Carolina, was expanded to become Korf Lurgi SteelTec Inc. serving the USA, Canada and Mexico.

Korf's new 'big brother' proved extremely useful because, by himself, Korf could only get peanuts from the banks. He'd previously founded a technology holding company in Switzerland, KORTEC AG, based in Zug. In June 1986, Paul Lachausse, deputy director of the Swiss Bankers Association, joined its board of directors. And the correspondence with Lachausse shows just how much more cautious banks had become about supporting Korf's new commercial ventures. For example, an internal memo from Korf KG reveals that KORTEC's credit line of 500,000 Swiss francs could only be even slightly exceeded with great difficulty, not to mention Lachausse's approval.

Diametrically opposed to this was Korf's unbroken determination to generously compensate his top executives, rather than look like the penny-pinching boss of a small business barely keeping its head above water. Korf still displayed a certain grandeur and believed that being a 'big spender' helped ensure his lasting popularity: "I don't have any image problems, quite the opposite, in fact. The reason for my insolvency – the fact that only big corporations received public subsidies – won me even more friends and sympathizers all over the world."

Korf also planned to recruit his staff from this supporters' club: "Many of those who left me after my fall are now coming back to me," he told *Capital* in delight. At the beginning of 1987, for instance, Otfried Forssman – formerly Korf's number one at the mini steel plant in Montereau (since been taken over in its entirety by Sacilor) – joined KORTEC as managing director. Glowing with the pride of the prodigal son's father, Korf gleefully informed Lachausse by letter: "Mr Forssman has decided to resign from his position in France because he sees no future in highly subsidized state enterprises."

Lachausse's reply to this letter was polite but distanced; his disapproval of the generous terms of Forssman's employment contract was plain. "I was overpaid for what I could do at KORTEC," Forssman freely admitted. "It wasn't justified because I couldn't make a difference there." In the end, he spent barely two years in Switzerland. Forssman had realized that Korf's finances were almost entirely dependent on borrowed capital, and developed significant misgivings about his new position. "Having seen that his financial future looked bleak, I began wondering how to escape. After all, I had a family to support."

In 1989, when Forssman received an offer from the Bavarian steelworks Lechstahlwerke, which belonged to none other than the newly formed Saarstahl Group, he left Korf for good. Forssman, who'd spent years working for Korf, lacked confidence that the EOF and the micro steel mill would succeed on the market. That's not to say he wasn't on Korf's side; he genuinely hoped the new technologies would be a resounding success. But, as time passed, he grew increasingly afraid that they simply wouldn't catch on and were destined for commercial failure.

Korf, of course, took a completely different view. For him, technology export was the trump card in his hand, which, in his estimation, already consisted of four, almost equally strong aces. He planned to focus on these four areas: steel production, steel trading, transport – and the technology business. After all, this last area had always been the profitable territory in his old, shuttered empire, making all those hoping to benefit from his bankruptcy salivate in anticipation.

It was no coincidence that during Korf's comeback, a raft of engineering companies was set up with powerful partners, in the space of just two years. He even teamed up with the Indian conglomerate Tata to found Tata Korf Engineering Services Ltd. in Calcutta; Korf had long suspected that the steel market of the future belonged to emerging countries. He had put forward this theory in a trade journal back in 1981: "The world's steel consumption will continue to rise due to population growth and the increase in global GDP. However, instead of in the industrialized nations, this growth is set to take place in developing countries, which will become new, important steel producers." And just before his trip to the Ganges, Korf told the press: "Steel must be made wherever customers need it. There will always be a market for mini steel plants with advanced technology. That's also why I went to Brazil. And at some point, I could certainly imagine going into business in Asia. After all, plenty of steel is required there, too."

This brought Korf to the second ace in his hand, steel production. Having lost almost all his steel mills and his lenders during the wave of insolvency, production was an area that now seemed closed off to him. Quite simply, he couldn't go back into steel without enormous capital investment. But Korf owned holdings in two micro steel mills – Pains in Brazil and Wallingford in the USA – and now he had allies who were willing to take risks. Soon, Korf found his old love for steelmaking rekindled, his entrepreneurial passion locked in a desperate battle with economic reason. Hadn't his low debt-to-equity ratios and the consolidation of his production plants brought the whole house of cards tumbling down last time? And as a result of his financial collapse, surely Korf's own capital was virtually zero?

Quotes reported by the media in the period following the insolvency of Korf-Stahl reflected this tension between his desire to start steel again and the practical reality of doing so. Korf was clearly keen, but he needed the right situation. Would he find it in Germany, or elsewhere in Europe, which was still saturated with subsidies, production quotas and red tape? Returning to an old chestnut, in 1985 he asked a press conference: "What good is it if I can make a tonne of steel 200 marks cheaper than my rivals, but they get 300 marks in subsidies?" Things had sounded much more optimistic just two years earlier: "Sure, my chances as a steel tycoon are better in

Brazil than in Europe, but I'm sure that in twenty years I'll still be a steel magnate in Europe." He would do everything he could to fulfil his prediction.

In January 1986, the first opportunity appeared on the horizon in the Ruhr Valley, the old industrial heartland of Europe and Germany, and stronghold of his bigger competitors. Korf hatched a plan to build a micro steel mill there, right on their doorstep, with an annual output of up to 300,000 tonnes. Turning scrap into reinforcing steel for the region, it would be a fabulous thorn in the side for Krupp, Thyssen, and the rest of the old barons.

Korf wasted no time pursuing his idea. He held an 'informal meeting' with Günter Samtlebe, the mayor of Dortmund. MG's subsidiary Lurgi was tasked with carrying out an extensive market study. Korf also got in touch with Knut Consemüller, the technical director of Hoesch Stahl AG, a potential local industrial partner. It turned out there were empty industrial units at Hoesch's Union plant on Rheinische Strasse – an irresistible magnet for Korf's imagination. However, his interest soon turned to Hoesch's huge Phoenix complex, where there were several attractive brownfield sites available, following the closure of various production units.

Dortmund's business development agency dared to dream of 200, 300, maybe even 500 new jobs created by Korf in the crisis-ridden coal-mining town. Their interest was piqued after someone had whispered that allowing Korf to invest there was a smart move. And that someone turned out to be none other than business consultant Karl Wienand, who'd conducted negotiations with the city council on behalf of Korf-Lurgi-Engineering. Once more, the old strategist and string-puller was fighting in Willy Korf's corner. And Wienand was most complimentary about the department head in charge of the project: "Congratulations to the council. This is a man of stature!" However, the magic must have quickly dissipated, for nothing was ever heard of the project again.

Nevertheless, Korf was undeterred from trying to regain a

foothold as a steel producer in his home region. His favourite book at this time was, significantly, an American publication that had inspired him to new deeds in Europe: *Up from the Ashes: The Rise of the Steel Minimill in the United States* by Donald Barnett and Robert Crandall. Like Willy Korf, the authors believed mini steel mills to be the future of a steel industry free from subsidies.

Lothar Späth later recalled Korf also planning a mini steelworks in Mannheim. The ministry of economic affairs in Baden-Württemberg wondered whether this new plant would end up being a rival for BSW in Kehl. Korf provided written reassurances that he intended to produce flat steel in Mannheim rather than structural steel, and so wouldn't be competing with BSW. But according to Späth, Korf kept changing his mind: "First he wanted to move the project to Hamburg, then he thought about relocating production to Brazil or Hungary and only keeping steel processing here. Then he considered shifting his processing operation to the port of Karlsruhe, or possibly even Kehl. In the end, he plumped for Hungary." Lothar Späth, the premier of Baden-Württemberg, who'd experienced dramatic ups and downs with Korf over the years, was able to do him one last service: "I was friends with Miklós Németh, the prime minister of Hungary. I got in touch with him on Korf's behalf. Korf had asked me to tell Németh that he was a good steelmaker."

Before his Hungarian plans could come to fruition, Korf launched another attempt to make a name for himself again as a West German steel producer – this time in Sulzbach-Rosenberg. This town in the Upper Palatinate was home to a steel company called Eisenwerk-Gesellschaft Maximilianshütte mbH, or Maxhütte for short, which Korf had had his eye on for years. He'd first tried in vain to buy into Maxhütte back in 1970, when it was owned by Friedrich Flick, and it was during those negotiations that he first came face to face with his later deputy, Wolfgang Bernhardt. When Korf renewed his interest in

Maxhütte, the steelworks was a jewel in the crown of German industrial history, despite being on the verge of bankruptcy.

Founded in 1853 by two Belgian entrepreneurs and named after King Maximilian II of Bavaria, Maxhütte had started out as a factory making rails for Bavaria's train network. It rapidly became the biggest industrial enterprise in the region, employing as many as 10,000 workers. A century after it was established, Maxhütte was mining and processing over 600,000 tonnes of iron ore annually; in the late 1960s, 11.5 percent of the ore mined in Germany came from its pits. Korf's long-time rival and one-time partner, the Klöckner Group, took over ownership of the plant in 1979. By the 1980s, though, after more than a decade of permanent crisis, Maxhütte's ancient blast furnaces were hopelessly outdated. And in 1987, when the uneconomical steelworks had reached the end of the line – after price collapses and the rising West German mark against the dollar – 4,500 jobs were on the line in the plant.

It was at this point that Korf arrived on the scene as a possible saviour. During intensive talks with the Bavarian government, he offered to get the plant back on track, as long as Bavaria provided the necessary financial backing. But while negotiations continued in Munich, Maxhütte went bankrupt. At first, this only strengthened Korf's hand, especially since the administrator appointed by the creditors' meeting was an old acquaintance of his: Jobst Wellensiek, the Heidelberg business lawyer who had wound up Korf's old steel group. For a brief period, there seemed to be a realistic chance of Korf taking over Maxhütte, with Schimmelbusch backing him up.

But once more, Korf was denied the opportunity to start making steel again. Perhaps his bold concept defeated the decision-makers' imagination. Naturally, he was banking on modernizing the plant with his miracle furnace, the EOF. After all, he'd been championing his own technology for years. "Korf promotes himself so skilfully", conceded one of Klöckner's managers at the time, who was marketing a rival smelting furnace system, "that the members of our supervisory board keep phoning me to ask how successful I've been." But this time Korf's sales genius was no use: the Bavarian government hesitated at the term EOF. Otfried Forssman, at that time the managing director of KORTEC and a member of the supervisory board of Maxhütte, remembered the negotiations stalling: "The officials in Bavaria trusted the 'old men from the Ruhr', who wouldn't give up trying to improve their traditional blast furnaces, rather than Korf and his unknown EOF."

Ultimately, it was decided that each of the five big German steel companies – Krupp, Thyssen, Klöckner, Saarstahl and Salzgitter – would each commit about 12 million marks to Maxhütte while Bavaria would put another 50 million or so into the successor company, Neue Maxhütte. "The project never really got off the ground," Forssman grumbled for years afterwards. In fact, Neue Maxhütte went bankrupt for the second and last time in 1998. It continued to produce steel for another four years under the supervision of the administrator without Wellensiek finding an investor, and it was finally laid to rest in September 2002. It was a sad end to a strand of German industrial history that had lasted a century and a half.

The lack of spectacular financial success made Korf more restless than ever. By the end of 1987, although his EOF system had already been on the market for a good two years, sales hadn't really taken off anywhere in the world. At Connecticut Steel in Wallingford, the planned demonstration furnace and rolling mill should have gone into operation in summer 1986, but there was a considerable delay. Trials in Pains designed to prove that an EOF could produce steel exclusively from scrap without the addition of pig iron were still ongoing, while other experiments on the EOF hadn't been completed either.

In Brazil, the main fuel used in steel production was charcoal, rather than the coke produced from hard coal like in Germany. Theoretically, compared to European coke, an EOF worked even better with fine charcoal, which had a high energy density and produced hardly any ash. Furthermore, Korf's technicians in

Pains were also developing a process to extract biomass from babassu nuts, which are abundant in Brazil, and turn it into coke in order to conserve wood resources. But despite spending month after month on the studies, there was no sign of a decisive breakthrough.

Korf's personal circumstances were very modest during this phase. His old friend and partner, the engineer Gerhard Fuchs, witnessed a depressing incident on a joint trip to the US. When Korf tried to settle his hotel bill, his credit card was declined. "Something like that is especially painful for a man like Korf. I felt sorry for him," recalled Fuchs. "I paid for him, and I also took care of his travel expenses related to my business. That was the right thing to do. He'd lost almost everything, and although he still lived in the villa, he was no longer in charge. He brought to bear what little he had left in an effort to save everything." It wasn't just Fuchs and Korf who got on well; their wives were great friends, too. Therefore, Fuchs, who still owed much to Korf from earlier times, felt obliged to take his friend back into the company they'd co-owned before Korf's insolvency. It was a good omen that solutions would be found.

Encouraging developments were already in the pipeline. An alternative site for Korf's first EOF in the USA was finally found: Rhode Island Forging Steel Inc. in East Providence. Originally founded by Washburn Steel & Wire in 1823, the bankrupt operation was bought by Korf with the help of MG and the Von Moos Steel Group in July 1988. Korf planned to turn it into a micro steel mill with the most advanced furnace in the world and an annual output of 250,000 tonnes, and rename it Ocean State Steel Co. The snag was that in the USA and Brazil, Korf was his own customer for these ultra-furnaces. He had received just one 'genuine' order for an EOF from Hungary. Another one ordered by the Indian Tata Group, with whom he'd set up an engineering joint venture, wouldn't go into operation until late 1990.

Despite the delays in selling his core product, which was supposed to replace the obsolete Siemens-Martin furnaces and expensive-to-run electric units all over the world, Korf again reported annual sales of around 500 million marks at the end of the 1980s. Now back on his feet, he'd accumulated some twenty company holdings and had 3,500 employees worldwide. International business was good with KORF, the smelting process using oxygen to boost the efficiency of the old Siemens-Martin furnaces. But in terms of revenue, Korf's top performer, accounting for more than 100 million marks, was the third ace in his corporate hand: the freight business with Korf-Transport GmbH in Kehl. He'd greatly expanded his old trucking business and even opened branches in France, Brazil and the USA. The result was a logistics network operating on land, sea, inland waterways, and air. Korf-Transport was extremely profitable.

So, when Willy Korf invited guests to celebrate his sixtieth birthday in August 1989, at a party "like the ones we used to have in the cheerful 1960s and 1970s", there was cause for both celebration and commiseration. For Korf, as usual, the optimistic view prevailed; he was only too happy to enjoy himself as a distraction from more depressing affairs.

The dinner dance was held on a sultry summer Sunday evening at the elegant Brenner's Park Hotel in Baden-Baden. Following a cloudburst in the morning, the sun symbolically appeared. The ladies fanned themselves to cool down. Brigitte Korf, in a red and blue floral dress, wore her hair shorter, and had long earrings resembling straw stars. The gentlemen wore dinner jackets; the ladies were dressed in long gowns. There were air kisses in abundance. As always at Korf's parties, a splendid five-course meal was served, including lobster with artichoke salad, consommé, saddle of venison, quail cream sauce, and baked Alaska. There were no steel celebrities among the guests; instead, there were ambassadors and theatre directors, barons and countesses – and, for the first time, many friends of Korf's now grown-up daughters. Willy Korf announced the arrival of his old family friend Aenne Burda like a guest of honour. Out on the terrace, there was dancing between courses, opened personally by Korf.

On Willy Korf's sixtieth birthday itself, Sunday 13 August 1989, the celebrations continued with a brunch in the garden at home. The attire was slightly less formal; Korf wore an open-necked blue shirt. A buffet was laid on, and the guests sat at round tables. Hostesses bearing barbecued sausages and glasses of pilsner passed through the crowd. A band played 1930s swing.

Finally, on the Monday, it was the turn of the staff at head office on Winterhalterstrasse. At eleven in the morning, they gathered for a reception followed by lunch. Korf himself stood at the lectern. Mindful of the few foreign guests present, not to mention the cracks appearing in the Iron Curtain, he declared: "The Korf Group means to continue its dynamic development, this time from the far west of Europe to the far east. I fervently hope that Europe will really grow together, and that its economic and political borders will be overcome." He then posed a question – "What will happen to Korf KG after the founder's sixtieth birthday?" – before answering it himself: "There can be only one reply: we intend to remain devoted to steel, to keep enhancing its production methods, and to defend our pole position in technical development." There was applause for his speech, before others stood to speak. Of the many words of thanks and praise that his friends and companions dedicated to Willy Korf, a native of Siegerland, one almost poetic sentence was particularly memorable: "The fires that went out in your homeland have been rekindled by you in many places around the world."

And with that, Willy Korf, the man of steel, had celebrated his last big party.

What followed was a great deal of arduous work, mixed with a hint of resignation. Willy Korf followed up his words about dynamic development "in the far east of Europe" with action. He judged Eastern Europe, which was finally starting to open up, to be an important future market for steel.

In 1990, he and MG (headed by Schimmelbusch) each took a 30 per cent stake in the Hungarian Ózd Steelworks. The Hungarian government remained the largest shareholder with 40 per cent. Making use of the political contacts he still had, and the new spirit of openness in the countries once hidden behind barbed wire, he began looking at Poland as well. But first, Ózd Steelworks was to be turned into a demonstration plant showing how EOFs and other new Korf technologies could transform ailing socialist factories into highly efficient steelworks fit for the world market. Unfortunately, this was the era known as the 'twilight of communism', which proved to be a chaotic transition to capitalism. Supply and service contracts with the Hungarians weren't worth much, as the Western partners soon discovered. As Heinz Schimmelbusch remembered with a shudder of horror:

> Someone told me, for example, that we'd been supplied with scrap metal pressed into large cubes with waste paper in the middle. It's said they even built a factory to make these cubes in order to collect the scrap price and get rid of their waste paper at the same time. With raw material like that, the steel mill's yield steadily declined.

Korf and Schimmelbusch derived no satisfaction whatsoever from their new acquisition. But a far greater worry for Heinz Schimmelbusch was his partner, Willy Korf. He was aware of the fact that despite the Korf Group's impressive appearance, it was under severe threat from a whole range of problems. He also knew about Korf's volatility, and was in a far better position to assess Korf KG's limited resources than Korf himself. Moreover, he'd started to notice signs of deep exhaustion in Korf, which seemed to be linked to his strained finances. "To be frank, he was broke," said Schimmelbusch. "He had shareholdings everywhere, and it was all too much for him. He had a lot of expenses, everything was fairly disorganized. He had company holdings that from a distance looked like an empire, but they weren't. You need cash flow to have an empire. Willy Korf had concluded that he couldn't go on like that anymore."

In 1990, that fateful year, Schimmelbusch and Korf still flew together to Warsaw to discuss modern steel mills with the Polish government. Korf insisted on flying on his only remaining aircraft, the leased Beechcraft King Air 200, even though MG kept a whole fleet of planes just for its business in Eastern Europe. Shortly after this unsuccessful trip to Poland, the two of them met again at Korf's urgent request, this time in the lobby of a prominent hotel in Frankfurt. Schimmelbusch knew that Korf was on his way to India to visit the boss of Tata. This was someone Korf found to be a difficult, stubborn business partner, and so he wasn't really looking forward to the trip. For his part, Schimmelbusch surmised that Korf must have had something very important on his mind if he wanted to discuss it so suddenly before heading for India.

Korf appeared at the hotel carrying an old-fashioned brown briefcase, which he kept on his lap as he sat opposite Schimmelbusch. While they were chatting, Korf kept fiddling with the briefcase in a strange manner, as if it contained something unpleasant that he was loath to reveal. Finally, he opened it and said: "Look, this is my financial situation. I've got it all sorted out: all the companies and holdings including Korf Lurgi Stahl Engineering. I'd like to ask you to look through it all. Let's meet again when I get back from India. I need to put my house in order, and if you make me a fair offer, I'll accept it."

Schimmelbusch immediately realized that their relationship was about to change. As the chief executive of MG, he'd just received an offer to purchase a stake in the Korf Group. "Our whole partnership was going to be restructured," Schimmelbusch recalled. "We also discussed whether Korf could become a paid executive of Lurgi. I didn't want to propose making him my employee, but perhaps chairman of a Lurgi subsidiary, and putting several consulting contracts his way. If he'd succeeded, his financial woes would have been largely over."

On that day in Frankfurt, Willy Korf was ready to draw a line under his entrepreneurial freedom.

A few weeks later, on Sunday 18 November 1990, secretary Renate Höing was at home in Baden-Baden. She dialled Willy Korf's private number. She hadn't worked for him for several months. The constant stress in the company had proved too much for her and she'd finally resigned. A while later, Korf had called her unexpectedly from Connecticut and asked her to come back to work. Although she flatly refused, she agreed to get back in touch with him at some point, hence the phone call that Sunday. "We had a long conversation. He told me how his children were doing. He didn't seem too busy. And he also said: 'I've just added you to the guest list for our Christmas party.'" And suddenly, the old Willy Korf was there again – the charmer who'd always managed to persuade his secretary to keep going through thick and thin. At the end of the conversation, they said goodbye to each other. It was the last time that Renate Höing would ever speak to Willy Korf.

Four days later, she saw the news: Korf's Beechcraft King Air 200, a burnt-out wreckage on the side of a mountain near Innsbruck. "Nobody who knew Korf well ever thought he'd die in bed with his boots off," said Höing reflectively. "That would have been unthinkable. We even told him that once to his face. He just laughed!"

CHAPTER 13
Willy Korf's legacy

"Where would you and all of us be without your dreams?"

Willy Korf's funeral was marked by a bizarre occurrence that would have appeared far-fetched had it been taken from the pages of a screenplay. Sometimes, truth is indeed stranger than fiction. After his coffin had been lowered into the ground, instead of scattering earth or petals, his elder daughter Astrid threw a cordless telephone onto the lid as a final farewell. This symbolic act was a reminder of the most precious tool used by her father, a man who'd seemingly spent his whole life on the phone. Then something happened that made everyone freeze in disbelief: the phone rang. There must have been a plausible explanation, but no one knew what. True, it hadn't been disconnected, but on the other hand it was clearly out of range, for the phone system was located in Korf's villa, about a kilometre away from the cemetery. Even though the incident remained unexplained, for a brief moment it shattered the sense of tragedy surrounding the funeral. It was almost as if Korf had personally added a final, humorous touch from beyond the grave.

Only once the shock caused by Willy Korf's death throughout Korf KG and the rest of Baden-Baden had ebbed somewhat did it emerge that he'd actually reached an out-of-court agreement with his creditors after the insolvency in 1983. Since then, all his available funds had been painstakingly scraped together to repay his creditors, which was also why Korf was as good as bankrupt shortly before his death. The plane crash had come at a time of modest consolidation, as Korf's adviser Bert Pfluger observed: "We'd promised to pay the settlement during his lifetime. Now it's grown even more complex." This was something of an understatement, since the amount owed still ran into the hundreds of millions – and concerned a suddenly ownerless corporate network, scattered across three continents, that was already as convoluted as Korf's empire had been before bankruptcy.

Alongside the amenability of some banks and government agencies, the fact that ways and means were found to meet Korf's remaining obligations – finally redeeming the disgrace of 1983 – was primarily down to three men: Bert Pfluger, Ralph Weber and Heinz Schimmelbusch. Pfluger, transformed from consultant to trustee, now coordinated the liquidation of Korf's immensely complicated estate. Weber, at that time a partner in Korf's Brazilian company IKOSA, took the reins of the Korf Group immediately after the tragedy. This was a role that fell naturally to him, given his contribution to Korf KG over the years and his detailed knowledge of the company from top to bottom. It soon transpired that this wasn't a permanent position, though. The company's financial situation was hopeless, and having been decapitated, it couldn't possibly continue to operate. "With Korf gone, the motivation was no longer there," recalled financial director Manfred Berner. "The engine was missing."

Using the lucrative Brazilian offshoot of the Korf Group as security, Ralph Weber worked with MG to salvage individual parts of the group, as Korf had already envisaged. "The marriage with MG was already well prepared," said Pfluger. "The engagement had already been announced, so to speak," he explained, adding that after the funeral, Schimmelbusch and Weber had discreetly taken him and a few other close colleagues aside to discuss starting the groundwork as soon as possible.

With share capital of 30 million marks and Weber as chief

executive, the successor company Korf GmbH was established at MG's head office in Frankfurt. Its mission was to administer everything of commercial value. It was supervised by MG, which was of course particularly interested in Korf's technological developments. Schimmelbusch bought Korf's stake in the joint venture Korf Lurgi Stahl Engineering GmbH and its subsidiaries. Later, when Schimmelbusch had been fired as chairman of the executive board and MG was restructured, these engineering activities were acquired by the large Brazilian Gerdau Group (a steel corporation owned by a German-born family), only to be taken over by Mannesmann shortly afterwards.

Many of Korf's other holdings and plants underwent a similar fate, being disposed of within the space of a few short years. The international steel business can be a revolving door of acquisitions, sales and mergers, spinning with brutal force. These relentless and rapid changes make it all the more significant that most of Willy Korf's steelworks were still operating successfully many years later.

Korf's former steelworks in Hamburg was taken over in 1995 by the steel magnate Lakshmi Niwas Mittal. A native of Calcutta who had opened his first steelworks in Indonesia in 1976, he rose to become the world's number one in the industry after acquisitions on four continents, being nicknamed the Bill Gates of steel. HSW was suffering serious problems when Mittal acquired it and, once he was in charge, he certainly lived up to his reputation as a tough restructurer and cost-cutter. The result was that nine years later, in 2004, HSW's sales were almost the highest since it was founded. And it continued to be regarded as a technical reference plant, just as it had been in Korf's day.

Despite negotiations with several potential buyers, the government of Baden-Württemberg was for years unable to find a suitable major investor for the BSW steel plant in Kehl, Korf's original steel mill. In the mid-1980s, Horst Weitzmann and his board colleague Hans Seizinger each took 50 per cent in BSW through a management buyout that was long concealed from the public. Continuing to downsize, they cut costs by two thirds,

THE STEEL REBEL WILLY KORF

and by 2004 were producing about 2 million tonnes of steel every year – over four times as much as in 1983.

In 1985, Otfried Forssman was recruited as plant manager of Société des Aciéries de Montereau by Sacilor, its new sole owner. Initially, the plant was highly profitable, enabling Sacilor to make substantial investments. But following Sacilor's merger with Usinor, long products such as wire rod and bars were completely dropped for strategic reasons, and the plant was sold to the Italian Riva Group.

Companhia Siderúrgica Pains was initially picked up by MG after Korf's death. When MG rejigged its strategy and dismissed Heinz Schimmelbusch in December 1993, Ralph Weber and Dalton Nosé had to find a buyer for the technologically advanced factory within two months. They succeeded, selling it to the Gerdau Group, and Pains remained one of its most efficient plants.

Connecticut Steel Corp, Korf's first 'new' plant when he got back on his feet, faced closure on two occasions. Swiss Steel AG from Lucerne bought the plant in 1990. Then there was a management buyout in 1999, after which the company became a big supplier on the American market, increasing its annual output to 400,000 tonnes.

Korf-Transport GmbH, always so close to the heart of its founder, had a far unhappier fate. It was sold to a former Korf company, the now independent Isar Baustahl GmbH based in Dinkelscherben, Bavaria, and the managing director Peter Koch was immediately sacked. The logistics company, once such a reliable source of income for Willy Korf, was later dragged down along with Isar Baustahl when the latter went bankrupt overnight. Isar Baustahl had squandered the corporate lifeline it had been given by Korf-Transport, leaving Willy Korf's beloved logistics firm to wither and die – for absolutely nothing.

At his home in Baden-Baden, Manfred Berner still kept a large framed black-and-white portrait of Willy Korf. This wasn't surprising, for Berner had joined Korf's company in 1964. And, strictly speaking, he didn't leave it until years after Korf's death. Having been head of finance and accounting at Korf-Stahl AG, and then financial director of Korf KG until Korf's demise, at the end of 2004 he was appointed liquidator of the last remnants of the old Korf Group.

Berner, working for Bert Pfluger, wound up Kehler Industriebau GmbH. This 'mini holding company', which took over everything that didn't find a buyer or was left over for other reasons after the closure of Korf KG, included two concrete plants. Following a tax audit, the modest Kehler Industriebau was unable to meet its high back taxes. A petition for bankruptcy was rejected for lack of assets, and so the group was put into liquidation. Accordingly, a chapter of German industrial history was closed on Berner's desk, and Kehler Industriebau became a thing of the past.

All told, Manfred Berner had worked with Korf or his companies for more than four decades, from 1964 to 2005. For Berner, it might have seemed like a forty-one-year struggle to get Korf to listen to him. But the financial expert, who outlived first the founder and then his remaining companies, bore it with a sense of humour, quipping: "I'm the last of the Mohicans!"

Willy Korf did not leave a will. This man, with his sights firmly set on his life and future projects in this world, had no thought for the next. In any case, there would only have been debts to inherit, for all the assets of the new Korf Group were owed to lenders. The private assets of Astrid Korf, the limited partner of Korf KG, were exempt from creditors' claims. Brigitte Korf renounced her statutory share of the inheritance to avoid unforeseeable disputes with creditors and looming estate bankruptcy. The beloved villa on Kaiser-Wilhelm-Strasse, which had remained in family ownership after the collapse of the first Korf Group, and which Korf had used so freely as collateral, finally had to be sold. When a private buyer was found at last, Willy Korf's widow, whose daughters were already living elsewhere, was the last member of the family to vacate the magnificent house.

Despite his financial situation, no one could argue that Willy Korf's industrial achievements disappeared without trace. Around the steel world, the technical innovations used by Korf to exert pressure on his rivals, following his invention of composite steel mesh, are remembered well – and many are still in use today.

"It's solely thanks to Willy Korf that the Midrex direct reduction process was invented and developed for the market," said his former deputy Wolfgang Bernhardt. Dieter Ameling, president of the Federation of the German Steel Industry, added:

> Korf deserves credit for being the first to combine the mini steelworks concept with continuous casting and the electric arc furnace. He was also the first person to produce sponge iron, a process that only ceased to be economically viable when the price of natural gas went through the roof. These days, although it's still expensive, the Hamburg steelworks is glad to have the resources to produce sponge iron because scrap is now even more expensive as a raw material.

Herbert Gienow, the former boss of Klöckner and sometime partner, sometime competitor of Willy Korf, regarded the principle of continuous casting introduced in Germany by Korf as a pioneering production method at mini steelworks: "Today's standards are all based on his ideas and developments. A small plant like Georgsmarienhütte near Osnabrück still benefits to this day from the way Korf organized his steelworks in Kehl and Hamburg."

Korf's winning idea of mini steel mills was so revolutionary that it reorganized the entire steel industry. Nearly all the large corporations ceased producing wire rod, bar steel, beams and rails, leaving these items to the 'minis', which were unbeatable in this line of work. On the other hand, mini steel plants were excluded from the production of high-quality special steels, an increasingly important commodity on the world market, due to the limited supplies of their raw material, scrap. Another factor that reshuffled the market was the abandonment of Korf's old enemy, the grotesquely high European steel subsidies of the early 1980s, which had severely distorted competition.

But while large corporations also discovered lean production structures, conversely, mini steel mills greatly expanded their product range. In some cases, they even penetrated the flat steel sector. One outstanding example is the success of Nucor Corporation in the USA, which is inextricably associated with F. Kenneth Iverson, a charismatic figure who resembles Korf in many ways. Nucor, today the largest steel producer in the USA, relied entirely on mini steel plants and, according to one industry expert, copied Willy Korf's wage principles, organization and technology. Operating out of Charlotte, North Carolina, Iverson could see Korf's model practically on his doorstep. Korf and Iverson were two pioneers of mini steelworks who, according to Korf's companion Dalton Nosé, had one thing in common: "Only by being a little mad will you succeed in changing anything."

But Korf did not only inspire such large-scale changes in the steel industry. Many manufacturing steps and process improvements, seen in modern mini steelworks to this day, can be attributed to him. Take, for instance, the water-cooling system for electric furnaces, which Korf perfected with his partner Gerhard Fuchs, and then supplemented with water-cooled lids and electrodes, working with metallurgist Hubert Knapp. "Very quickly, everyone adopted his method," said Knapp in retrospect. "And even today, water-cooling is still the state-of-the-art procedure used for furnaces." These days, however, electrodes are cooled with spray water to slow down the development of mill scale.

Korf was always quick to spot emerging developments in his industry – as well as to adopt solutions that enhanced them. When he put his best minds to work on the Electric Furnace for the Year 2000 in the late 1970s, one aim was to separate the metallurgical part of steel production from the pure smelting process in the electric furnace and thus gain valuable production time. "Until then, the scrap was melted down in the furnace. The steel was also refined in the furnace with the addition of coal. And that took time," recalled Werner Marnette, who participated in the trials. Instead, Korf had the molten pig iron processed in a separate ladle furnace. Marnette noted: "That's how it's still done currently. Although Korf didn't invent it, he promoted innovations like this."

Korf's role in popularizing direct reduction of iron lives on, even though this enormous capital was taken out of his hands when his first group of companies collapsed. Midrex is still a trademark used for direct reduction of iron. Probably no one believed in the potential of this process earlier than Korf, who was initially ridiculed by his big competitors. But Midrex wasn't a universal solution, for its advantage is cancelled out in situations where natural gas is expensive or in limited supply.

Korf's 'miracle furnace', the EOF (Energy Optimizing Furnace), and the KORF (Korf Oxy Refining Fuel) process, which was intended to elicit more output from old Siemens-Martin furnaces, failed to catch on permanently. But the KR process, the coal-based direct reduction method developed by Korf, which eliminated the need for electric furnaces and coke, and produced liquid pig iron instead of sponge iron, is still used. Having been adapted and refined, it continued to be marketed as the Corex Process by Vöest-Alpine, Korf's former development partner. It's still used in countries like South Africa and South Korea, where coal is cheap and abundant.

Last but not least, Korf showed considerable foresight regarding the role of emerging countries in the steel industry of the future. He once described steel to business weekly *Wirtschaftswoche* as a "considerable growth industry, albeit not so much in the traditional industrialized countries as in the under-industrialized – not underdeveloped – countries." This sentence, which today sounds obvious, was actually spoken by Willy Korf back in 1973. Korf backed up his analysis by expanding to India. As he declared shortly before his death: "India has the potential not only to become self-sufficient in the steel sector, but to compete in the world steel market like

South Korea and Brazil." In a similarly perceptive move, Korf had already set his sights on the other new steel mega-market, China, as early as the mid-1980s.

Korf's general qualities as a businessman also remain, perhaps minus one or two characteristics that became pitfalls for him. The tremendous willpower and energy he exuded can hardly be overestimated. Always a challenge to those around him, they were like a forcefield that empowered Korf to walk through walls. They made him act in a truly entrepreneurial manner – able to do things that were unprecedented because they had seemed impossible before he attempted them.

Willy Korf's life even inspired a novel. Written by Werner Möllenkamp and published in 1989, it dealt with a fictional German entrepreneur named Georg Ruff, whose adventures bore tongue-in-cheek resemblance to those of the real steelmaker – even if the author clearly had little understanding of the industrial reality! Nevertheless, this work of fiction proved just how much material for epics and dramas Korf provided, for he was a bubbling source of creativity, and not just for writers.

The originator of all these stories may have polarized his audience at times, but he left no one in doubt about the changes he wrought – and the disruption he caused – to the steel industry during his lifetime in business. "Korf helped to destroy the myth of the old conglomerates," a former Klöckner manager admitted in 2005 without envy. "He showed that you didn't have to have been born in 1830 to be a successful steel entrepreneur. He introduced modern management methods."

"He was the person to whom I owe almost my entire career," said Manfred Berner. "He was an entrepreneur with heart and soul, and he sacrificed everything for his vocation." And Berner certainly knew what he was talking about, having worked with Willy Korf longer than anyone else.

"He impressed me with his dedication, his ideas, what he built up over the years. He was a man who really made a difference." This description came from none other than Jobst Wellensiek, the insolvency administrator of Korf-Stahl AG. But he tempered this remark with a stark assessment: "What he lacked was an awareness of the costs. After all, the losses were ultimately borne by others. It wasn't funny for them."

"I'm in two minds about Korf," said Lothar Späth, the erstwhile premier of Baden-Württemberg, who later became a successful businessman himself. "I've got a certain admiration for him for showing what a difference a man can make. Sometimes you wanted to slap him, but when he looked at you, you thought: What a great guy!" Späth mentioned a valuable lesson from Korf's fate: "You need business magnates like him, but you also need regulators to make sure their activities don't get out of hand."

Edgar Georg, Korf's old friend from his youth, emphasized the positive sides of Korf's risk-taking mindset. "There are too few entrepreneurs of his calibre. In this day and age, people are obsessed with playing it safe rather than entrepreneurial vision. People from outside Germany like Lakshmi Mittal don't shy away from risks. If businesspeople like that weren't around, many companies would cease to exist."

Otfried Forssman summed up his view of Willy Korf as follows: "You shouldn't always waste time beforehand wondering whether something will go wrong. You have to follow your instinct. Don't complain, just do it!" And he also had this to add: "He believed in the good in people. In a way, his optimism was also naive."

Willy Korf is still held in admiration in the USA, the spiritual home of both naive optimists and hard-nosed money-makers. Korf is more often held up as an example to young steel managers in the US than he is in Europe. Focusing on mistakes, where value has been created and visions pursued, does not suit the American mentality. Every June, Astrid Korf Wolman presents the Willy Korf Steel Vision Award in New York for the metals market information resources *American Metal Market* and *World Steel Dynamics*. Many of those disruptors who, like Korf in his day, keep the steel industry on its toes have already accepted the award with pride, including Lakshmi Mittal, and head of the Gerdau Group, Jorge Gerdau Johannpeter.

At the same event, Korf Wolman also presents the Korf Award for Young Excellence to promising young scientists working in metals. Researchers from RWTH Aachen University, the institution that gave Willy Korf an honorary doctorate, have received this award, too. Last but not least, scholarships are presented to exceptionally talented engineering students by the Willy Korf Memorial Fund of the American Association for Iron and Steel. It's safe to say that the name Willy Korf won't fall into oblivion or disgrace any time soon.

Autumn in Germany, 2004. The former Korf Villa on Baden-Baden's Kaiser-Wilhelm-Strasse is empty. The imposing listed building and its small park are being renovated again. Holes have been dug in the garden paths. Workmen are inside the house, the noise of their tools echoing through the corridors protected by dust sheets. Obscene graffiti can be seen on the wall in the stairwell. Rumour has it that the property has been bought by a group of Russian investors. Even the foreman doesn't know (or pretends not to know) the identities of the new owners. It has taken some time to find a worthy buyer for the place, whose grandeur refuses to be tarnished, even by graffiti. Initially, it was sold to a finance broker from Heidelberg who planned to remodel the entire building. After this project was abandoned halfway through, a bank bought the villa at auction on behalf of an unknown client.

It's a pretty walk from the house to the cemetery, nestled on a steep incline with old trees and wafting the scent of the Black Forest. Willy Korf's simple headstone is only engraved with his name and the dates of his birth and death. His mother is buried alongside him. Nearby are the final resting places of other great families from Baden-Baden, the Richthofens, the Grundigs: a neighbourhood of pioneers, even in death.

Korf's grave isn't adorned with a motto. But if one were to think of a maxim by which he lived, then these five words – once spoken by Korf to a reporter – perfectly capture his attitude to adversity: "A true magnate never surrenders!"

PHOTO CREDITS

page II Photohandlung u. Atelier Passerah, Wissen-Sieg; page IV Pförtner's Sylter Photohäuser, Westerland-Sylt; page VI Photohaus u. Atelier K. Strobel, Bad-Ort; page IX Photo-Sierek, Velden am Wörthersee; page XI H.H. Neuendorff, Baden-Baden; page XIII Carol Lee; page XV Wolf P. Prange, Köln; page XVI J.H. Darchinger IFJ, Bonn; page XVIII Kuhnigk; page XXII Bundesbildstelle, Bonn; page XXIII Bundesbildstelle, Bonn; page XXIV Pressefoto Kraufmann u. Kraufmann, Stuttgart; page XXV Pressefoto Kraufmann u. Kraufmann, Stuttgart; page XXVII Jerry Kennelly/NEWSFAX; page XXIX Wolf P. Prange, Köln

---

[1] The quotations preceding each chapter are taken from the speech marking Willy Korf's fiftieth birthday given by Wolfgang Bernhardt, who at that time was the deputy chairman of the board of Korf-Stahl AG.

Printed in Great Britain
by Amazon

81625784R00159